Three Rivers Form An Ocean

...vignettes of life in Charleston, SC

By

James Funk

This book is a work of non-fiction. Names and places have been changed to protect the privacy of all individuals. The events and situations are true.

ISBN: 1-4140-1859-2 (e-book)
ISBN: 1-4140-1858-4 (Paperback)
ISBN: 1-4140-1857-6 (Dust Jacket)

Library of Congress Control Number: 2003098153

This book is printed on acid free paper.

Printed in the United States of America
Bloomington, IN

1stBooks - rev. 12/11/03

FOREWARD

This story is possible because of the research and professional writings of many people. I am not a historian, and therefore, relied heavily upon the works of the many source documents listed in the Selected Bibliography at the end, and more. I want to express my thanks and acknowledgement to the authors, for I have borrowed heavily from their craftsmanship in telling the story of Charleston.

It is my hope that this work will be an easy, enjoyable read for many. If the story can incite some interest in learning more about this unique city, my purpose is served. Charleston's glorious past has played a role in America's formative years, like no other city. And, her future, perhaps, may be even greater.

But a city's history is really just a collection of the stories, one by one, of its citizens and their day-to-day life in the city. I have tried to capture some of these stories of life in Charleston. Each of you are invited to come, and experience 'Charleston' first-hand. If you do, say hello by just saying "hey"...or, if it's morning, just a friendly "morn" will do, and the citizens of Charleston will return the greeting with a smile.

James Funk

TABLE OF CONTENTS

DEDICATION

Thanks, and gratitude forever, to Marilyn...my friend, partner, and companion.

And, to our children and grandchildren.

And, to my mother and father.

For them, this book became a labor of love!

PROLOGUE

For three centuries Charleston's citizens have shown courage, resolution, and tenacity. Jim Funk does a wonderful job of telling their story in his book *Three Rivers Form An Ocean*.

Charleston has survived the shelling of two great armies, and their occupation…first, by the British during the Revolution, and later by Federal forces during the siege and occupation in the Civil War. Also, fires, hurricanes, earthquakes, and deadly disease have devastated the city.

But, time and again, its citizens have rebuilt, until Charleston stands today as a national treasure. It is that strength of character and resiliency of its citizens that makes me optimistic and confident that Charleston's future will be even better than its glorious past.

Joseph P. Riley, Jr.
Mayor, City of Charleston, SC

ONTO CHARLESTON: CHAPTER 1

Charles Kuralt, the noted journalist and television personality, wrote of Charleston, South Carolina, in his acclaimed book *"Charles Kuralt's AMERICA"*. In describing the city's people, he wrote that Charlestonians are so smug that they describe 'their Charleston' as the place where the Ashley, Cooper, and Wando Rivers "come together to form the Atlantic Ocean".

Yet, despite their smugness, or even aloofness, Charlestonians are repeatedly voted the "friendliest people" in America by their visitors. It is this seeming dichotomy, aloofness on one hand and friendliness on the other, that signals the breadth, diversity, and uniqueness that is so compelling when one gets to know Charleston, and her people.

We stumbled upon Charleston. As northerners all our lives, my wife Marilyn and I found our roots firmly entrenched in the Midwest. Our transplant started with the urge to restart our lives, and the Southeast and its warm year-round climate seemed to beckon. Since our marriage in 1983, Marilyn and I have been best-friends, and true partners in all our decisions. My career had all the security developed over 17+ years with Ford Motor Company in car and truck product planning and

1

product development, while located in Dearborn, Michigan, just outside Detroit.

All of this began to change in 1985 during the long hours of driving north as we returned from a trip to Florida along Interstate-75. Marilyn and I used the drive time as an opportunity to formulate our decision to leave all the security of a career with Ford Motor Company, for the uncertainty and risk of starting our own business. We decided to go for it, and within the next 11 years, our trail moved through real estate development, building homes, selling homes, and ultimately purchasing and developing a golf course. What an adventure it was, and what a learning experience.

But, after all this, we decided to uproot again. Why not go boldly we reasoned, mothball our business, pack up, and head south to the lure of great weather, and new challenges! Atlanta and Charleston seemed to be possibilities. In Spring 1995, we visited Charleston for the first time. We checked into the Comfort Inn hotel in Mt. Pleasant, SC, just at the foot of the Cooper River bridges leading into downtown Charleston. And, we were happy that any room was available. Everything seemed to be booked for the weekend…for you see, unbeknownst to us, this was the weekend of the internationally acclaimed "Cooper River Bridge Run"! Over nearly 20 years, the run had grown to 10,000 participants.

Championship runners from all over the world, local amateur runners, and even "walkers" who just wanted to be part of it all, signed up for this annual Spring ritual. Each participant, of all ages, was eager to face the challenge of this difficult 6K run. Beginning at the Mt. Pleasant foot of the bridge, the route was up the "Silas Pearman Bridge" which rises 160+ feet arching over the Cooper River and Charleston harbor, and then into old downtown peninsular Charleston, to the race's end at Marion Square. Roads were blocked, crowds were enthusiastic, and a feeling of energy and fun filled the air. This was our baptism to

Charleston. Something is always happening in this city! In that one weekend of job interviews, driving and exploring, we fell in love, again, and suddenly our decision was made...it was Marilyn, Jim, and now Charleston!

In July 1996, we loaded our trusty 10-year old 1985 Bronco II with my belongings from our Fenton, Michigan home, and Marilyn and I drove in a two-car caravan with my father and mother, Les and Fern Funk, following toward Charleston, and our new life. We headed our two cars down Interstate 75, and out of Michigan and Ohio, through the vivid green rolling hills of the horse farms of Kentucky, and into the mountains of Tennessee. From Knoxville, a turn east on Interstate 40 took us across the gorgeous fiords criss-crossing the Blue Ridge Parkway, and onto Asheville, North Carolina. From Asheville, we traveled south on Interstate 26 into South Carolina's capital of Columbia. As we headed southeast, we entered South Carolina's so-called "Lowcountry", and our new home at the mouths of the historic Cooper, Ashley, and Wando Rivers...Charleston, SC. It is called "Lowcountry" because everything east of the mountains of Kentucky, Tennessee, and Georgia drains downward, eventually with all water runoff making its way to the Atlantic Ocean. Rivers, streams, creeks, and tributaries wend their way downward, eventually through the marshes and tidal creeks that comprise the Lowcountry landscape around Charleston. Marilyn and I shared excitement, apprehension, and trepidation over the unknowns that would face us. But, here we were, and we looked forward eagerly to the new opportunities and challenges.

A CARRIAGE HOUSE BECKONS: CHAPTER 2

A year passed. My new job was underway building new homes for CENTEX HOMES in Charleston. Marilyn had rejoined me, after returning to Michigan for four months, bravely and on her own to sell our home. We were happily settled in an apartment at "Palmetto Plantation" on Highway 17 in Mt. Pleasant. I would commute 25 minutes across the Mark Clark freeway that rings the greater metro area, crossing the Wando and then Cooper Rivers, to work at the CENTEX HOMES Whitehall South community in North Charleston. Our lives were much simpler than in Michigan. Weekends were free for Marilyn and I to explore, and we did.

A typical weekend would involve going somewhere for breakfast, or a cozy cafe for just coffee and a bagel; then, perhaps a walk on the beach at either Isle of Palms or Sullivan's Island, just 5 minutes drive over the "connector" which bridges across the Lowcountry marshes to the nearby barrier islands. Or, we could choose a day of walking the streets of downtown Charleston, awed by the newly found history so evident in the buildings and streetscapes, or by a glimpse over a wall or through a gate to a breathtaking garden beyond; or, perhaps a game of golf at the new golf club we joined at Snee Farm, just a 5 minute walk across Highway 17 from our apartment.

Our plan had been to go slowly, stay in our apartment, learn the new area, and then after 2-3 years, buy a home. But that was not to be, and it is here that our story really begins.

Marilyn had met the MacLean's, Neil and Jocelyn, who had recently purchased a home on a quaint one-block long street in downtown Charleston, aptly named Short Street. The MacLean's told us of Beth Simmons, an able realtor who was born downtown, knew the City like her hand, and just simply oozed 'Charleston'. Marilyn could not resist; she contacted Beth and enlisted her help. Marilyn told Beth to "start looking, but we are in no hurry, because Jim wants to take 1-2 years". Well, Beth must have thought Marilyn said 1-2 weeks!

Beth Simmons arranged with Marilyn to "spend a couple hours" the next weekend just looking around; Marilyn set out to convince me, and gain my consent. I conceded, and destiny was set in motion. For, soon, we would be owners of the so-called "Charles Kuralt home", the very place he stayed during what had become his immortalized visit to Charleston.

Charles Kuralt

Charles Kuralt was the folksy CBS newsman who traded the drama of his early journalistic career covering far-off wars and national elections, and turned instead, to chronicle for twenty years small town America and offbeat stories of its people. From his motor home touring America, the **_CBS Evening News_** series **_On the Road_** became a television institution. While never wearing patriotism on his sleeve, Charles Kuralt genuinely seemed to love America, and its people. He once explained, "I keep thinking I will find something wonderful just around the bend".

With his trademark soothing voice and reassuring manner, Charles Kuralt would search the back-roads of America for stories. His **_On the Road_** odyssey, Kuralt explained, was a search for the "unimportant", "irrelevant", and "resolutely insignificant". He and his crew would log more than 1 million miles in his battered motor home in search of just such simple stories, seldom otherwise represented by the national media. His balding and paunchy appearance and trademark voice were comfort food to the everyday American, because he lacked pretense and was never pompous.

Kuralt was the author of numerous books, including his memoir, **_A Life on the Road_** which was a No.1 nonfiction best-seller in 1990. He retired from CBS in 1994, and went on the road himself to write **_Charles Kuralt's America_** in 1995. For one year, he took off again to revisit some of his favorite places, in their favorite seasons, to rediscover slices of America closest to his heart. With warmth and humor, he showed them to his readers in this book which chronicled his journey. He chose 12 spots, and in each he stayed one month.

Charles Kuralt wrote of Charleston in March. He wrote of a "cocky mockingbird perched in the next door garden"…"on a real moonlit night on Montagu Street". He went on to say, "The mockingbird and I resided together in style, he in his tree, I in a rented three-story 'carriage house'…with a 'garden view' (screened porch)

6

opening onto the courtyard". He then went on to explain the home in some detail. That was it! That was the carriage house at 29 ½ Montagu Street!

Charles Kuralt was invited to return to Charleston someday, and he mused, "Perhaps I will. I hope so...I hope a mockingbird is singing". Charles Kuralt died in 1997, ironically on the 4th of July, Independence Day, perhaps giving Charles Kuralt the patriot a last delicious sense of completion.

Often I sit to pen words that recall our story, only to reflect with wonder that I am sitting in the same location where Charles Kuralt sat to write words so descriptive and captivating in their charm. If only I can conjure up the help of Charles Kuralt, as I search for the best words to describe how Marilyn and I came to share his former domain. Marilyn and I talked about completing our task, and then inviting Charles Kuralt back to Charleston; but, then, suddenly he died. But, you know, that 'cocky mockingbird' is still singing outside our door. The mockingbird, with its breast and belly of light gray, and wings of brown flecked with white, was named for the Indian word that meant '400 tongues', because its call could change to imitate all birds from the hummingbird to the majestic eagle. Perhaps, like the mockingbird, I can find the 'tongues' to tell this story...or, perhaps, just perhaps, Charles Kuralt and his favorite mockingbird are still here to help me.

So, let me continue with our story. We met Beth Simmons on a Saturday afternoon in late-March 1997, and loaded ourselves in her BMW car, with more than some trepidation, and excitement. Beth was dressed head to toe in black, wearing a

7

long dress, which is in fact 'Charleston'; we came to realize later, this was always how Beth dressed, black being her favorite color. Beth is high energy, and take-charge, in a most pleasant and friendly way. What you see, is what you get...no pretense, and talk that comes to you in the same candid, straight forward way. Refreshing it is.

After showing us a couple teaser houses, Beth quickly pointed out that she was making a mistake by showing us the first day of our search the best house she could envision. But, she said, "it just fits what ya-all describe", and this special carriage house just became available for sale.

The listing in that day's *Post and Courier* newspaper classified real estate section read:

"New Listing—Wonderful carriage house loaded with charm. Charles Kuralt stayed here. Private garden."

Beth Simmons/Bob Rymer.

As we turned the corner from Smith Street onto Montagu Street, Beth pulled curbside. An old black wooden gate, with arched top and see-thru ornate metal grate, stared back at us, and its simple brass numbers read "*29 ½*". The numbers were just above the see-thru grate in the door which allowed a passerby to peek into the courtyard to the rear; below the grate hung a black-painted metal box with lid to deposit mail. The narrow wood gate, like most structures in Charleston, showed many coats of paint applied over its many years. A stucco arch reached over the gate marking "*29 ½*". To its left side, stood a massive wrought iron gate with intricate artistic detail, that served as an entry for the imposing 4-story structure next door, a house with double piazzas to its side and overlooking its close neighbor at '29 ½'.

The gate next door shouted of pretense, while the gate at '29 ½' was modest and understated. The stucco arch that separated the contrasting entries was covered with fig vine, a vine that obviously had been happily ensconced at this gate for many, many years. The gate was a mere 15 feet off the street, with only an adjacent sidewalk passing by to separate the house from the street. The narrow gate was the only entry from the street, and as we peeked inside, it led to a narrow brick-lined walkway to the rear garden beyond.

The towering three-story tan stucco wall of the carriage house was covered with fig vine, overgrown, and partially concealing eight windows, each with side shutters, providing a look down to the street and sidewalk below. The carriage house roof was surfaced in charming old slate, and jutting into the sky were two chimneys rising on each side...obviously the slate roof and brick chimneys were original to the house. Curbside, two crepe myrtle trees were resplendent with lush pink flowers in the peak of their blooms.

Through the creaky gate, we entered a narrow 4-ft. wide walkway, shaded by the side wall of the carriage house towering three stories overhead. To the left of the walkway, stood a 8-ft. high stucco courtyard wall, with exposed brick capping its top, covered with fig vine, and canopied by a tree rising from beyond the wall within the compound of the imposing four-story mansion next door.

From the open gate at street level, one step up, and we followed Beth toward the rear courtyard along the old brick walkway coursed with moss from its shady existence. We walked rearward one room's depth, and were at the rear courtyard. The courtyard was enclosed completely by the 8-ft. high stucco wall, except for a lone intricate wrought iron gate fixed in the center of the rear wall. Flanking the iron gate on either side, were circular decorative portholes in the wall. The neighboring courtyard, and separate old kitchen house, were visible as we peered through the sculptured wrought iron.

The courtyard of '29 ½ Montagu' was overgrown, and obviously in need of gardening attention. Very little sunlight was finding its way through the dense canopy of trees in this courtyard, and in the adjoining properties. Yet, a certain charm seemed to resonate immediately to us, and 'promise' seemed quite possible.

Beth led us to a door at the rear of the carriage house that opened into an old, somewhat dilapidated single story screened porch, overlooking the courtyard. The screened porch's roof was covered by folded metal sheeting. Through the creaking screen door, we stepped into the porch and onto cobblestone-like brick, set simply into the ground without mortar grout. Beth mentioned, coyly, that this was the screened porch where Charles Kuralt sat to write of his whistles to the mockingbird, and the mockingbird's mimic back to him, and of the creaking old screen door. Beth was setting the hook…she could sense our growing interest, and excitement.

From the screened porch, the carriage house could be entered from either of two pair of double French 10-lite doors. We surmised the doors were originals. We could tell from the patina of layer upon layer of paint, waviness and imperfection of the glass, and gnawed look of the window sashes. We wondered, what humanity had passed through these doors over the structure's 150 years, and what stories could be told? Beth told us the carriage house was built in 1850, ten years before the Civil War's start.

From the centermost pair of French doors, we entered the small foyer, with a stairway in front of us, and noticed the bronze head of a horse ornament mounted to the top of the first newel post to the stairway's railing. To the right of the foyer, an archway provided access to one room, now serving as living room. Inside, stood a fireplace flanked by higher level windows on each side looking onto the street. On the opposite side of the living room, a window looked out onto the brick walkway leading streetside. Flooring appeared to be original heart pine.

Left of the stairway, we found another same-size room, serving as dining room, and again with fireplace. Through the dining room, an entry opened to the rear into a very small, and less than appealing, kitchen. The kitchen was tired and dated, with just enough room for a small circular table, placed just to the side of another 10-lite French door that provided a second exit to the rear courtyard. The kitchen was like the screened porch, with a folded metal roof, both rooms being added at a later time to the original rectangular-walled house. (A kitchen was not part of the original building, because fire prevention laws in the mid-1800's required that kitchens be located in separate structures away from the house itself.)

Up the stairway to the 2nd floor, we found on the left a bedroom with its own fireplace, and a duplicate size room to the right, with 4th fireplace in the house. A small bathroom, with old cast iron tub, faced us at the top of the 2nd floor landing, and extended to the rear of the house.

The 3rd floor consisted of a semi-finished attic with landing and dormer window at the top of the stairway. A small, loft-like bedroom space was to the right, and bathroom to the left. All ceilings were sloped at the outer roof lines, resulting in reduced headroom. The doors into the two attic rooms were made of crude planks joined together, and of a height such that someone tall would have to duck to pass. Flooring was crude painted wood, and not equal to the finished heart pine on the first two floors. A window in each room jutted out from a dormer to overlook the rear courtyard.

Our tour was complete. Beth summarized the carriage house as having a little over 1,600 sq. feet, three stories (including partially finished attic space), four fireplaces, a screened porch, and the 'charm' of being inhabited by Charles Kuralt. There she was…again, setting the hook so subtly.

Beth showed us two other, nice but rather conventional, Charleston homes that day; but, Beth had set the hook well, and she knew it! Almost from the moment we first passed beyond the gate at '29 ½', Marilyn and I started conjuring ideas of what could be done to this special 'carriage house'. We had worked together before. Marilyn and I were no strangers to renovation…or, as they say in Charleston, "restoration". We started with small projects on our lakeside cottage at Lake Missaukee in northern Lower Michigan. Then, we renovated a 100-year old horse barn into commercial offices in Fenton, Michigan. This was followed by complete gutting and rework to an 800 sq. ft. brick gatehouse at our lake property in Fenton, Michigan. We lived in the quaint, though small, gatehouse as we worked on a massive rework project on the lake home at the rear of this same property. The end result was a gorgeous French-chateau looking home that we loved, because it was positioned on the finger of a peninsula offering a 180-degree view of Lake Fenton. These last two projects comprised three years of great effort from both of us…the fruits of which we left for the promise of South Carolina, and Charleston. But, were we ready for another great challenge?

We both soaked on the idea for the next week, each day generating stronger and stronger vibes…but, at the same time, somewhat wishing that the charm of that carriage house at '29 ½ Montagu' Street was not so near to our liking. We tried to convince ourselves that it had probably had already been sold to someone, making our decision easy.

Finally, at week's end, we decided to call Beth...just to see if we could get one more look. To our amazement, it was still available, and Beth arranged for our visit with its owner, David Kludt.

David Kludt was quite a character. When we returned to '29 ½' with Beth, David greeted us with what we would come to know as his ever-present twinkle in the eye, warm smile, and handshake. He presented his business card; and, it read:

<u>LOTSA STUFF</u>

Major advertising agency writer and creative director;
Interior designer; actor; real estate maven; sparkling conversationalist; dependable dog keeper; passionately steadfast friend; and a few things off the pathened beat.

What an unusual business card for a highly unusual and refreshingly candid man with warmth in his heart, and more than just an inclination toward the romantic.

David had retired and relocated to Hilton Head, SC, only to be subsequently drawn to Charleston. He grew to love Charleston, and acquired '29 ½ Montagu' as a weekend getaway spot. David had thrown himself into making improvements to the property, and it had become dear to him.

Visitors to Charleston could arrange stays at '29 ½', but only after careful screening by David. Not just anyone could qualify. It was in this manner that Charles Kuralt had become an acquaintance and special guest of David's; Charles Kuralt's stay at '29 ½', and his subsequent widely read recollections of its charm, only fueled the love David held for this special carriage house.

Beth told us that David was not exactly thrilled to be selling a place he held dear, so he would only agree to sell to someone he judged would likewise place it in lofty regard. If we were really interested, Beth cautioned, we would have to approach David with sensitivity, and forethought.

David had agreed with arrangements for Beth to show us '29 ½' one more time, and it was upon this occasion that we learned more of David's wit. After David bid us farewell to give us time alone with Beth, Marilyn and I toured the house for the second time. In the foyer, I noticed a trap door in the wood flooring, covered by a loose rug near the stairway. Of course it provided access to the crawl space below the structure, so I was interested to see under the house. I lifted the trap door casually, while the two ladies conversed nearby. As I peered into the eerie darkness of the crawl space, I thought I made out the likeness of a slithering creature, about three inches in girth, which lay coiled in the sandy floor of the crawl below.

I reeled away, and obviously my expression showed some fright, because Marilyn and Beth caught my look immediately. Marilyn has a mortal fear of creepy, crawly creatures, to the extent that she could never think of herself co-inhabiting a home with such critters. She immediately shrieked at my reaction, and fled out of the room to a nearby chair on the screened porch. Beth's reaction was much cooler; each questioned what I had seen. Beth and I managed to calm ourselves somewhat, and we decided a flashlight was needed for another peek at what lie below. A flashlight was located, and with some trepidation, Beth and I approached the trap door for a second look. As I slowly lifted the door again, and pointed the beam of light to the sand below, the mystery was revealed. It was a snake all right, but certainly not alive!

It was an inflated likeness of a snake, carefully placed by the perpetrator, coiled realistically in the sand, with the clear objective of scaring the "begeezes" out of whomever would open that trap door. The three of us shared the heartiest laugh at the gag played upon us; as laughter died down, and relief overcame us, Beth said "wait until I get to David Kludt and tell him how close he came to losing us!"

Later, David would tell us, "the crawl space is an inscrutable mystery", since I've never been down there. The closest I ever came was to drop that fake snake into the crawl, which I felt was a "suitable reward for any guest curious enough to snoop".

Well, it seems the story has an even funnier ending; for, you see, not more than weeks after our incident, a guest of David's "snooped", but took no chances with the creature...the guest shot the snake with a handgun, only to watch with sheer amazement as the harmless object lost all its inflation, crumpling with a hiss of air as it came to lay in a final deflated heap, a threat no more!

As even that incident could not dissuade us, Marilyn and I decided to make an offer to purchase '29 ½'. With Beth's counsel, we agreed to approach David Kludt via a letter drafted carefully to convey our feelings for his '29 ½', and ask him to share it with us. In early April 1997, we wrote:

"Marilyn and I found your carriage
house at 29 ½ Montagu Street to be
a special place, with so much

charm...we are very much looking forward to it becoming our home".

David replied within two days with a letter we will keep forever. He wrote:

"I can't tell you how grateful I am that someone attuned to "29 ½ 's" charm is hopefully its next owner. At the time I bought it, another person bid on it almost simultaneously. The horror was that he intended to tear off most of the rear wall and build a two-or-three story glass wing...ala the beach houses at Wild Dunes. The carriage house is a gentle antebellum jewel that just doesn't lend itself to that kind of groovy butchery. And, I gather from your comments that you share that view".

He closed the letter by saying:

> *"Again, I can hardly tell you how pleased I am that Beth found you. Until recently, I never intended to sell the Carriage House; it was to be put in the pyramid with me when I died. But times pass, and I'm not getting any younger. So maybe now is the time to say goodbye to a treasured friend. I hope you enjoy it as much as I did.*
>
> *W. David Kludt"*

What a letter, filled with such strong emotion. David Kludt would become our lasting friend; hopefully, we could become a friend, and caretaker, to his '29 ½ Montagu'.

We closed on the purchase of '29 ½' on May 9, 1997. It had stood proudly, and witnessed much humanity pass within its walls during two centuries; it was now up to Marilyn and I to get it ready for its third century!

CHARLESTON'S BEGINNING: CHAPTER 3

Marilyn and I began to prepare with excitement for our new beginning, for neither of us had ever lived within the downtown of a cosmopolitan city. Our living experience had been mostly in the neighborhoods within the suburbs of large cities, like Detroit and Chicago, although Marilyn grew up on a farm outside small town Clare, Michigan. We were unsure what to expect of life in a city such as Charleston. But, we promised that we would immerse ourselves in getting to know the history of our new house, its neighborhood, and this proud city…a city which at times perhaps appears arrogant in its resiliency, always aristocratic and noble, and seemingly defies history, time, and adversity.

We would read about all of this through many trips and hours at the magnificent new county library on Calhoun Street, just a brisk ten-minute walk from our new home; but, walking was an even greater experience, and we looked forward to long walks all over the City. Our new home, after all, was in a wonderful central location: five blocks to the west on Montagu Street was the Ashley River, and the City Marina; to the east three blocks was the College of Charleston, and two blocks further east the heart of downtown Charleston, King Street; within a 15-20 minute walk we could be at the tip of the peninsula at the so-called Battery, or east to the Cooper River, enjoying the thriving tourist areas of Market Street, Meeting Street, and Broad Street.

One of the first of these walks took us out our gate left onto Montagu Street, one block to Rutledge Street, and another left following Rutledge past Colonial Lake, and onto Murray Boulevard which meanders from the Battery and White Point Garden along the Ashley River. Today a concrete seawall catches the lapping waters of the Ashley River, and the railings at the walkway on the seawall's edge are a wonderful spot for pausing to view gorgeous sunsets glistening across the water. As we lean against the railing, and peer across the rivulets of water as the tide is receding, our imagination can make history come alive for us.

The Spanish were the first to attempt settlement of the Carolina coast. In 1520, the Spanish reached the coast to obtain slaves, and returned to Spain with 70 Indians. Six years later, Lucas Vasquez de Ayllon departed Spain to establish a settlement, with six ships, and more than 500 men and women on board; but, his largest vessel ran aground, supplies were lost, and within months he died of fever and his men mutinied. The French also visited the Carolina coast, beginning in 1524. But, no venture would prove successful for nearly another 150 years, and then it would be an English venture.

My thoughts go back to April 1670, when at this spot on the shore of the Ashley River, two small, wooden ships entered Charleston Harbor. The ships had set sail in late November from Barbados, bound for Carolina, with 100 colonists (including 19 women). After nearly four months of terrifying travel, in such close quarters at sea, land must have been a reassuring sight. The occupants of those two ships must have been filled with emotion as they gazed upon huge gleaming white banks of oyster shells discarded by the Indians, and now glistening white in the sun's reflection.

Imagine as they pressed close to the shoreline, hearing the sounds of hundreds of birds calling from thickets of oak and tall palmetto palms. Perhaps, they were even close enough to smell fragrant flowers and sweet myrtle. Seagulls and herons soared overhead as they passed the rocky shoal that would become Fort Sumter a century and a half later. They proceeded past what would become known as Oyster Point, because of the glistening white banks of oyster shells piled high. Five miles further up the Ashley River, they landed at Abemarle Point, now called Charles Towne Landing. Charles Towne Landing is now a county park which can be visited, complete with replica of the one of the ships, the 200-ton three-masted frigate called "Carolina", that can be boarded today to bring that long ago day into better focus for one's imagination.

The settlement was named Charles Towne, in honor of England's King Charles II. The King had granted land to eight so-called Lord Proprietors, the most prominent being Anthony Ashley Cooper, later Lord Shaftesbury, who had convinced the others to pool 50 lbs sterling apiece to finance the expedition. One third of the first colonists were freemen of property, who were promised by the Lord Proprietors 150 acres each, and an additional 100 acres for each able-bodied man servant they brought with them; as such, two-thirds of the persons on board were indentured servants, bound to serve their owners for 2-7 years in return for their passage to Carolina.

A fortification was erected, more to protect against the threat of Spanish raiding parties from their colony in Florida, than from the native Indians. Early settlers soon numbered about 155, and included English, Irish, and island immigrants from Barbados. At that time, inhabitants of Barbados had swelled to

50,000 whites and 80,000 blacks, so spillover and migration to Charles Towne came naturally and from the beginning. The tradewinds played a role, because sailing ships were drawn south from Europe by the prevailing winds, and Barbados was in the path on the route to the Carolina coast. The heritage from Barbados would have a strong influence on this new colony.

In 1671, the Grand Council appointed a committee to "examine the banks of the Ashley and Wando rivers" to determine the best places to "situate towns upon".

By 1680, the early settlers moved the town to a more defensible location, on the peninsula, and just north of that oyster bank they passed on their first arrival. The chosen site was bounded on three sides by water: the Cooper River to the east, north and south by large creeks, and to the west an earthen wall was built. The fortified city quickly became a thriving trading center because of its harbor, and wharves and ships soon dotted its landscape. By 1690, in just 20 short years, Charles Towne had become the 5th largest city in America, with a population of 1,000 persons, and 100 wood dwellings.

Indian trade was the first to develop. Between 1699 and 1715, more than 53,000 deerskins worth 30,000 lbs. sterling would be shipped to England by some 200 traders. But, soon other goods would become even more important than deerskins. Tar and pitch from the sap of pine trees would grease wagon wheels, waterproof ship's cordage, and caulk the ships. The growing season was long, costs low, and raw materials abundant. Twelve laborers, working about 2,000 acres, could gather tar and pitch worth 500 lbs. sterling. Lumber products reached the West Indies, or Europe, from Charles Towne. The English placed growing importance on Carolina naval stores, and market prices rose, because wars with France had disrupted supply from England's usual sources. In 1705,

Parliament granted a subsidy on colonial tar and pitch, to encourage even greater trade.

The main threats to the prospering city were the Spanish, disease, pirates, and Indians, including the Yemassee and Creek tribes. In 1682, the Indians spread the alarm that a force of 800 Spaniards was marching toward the city, and defensive measures were taken, but the impending raid proved to be a false alarm. As further defense, the Provincial Council in 1690 established a "great gun" with lookout posted on Sullivan's Island to signal Charles Towne of approaching hostile vessels.

Sewee Indians

A tragic but great story involves the Sewee Indian tribe, who inhabited an area of the Carolina coast, along what is now Sullivan's Island and Isle of Palms.

You see, the Sewee Indians were one of the more advanced thinking tribes of their day, and utilized a democratic form of government, relatively unheard of among fellow Indian tribes.

Their final destructive undoing came as a result of a great trading scheme, hatched by someone given a voice in the 'democratic' way. The tribe's hunters and trappers decided to 'eliminate the middle man'…the traders. (This may give a tongue-in-cheek lesson to today's marketing professionals.)

The Sewee tribe decided to cross the sea directly, themselves, instead of utilizing the large sailing ships of the traders, who were profiting on their products (deerskins).

Every able bodied Indian brave loaded their cypress dug-out canoes, and pushed off from the shore, headed for the great marketplace in Europe. As they barely faded out of sight over the ocean's horizon, a great storm broke, nearly destroying the entire fleet of canoes. The few survivors were 'rescued' by a British trading ship, but sold as slaves in the West Indies. They were gone...the entire male adult tribe of "entrepreneurs"!

You can stand today on the beautiful beaches of Sullivan's Island or Isle of Palms, and imagine bidding farewell to the anxious braves as they pushed off their canoes for the great voyage...a trip that would be the last voyage of their nation!

These are the same beaches that would later be frequented by pirates and privateers.

Disease always was a threat to the early settlers. In the summer to winter months of 1697, small pox raged for the first time, killing 200-300 persons; disease would be a recurring peril to the city time and again, with its threat literally changing the way people lived. In 1699 yellow fever struck, claiming 14 lives in one day in September. The town was almost deserted, except for an occasional someone scurrying by with medicines, or death carts rolling by heaped with the dead. The epidemic ended only as colder weather arrived, but 180 persons perished. Other diseases were dysentry and malaria, but unlike these two, yellow fever either killed its victim, or usually rendered that person immuned from further attacks. Blacks having come from regions where yellow fever and malaria were common, possessed considerable immunity, whereas whites did not. It would take nearly two centuries before yellow fever would be connected with mosquitoes.

The Yemassee Indian War erupted in 1715 when traders, financed by Charles Towne merchants, plundered, killed, and enslaved Indians from the backcountry. The Yemassee were joined by Creeks, Choctaw, and Catawba tribes. Indian raiders struck along the upper reaches of the Ashley, Cooper, and Santee Rivers, murdering, pillaging, and burning in their attacks. The 'War' ended in 1716 when the Cherokee Indians came to the aid of the colonists by attacking the Creek Indians.

Pirates plied the coastal waters from the Caribbean to the Carolina shores. 'Blackbeard' (Edward Thatch), and Stede Bonnet the 'Gentleman Pirate', became famous, as well as the infamous lady pirates Mary Reed and Ann Bonny. Pirates and privateers would defiantly lay anchor just outside the harbor, or frequent the beaches of Sullivan's Island or Isle of Palms, lying in wait for their prey.

In 1718, Colonel William Rhett sought to rid the area of the pirates.

Colonel William Rhett

Colonel William Rhett had come to Charles Towne in 1718 with his wife Sarah and their children. His father was Dutch, and went to England to help the monarchy. Because of his service to the crown, his son, William was made a colonel in the British army by the King. Then 'Colonel' William Rhett was dispatched to the Charles Towne colony, as commissioner of customs.

Enmity soon developed between William Rhett and the de facto ruler of Charles Towne, Judge Nicholas Trott. The rumor lingers that Judge Trott dispatched Rhett to capture pirates, thinking him not up to the task, and therefore setting him up for his demise.

Pirates, you see, were besieging Charles Towne, because some in the colony were encouraging the pirates to visit and spend their loot in the town, as the story goes. (Some would say, this sounds like present day Charleston's tourist situation!)

Well, Stede Bonnet had changed his life in 1717, opting to become a pirate. Before this transformation, Bonnet was a retired British Major in the King's Guards, who lived with his wife on a large estate in Barbados. He earned the nickname 'Gentleman Pirate' because of the cultured image he continued to portray; he was well groomed, wore fancy clothing, and a periwig. Bonnet bought a sloop and outfitted it with ten guns, purchasing it with his own money (hardly the act of a real pirate!). He christened his new sloop 'Revenge', recruited a crew of 70 citizen-pirates, and set sail for the pirate life. He quickly proved to know nothing of seamanship, and he was not a very good pirate either.

The 'Gentleman Pirate' participated with the famous pirate 'Blackbeard' in a siege of Charles Towne, where they kidnapped private citizens and held them for ransom. Soon, however, 'Blackbeard' found Bonnet to be inept, and left him, along with Bonnet's share of the plunder.

> Rumor has it that Colonel William Rhett was sent to capture 'Blackbeard', but came upon Stede Bonnet instead. In a quick rout, the 'Gentleman Pirate' and 54 of his crew were captured off Cape Fear on the North Carolina coast, and brought back to Charles Towne by Rhett.
>
> Colonel Rhett's home at 54 Hasell Street, is believed to be the oldest house in the city, built c.1712.

The 'Gentleman Pirate' and his crew were held prisoner in the dungeon of what is now the Exchange Building, at the foot of present Broad Street on East Bay Street. But, the pirate Bonnet, dressed as a woman, and rumor says with the help of sympathetic citizens of the city, somehow escaped and hid, only to be recaptured on Sullivan's Island. Despite pleas from the city's citizens, Bonnet and 34 of his crew were tried, convicted, and hanged in 1718 at White Point in Charles Towne, and a monument marks that occasion in the park today.

As Marilyn and I read that monument memorializing this gruesome event, we let our imaginations run wild. It's December 10, 1718. A fairly large crowd probably gathered to witness the execution of the 'Gentleman Pirate'. Our minds pictured a mix of different people, probably boisterous and shouting remarks; others were reserved, and sad, because Bonnet was also popular among many citizens, enjoying a reputation as a bit of a 'Robin Hood' among the townspeople. We could see the gathering crowd around the hangman's gallows.

> Poor people were dressed in course homespun material...the men with woolen stockings that came to their knees, guarding against the chill in

the air, whereas in summer's heat they would go barelegged and barefoot. Several frontiersmen gathered, and servants of the gentlemen and ladies assembled nearby...each dressed in leather breeches and leather jackets.

The colonial gentlemen wore silk stockings, and breeches made of velvet, some of silk and some intricately brocade. Broadcloth coats extended to their knees, and the coats were collarless and unfastened, but decorated with fancy buttons and embroidery. In the prior several years, dyes had improved, so several men were fashionably attired with new red coats. Some men had the new yellow stockings, while others wore traditional white. Some had shoes with colored laces, and even red heels. Most of the gentlemen wore wigs because they were out in public, whereas in the privacy of their home they would remove their hat and the uncomfortable wig, and at night don a sleeping cap to protect their shaven head.

Several ladies accompanied the gentlemen. The ladies wore elaborate hooped skirts of handsome material. Their hair was not powdered, but brushed back simply. A fashion for the ladies of the time was a mask to protect their face when out riding. Several of the women, and a young girl, wore full length hoods of red. Children were dressed like their parents.

Then, the pirate Stede Bonnet was brought forward in a cart, manacled and clutching a bouquet of wildflowers, as the story goes. The executioner dropped the noose over his head and around his neck. Bonnet swung off the cart, as the crowd gasped, left to die the agonizing death of strangulation. After the hanging of Stede Bonnet, and his crew, their bodies were left swaying in the breeze, to decay in the sun for days, as a gruesome visible warning sign to ships incoming the harbor. In all, 49 pirates were hanged in Charles Towne that year, and many are thought to lie buried to this day near White Point.

PLANNING FOR 29 ½'s THIRD CENTURY: CHAPTER 4

The structure known as '29 ½ Montagu' was part of an extensive in-town estate, built c.1850 by Ettsel Adams, a wealthy merchant. Ettsel Adams and his family built, and occupied as his residence, the adjacent large house at 29 Montagu Street. Our new home to be was a structure built separate from the Adams' residence. Today, people refer to houses of this type as 'carriage houses'. But, this house stored no carriages, or horses. This structure served as a 'dependency' for the main residency, housing the household staff in four small bedrooms, each with its own fireplace for heat, and a third floor loft.

Typical of its day, the house was built around a central stairway, with entrance to the rear off the street, so the masters could oversee and control who was coming and going. To each side of the stairway were two rooms (which served then as bedrooms) on each of two floors. Each bedroom probably housed several people per room. This so-called 'dependency' structure was separate and apart from another structure or "kitchen house", which was built apart from the main residence and other outbuildings, for fire protection. All meals would be prepared in the "kitchen house", so no provision was made for cooking in our "carriage house" at 29 ½ Montagu until years after its original construction.

We observed that the walls of this house are 18" thick, built of brick, with a stucco overlay. Many of the windows and glass appear to be original. The four fireplaces were small, and built for burning coal for heat in each room. Later, heat registers were added to this house to 'modernize' the heating. Today, central heating and air conditioning give the house its third version of heating system.

As new owners of 29 ½ Montagu, Marilyn and I were eager to get started with plans for restoration work. We agreed on two objectives: we did not want to lose the historic charm of this long standing structure by "groovy butchery" as David Kludt had warned, and we wanted to limit our spending to keep within our budget. First priorities were to improve the kitchen and gain more space in the lower level, and to redo the bathrooms on the second and third floors. Later, we would tackle the courtyard, after we moved into our home.

Our first step was to measure the size of all rooms, and draw a rough scaled layout of each of the three floors. Working from that plan, we would fashion a plan for our restoration. The kitchen was the biggest challenge; it was small (8'x 12') and quite out of date…everything had to go! A wall separated the kitchen from the rear entry to the house via the screened porch. The screened porch had a pair of old French doors, one set leading into the house at the foyer to the stairway, the other set as an entry to the living room.

We wanted to enclose the screened porch area (7'x17') and make it into a year-round room, keeping the French doors open to the house, and in this way increase living space; the porch area would also provide a great visual setting overlooking our future garden/courtyard. Therefore, the wall separating the existing kitchen from the porch just had to go…this, in one bold move, would open many more possibilities for the new kitchen, would improve traffic flow allowing two accesses to the kitchen, and create a much brighter, open feel to the home. It would certainly prove to be our best idea for the restoration!

'29 1/2' Before Restoration

We are inspecting the rear courtyard at '29 1/2' with our friend, Sheila Spung, before restoration work began.

31

The question remained how could we make it happen…was it feasible? As we probed the wall to get a clue, its hollow sound as we knocked gave some assurance that the wall was of hollow frame construction, probably added to the house when the kitchen was built as an add-on to the original, rectangular 18" thick brick and stucco structure. But, what kind of structure was within the wall supporting the second story bathroom, and what if any, plumbing or electrical work resided within that wall? You have to be a little gutsy, some would say crazy, to plow forward with such unknowns…but, that is what Marilyn and I had experienced with our prior work, and plow ahead was what we did!

The new kitchen and year-round porch, or sunroom, would give us a space of about 29' long x 8' wide with which to plan. I began to draw layouts. The windows in the existing kitchen would have to stay where they were; likewise, the door to the dining room and door to the courtyard would be kept, and the location for the electric panel where service entered the house in the corner of the kitchen would have to remain. All of these had to stay in order for us to meet our budget.

I drew a new kitchen sink located beneath the window overlooking the courtyard, with a new dishwasher space to its right. The refrigerator, within easy reach to the right of the sink, would work nicely, located to the side of the electric panel, and just underneath a high window that let light stream from the west side of the house adjacent to our neighbor's rear veranda. Cabinet space would work on either side of the refrigerator. The new range/oven/microwave would be handy located just behind the back of someone working at the kitchen sink, and cabinet workspace would just barely fit to its right, and still allow enough access room to walk from the new sunroom into the kitchen work area.

Dividing the sunroom from the kitchen would be countertop with room for two bar stools, providing a great space for eating snacks, serving space, or just an area to sit and converse with people working in the kitchen. Overhead, serving as a partial space divider, cabinets with front and back glass doors would give added storage, while still allowing bright sunlight to pass thru and create a feeling of openness. Finally, just to the left of the sink in the corner, we could utilize a pantry-style cabinet to conceal the water heater; it was clear that every inch of space had to be carefully utilized, and locating a spot for the water heater was a welcome solution. With that, the overall layout for the kitchen seemed to fall in place, and Marilyn was pleased that it would work well.

Conversion of the screened porch to a sunroom would be relatively straightforward. We wanted to get as much open glass as we could to allow daylight, and create an open panorama view of the courtyard. The roof would stay unchanged, and we certainly wanted to keep the wonderful old historic brick that served as its present floor. The new windows and doors would have to be selected carefully so they would blend, as much as possible, with the existing wood divided pane windows of the original structure. I determined that two double-unit windows would fit, alongside a double French door at the rear wall facing the courtyard; a similar double-unit window could work on the end of the sunroom looking out onto the side brick walkway. To match, we could replace the existing door to the courtyard from the kitchen with a new divided light door in the same style as for the sunroom. We were excited that all of this seemed to work nicely, and we could visualize a truly dramatic new look to the rear entry of our new home. And, a wonderfully landscaped garden courtyard would be just right.

The living room and dining room would not require major construction...just some added detailing with moldings, trim, and painting. All of the original heart pine floors would require refinishing, but that would be a last step. This would complete our planning for the first floor restoration.

On the second floor, the two rooms on either side of the central stairway would stay, except for adding closet space, moldings, trim, and painting. We wanted to use one room as our master bedroom, while the other room would serve as a reading/TV area, creating a full second floor bedroom suite. We wanted to keep all existing windows to protect the house's historic integrity, because much of the glass was crinkled, imperfect, and obviously original; most of the windows would not open or close, and this would be a problem for later, because we wanted the fresh air and wonderful sounds of the street below to lull us to sleep.

The bathroom at the head of the stairway, was another matter, and a major challenge! An old cast iron tub and out-of-date cabinets and fixtures made the room pretty dismal...not to mention the wallpaper which would have looked more at home in a bordello. We had to totally gut this room, but our dilemma was where could we get space for a washer/dryer? An existing washer/dryer were in the bathroom on the third floor; but, Marilyn was adamant...going up and down stairs to the laundry would never do! The only solution was to locate this equipment in this bathroom...but how?

We struggled with this question for several days. One problem was space; another was that the plumbing and electrical for the washer/dryer was on the third floor, while we needed it on the second floor. After some agony, we agreed that a stacked apartment-size washer/dryer could fit if we gave up on a tub, settling instead for a shower only. This became a good compromise; the laundry would be handy in the living quarters, a shower would work just fine, and we would keep the tub in the third floor bath for the times it was desired. New fixtures, cabinet and countertop would complete the new bathroom, and we would keep some of the old charm by utilizing an old linen closet and medicine cabinet that had the patina of many coats of paint and evidenced its use by humanity over the many years.

At the top of the stairway to the third floor, wood flooring was crude, and repairs would be needed. To the right, a small bedroom would serve as our guest quarters, complete with the charm of low sloping ceilings at either end following the roof's gable. Perched from a dormer out and over the slate roof, a window yielded a breathtaking view over the treetops and our rear courtyard to the magnificent rooflines of the huge Wentworth Mansion beyond. This room would stay unchanged, except for tidying up and repainting. Across the stairway landing was the third floor bathroom. With the existing washer/dryer removed, plenty of space would exist for new cabinets, new flooring, and basic freshening. The existing bathtub and toilet would do just fine. Off the rear of the bathroom was a small walk-in storage space formed by the sloped ceiling of the gable roof streetside; one of our early tasks would be to fix a leak that was evident from the stained and ragged plaster adjacent to the chimney area of the roof.

With this planning stage complete, we had rough scale drawings of our proposed restoration, and the next step was obtaining city approvals for permits. In early June, I was ready to approach the city building and planning departments with our proposal. That morning Charleston had experienced a not-so-unusual sudden deluge of rain, and when combined with high tide, the result was predictable flooding in some of the low-lying streets. The corner of Calhoun and East Bay Streets was just such an area, and the morning's rain had made it impossible for city employees to enter their offices. This was just the opportunity I needed.

You see everyone gets kind of antsy when their usual day has been disrupted, and they are more than anxious to have the crazy day end, and get to their homes early if possible. This seems to really apply to government employees.

With this situation in mind, but not knowing exactly what to expect, I climbed the front steps of the imposing building on Calhoun Street which housed City offices, across from the new Charleston County Library. It was just after 3:00 PM in the afternoon, and my timing could not have been more perfect. I found my way to the counter of the Building Department, and after brief introduction, proceeded to review my sketches and outline our restoration plans. Everyone was extremely friendly and courteous, but it became clear that they really wanted to dispose of this matter quickly, and end their day, and head home. The magnitude of what we were proposing was not all that substantial, because our changes could be accomplished under existing roofs, and the streetside appearance of our home would not change.

You see, the City of Charleston has extensive requirements for approval of any change to a historically significant building. These requirements come under the watchful scrutiny of the Architectural Review Board. I had been apprehensive, not knowing whether or not we would become entrapped in a bureaucratic nightmare of meetings before a Board, or not. I was quite relieved when the building official told me our changes could be approved by Staff, who were there and on-duty at the time. I had a paint chip of the color we wanted to use to repaint the exterior; because the color was coral, and in keeping with Caribbean-like colors used on many historic Charleston structures, a staff person was located who could represent the Architectural Review Board, and our paint color was approved.

Next, the planning staff member had to review the construction changes to assure that everything met zoning and building code requirements. The hurdle here was to assure the planner that enclosing the screened porch would not violate fire code requirements, by being too close to adjacent neighbor's property; when I used the lot survey drawing to demonstrate our entry walkway was at least 4' wide, I was home free. All that remained was for the clerk to type the permit, and me to pay the fees.

Just like that, I was walking out, permit in hand, and it was just going on 4:00 PM and City staff could leave on-time, and make their way homeward. I could not have been happier, or more excited to get back and share the news with Marilyn. We were ready to start restoration!

CHARLES TOWNE...THE WALLED CITY: CHAPTER 5

Charleston today is a walking city, much in the European sense, and therefore unique in America. Walks in Charleston are best when the enjoyment of the present is combined with appreciation of the past. The great expanse of surviving architectural monuments within the city allows that past to come alive. One such of these monuments is the Old Powder Magazine on Cumberland Street.

The Old Powder Magazine at 79 Cumberland Street (what was then the northern boundary of the city) is the only public building remaining from the era of the Lord Proprietors' ownership and rule of the province of Carolina. It has been restored, and can be toured today, which gives us a wonderful glimpse into the early walled city's past. The Powder Magazine was crucial to the defense of Charles Towne as the 1700's began, helping protect against the threats of marauding Spanish naval vessels from St. Augustine or pirate or Indian attacks. It was built between 1703-1707, as part of the "walled city's" fortifications against enemies by land or sea. With its 32-inch thick brick walls, and gabled masonry roof, the building stored gun powder for the city, and although replaced by a newer magazine in 1748, it would serve the city effectively through the American Revolution.

The original 'walled city' was probably protected by earthen berms, but the berms were soon replaced by brick walls that comprised an engineering marvel for its time. Construction of a seawall began in 1704. The brick wall was constructed on a 'grillage' or raft foundation to spread the weight of its walls on the unstable lowland marsh soil, and when completed, the wall would be 15 ft. in height, and enclose a roughly rectangular area three blocks wide by nearly a mile in length. The wall extended along what is East Bay Street going north to Cumberland Street, just before present Market Street; with Cumberland Street as it north wall, it turned along Meeting Street, until it crossed Broad Street where a moat was dug, and drawbridge built over it. At its corners were protective areas, called Bastions, each named for four of the Lord Proprietors. Just outside the northern wall, a creek ran east to the Cooper River, along present Market Street. The creek served as a type of moat, guarding against land attacks from the north. Likewise, to the south a creek ran from present East Battery along what is now Water Street.

Covering roughly 80 acres, Charles Town (the "e" on the end began to be dropped about this time) had become a fortified city-state unto its own. Main street was Church Street, with Meeting Street and East Bay Streets running parallel; Broad Street, Queen Street, and Tradd Street crossed. Tradd Street was named for Robert Tradd, thought to be the first white child born in Charles Town. King Street became the road into town from the north. Charles Town was connected to the frontier through the old Indian path of the Cherokee. It ran up the so-called Charles Town "Neck" to Monck's Corner, and then along the west side of the Santee River past the Eutaws to Longaree Fort, and then to the lower towns of the Cherokee. Another route was the wagon road, that would develop later, from Charles Town to Philadelphia; this route left the Cherokee Trail at Nelson's Ferry on the Santee River, and proceeded through Camden and the Waxhaws northward. Pack horse trains would soon be bringing 50,000 deerskins annually to Charles Town from the Indian nations and traders.

By 1706, 3,500 people lived in Charles Town in 250 dwellings, and nearly 500 of these citizens were involved in trade. Trade with England, Jamaica, Barbados, and the Leeward Islands flourished, and Charles Town was becoming a major trading center in America. Over 80 ships would clear the harbor each year, including ships with imports of African slaves, and exports of Indian captives, as well as deerskins and naval stores.

Immigrants came from everywhere; from the British West Indies (the Middleton and Lowndes families are examples); the French Huguenots (the Manigault and Legare families); the Dutch (VanderHorst, and later Nathaniel Russell families); the Scotch (Moultrie and Pringle families); the Irish (Rutledges); and Jews (Cohen and Tobias families); and, of course, the English. Many would arrive in "pitiful condition", poor, and seeking to renew their lives and fortunes in Charles Town.

With diversity of backgrounds, Charles Town became a cosmopolitan center, accustomed to interweaving many different viewpoints and cultures. The turmoil of constant threats from wars, disease, fires, and natural disasters, would become even greater catalysts for change, and with change the opportunity for rebuilding. Life was short in Charles Town; mortality was high. These factors would shape this port city over its three centuries.

Religious diversity accompanied ethnic diversity. Religious tolerance flourished, and churches began to be built from Charles Town's early beginning. Boston was founded by Puritans; Philadelphia by Quakers; whereas, Charles Town was founded by traders and businessmen. Religious diversity was tolerated early, if not encouraged, as a way to generate greater immigration and growth for the Lord Proprietors' colony. Anglicans (Methodists), Presbyterians, Huguenots, Baptists, Jews, Quakers, and even non-believers were welcome in Charles Town. By 1710, Anglicans and Presbyterians represented the majority, in about equal numbers, but others were certainly growing. New congregations flourished, and Charles Town was on its way to earning its reputation as the 'Holy City' for all its gorgeous church structures.

The first English church was St. Philip's, part of the Church of England, located on the present site of St. Michael's Church at the corner of Meeting and Broad Streets. Then, the Circular Church of Presbyterians, the French Huguenot Church, and a Baptist church followed. In 1711, construction started on the new St. Philip's Church, where it stands today on Church Street, just north of Queen Street. Its construction was interrupted by a hurricane which ravaged Charles Town in September 1713, in which about 70 persons were drowned, and the storm severely damaged the new church under construction. By early 1721, construction resumed and repairs were underway. Its massive brick edifice with lofty arches and high pillars, was topped by a tower that soared 80 ft. above the Charles Town skyline, and gave comfort as it was sighted by ships approaching the harbor. This grand church stood as a tribute to Charles Town's growing wealth and power.

The streets of Charles Town were teeming with a mixture of merchants, indentured white servants, sailors, planters, fur traders, African and Indian slaves, and prostitutes. The scene was a mix of nationalities, racial and religious groups, and languages, making a cacophony of sights and sounds on its streets. Charles Town became a city of "tippling houses", for the taverns and inns were the social center, providing drinks and entertainment. The city was a seafaring town. By 1720, at the peak of the shipping season in February and March, 500 or more seamen would come ashore.

Boarding houses and rental properties were being built to accommodate sailors, traders, legislators, and planters coming into town. Taverns and public inns sprouted along the waterfront, and onto Church Street, while prostitution, disorder, and public drunkenness grew.

Charles Town soon had the reputation of a free-wheeling city, open to all, including residents, outcasts, and visitors of all types. Free spending sailors and Indian traders would jam these taverns, where they would drink away the nights with beers, cider, rum punches, brandy, and Madeira wine.

In winter 1712, the city suffered through the "worst and longest sickly season" in its history, being ravaged by epidemics of both yellow fever and smallpox. Dr. Francis Le Jau, a missionary, wrote of the terrible conditions plaguing the city; "we have lost a great number of white people and 300 to 400 slaves in the province within four months. The town is deserted. The distemper seizes suddenly; it is like pleurisy…I have used large doses of snake root…with good success".

And, with stout hearts and courage, the survivors would continue their lives.

By 1717, resentment grew against the Lord Proprietors, who had failed to protect the colonists, particularly following the Yemassee Indian War of 1715-1716. Representatives lobbied Parliament for South Carolina to become a British royal colony, rather than a proprietary colony. And, their efforts were successful in 1721.

Trading was the economic life blood of Charles Town. By 1717, the market for deerskins and naval stores reached their peak; that year, nearly 44,000 barrels of tar and pitch were exported from Charles Town. In a few years, however, overproduction of naval stores, and Parliament's removal of its bounty in 1724, led the naval stores industry to collapse.

British merchants succeeded in getting the bounty restored in 1729, but by then another crop was beginning to overshadow the importance of deerskins and naval stores.

Rice was becoming more important. As growing techniques were being mastered, the importation of slave labor allowed more and more land to come under cultivation. By 1722, a little over 1 million acres were under cultivation; in just 20 years, that would double. In 1690, 1,500 slaves were in the area, and by 1710 the number had grown to 4,100 slaves. In the next 10 years, that number tripled, and by 1730, 20,000 slaves were in Charles Town and its neighboring plantations, with slaves outnumbering whites by a 2:1 ratio.

Independent traders like Samuel and Joseph Wragg found a way to break the monopoly on slave trade held by the Royal African Company, and cargoes of African slaves regularly landed. At the same time colonial land policies made possible the formation of large landed plantations for rice production. The so-called 'headright system' permitted one man the capability to acquire large tracts of land. A 'headright' for 50 acres of land could be granted for each slave purchased.

The slave trade required enormous outlays of capital, so the traders used Caribbean or English creditors, and made their profit by auctions of slaves at wharfside to the planters, who paid in rice. The trader or merchant would keep 10% of the rice as commission, and ship the remaining rice to his creditors. From his commission, the merchant paid duty on the slaves imported, as well as paying the wages of the slave ship's crew while they were in port. The duty on slaves was '50 lbs. Carolina' for slaves over 10 years of age; and, '5 lbs. Carolina' for younger slaves. The duty alone provided Charles Town with nearly half of its needed revenues for operation. The merchants assumed the risk for bad debts on their credit extended to the planters, and the planters mortgaged both their land and their slaves to the merchants for the credit.

Easy credit could be a quick road to ruin for some merchants and planters; but, for about 30 merchants of Charles Town, the profits proved to be enormous. Likewise, the Lynches, Horrys, and Alstons to the north, and Heywards, Barnwells, and Elliotts to the south became great rice planting families.

In shallow boats, manned by slaves, rice would come down the Ashley, Cooper, and Wando Rivers, to the wharves in Charles Town. From 1730-1735, the export of rice averaged 40,000 barrels annually. Meanwhile, the market price was rising from 6 shillings/100 pounds, to 10 shillings, with one barrel of rice weighing 420 pounds. Major exporters were also the importers, and English-made fine goods were brought in, as well as wine, sugar, molasses, and rum from the West Indies.

Rum was Charles Town's favorite drink, and about 134,000 gallons were imported in one year alone; but, slaves were the most profitable commodity.

The combination of low cost slave labor and the capability to accumulate large tracts of land allowed rice production to become an economic engine that would drive Charles Town's economy to levels unprecedented.

Even greater fuel would be added when the British Crown bought back the rights of the Lord Proprietors, and made Charles Town a British Crown colony in 1721. This action removed a source of political uncertainty, and laid the groundwork for Charles Town to become a trading center of the British Empire for the next 40 years. A strong market demand for rice in Europe in the 1720's to 1730's would jumpstart Charles Town to become the wealthiest of the American colonies, thereby creating a lavish lifestyle for a handful of its most successful planters and merchants.

Colonial Newspapers

The *South Carolina Gazette* was one of the first newspapers in Charles Town, starting in 1732. It came out every Saturday, until two years later, when its publisher died of yellow fever, as did so many colonists of that time. The newspaper would soon be re-published. By the Revolution, it was being published by Robert Wells, a Loyalist, first from offices on Bay Street, and later at 71 Tradd Street. By then, it was one of three newspapers being published in Charles Town.

Today's *Post and Courier* newspaper can trace its lineage to the *Charleston Courier* published in 1803.

On the verge of unprecedented prosperity, Charles Town in 1734 was a small town, consisting of 500-600 houses, most uncomfortable and of poor construction. Its major problem was care of the poor and sick, a task which fell to each church parish. But, more often than not, the task was too large for the parish officials, and care was far less than adequate.

In 1738, smallpox struck Charles Town, carried from a boat from Guinea. The epidemic spread quickly, to nearly every house, and hardly any family escaped from one or more deaths. The first smallpox inoculation was attempted, and with some success, although the practice was considered highly controversial and caused heated debate. In September, Lt. Governor Bull convened the General Assembly at Ashley Ferry, and passed two laws to prevent the spread of smallpox. One law prevented anyone with the disease from coming within two miles of the city. The second law required each house, or plantation, to place a white flag at its entrance if smallpox were present.

Times were tough in Charles Town, but that was all about to change.

RESTORATION BEGINS ON 29 ½: CHAPTER 6

Marilyn and I were in agreement on what we wanted, and we had our City approvals and permit in hand; so, with first steps complete, we were ready to get restoration started on '29 ½'.

First, planning was needed to select window and door units that would be just right for the conversion of the existing screened porch into a year-round sunroom. We wanted the window units to blend with the existing, original 150-year old windows, and not look "added-on". We were constantly mindful of David Kludt's warning for us to avoid "groovy butchery".

After much research, we found a window manufactured out of wood with the divided panes of glass separated by wood mullions, much like the look of our original windows. A similar construction for a two-door French door unit would be perfect for the new rear entry to the sunroom. The dimensions of these window units were selected to get as much sunlight into our new room as the wall space would permit. We wanted to build a new, landscaped rear garden that would feel like it was simply an extension of space from our sunroom into the outdoors.

Likewise, supplemental heat and air conditioning would be needed in the new sunroom space. A self-contained unit was found with integral heat pump/AC capability that would fit in the wall just under the new window units. The dimensions for the window and door units, and the heat/AC, allowed us to layout the screened porch area.

Now we were finally ready to start the actual restoration work. Getting started is never a pleasant task. Restoration's first step is peeling away all things that must go, before new construction can begin. This is really no fun. It would be a mess. But, 'start' is what is needed, and then sheer determination and grit get the job done.

Our first step was to remove the grass cloth wallpaper from the dining room and living room. You never know what to expect…could be easy, could be impossible. We armed ourselves by renting a steamer; we bought liquid wallpaper remover, and a ratchet roller that literally scrubs wallpaper off the wall. Marilyn and I started early on a Saturday morning. The trick was to get the wallpaper off the walls, without at the same time pulling the centuries-old plaster off its original wood lath and screen base.

The steamer is used to soak the wallpaper, and loosen the glue beneath, but grass cloth does not cooperate because the moisture will not permeate beyond the outer surface easily. After soaking, and with clouds of moisture hanging in the air within the rooms, we found ourselves sweating as much as the wallpaper. Some pieces of wallpaper pulled off the walls easily; others just teased us with their tenacity to cling. After utilizing every possible instrument and scraper, we made headway. Gradually we began to see progress as the old plaster walls, with their cracks and scars, became visible. This was our first weekend, in an exhausting, but rewarding, trek into discovery.

As we headed home, late on a Sunday evening, our muscles and backs knew we had done battle, but the job was complete. A nasty first step was behind us, and self-satisfaction was a reward Marilyn and I shared that evening.

The longest journey begins with a single step, and our first step was complete. We were on our way. Step two was to remove all the old wooden cabinets and nasty countertops in the kitchen. This is just a brute force, dirty job. The old cabinets were the first to go. Brute force is required in demolition, and one must simply plow forward with little regard for dust, debris, and sometimes even flying objects breaking away from their prior security. Fear has no place in demolition!

And so, we proceeded with the nasty job; I would wield the pry bar and hammer; Marilyn became the 'expert' in debris removal, and cleanup. The work is extremely backbreaking and tiring, and only the strongest of partnerships will survive such an endeavor. Marilyn and I have done this before, and know how focused you must stay on getting the task complete. We seem to just get stronger as a partnership, as the challenge gets larger.

A little muscle, and the cabinets pried off the walls, breaking loose chunks of old plaster, which revealed the long-gone construction method of applied plaster over 2" wide rough wood lath strips, with wire mesh attached over the lath. Dust was everywhere, and we were not sure what creature would come out of the walls, now exposed to the outside air for the first time in a century and a half. The smells were old and musty.

One great discovery came from all of this...behind wall cabinets, we saw that built-in shelves had been covered over. These shelves had been built earlier, probably when the kitchen was first added to the original building, to fill the void where an original window had existed. This type of find is a magic discovery in any restoration...you find something unexpected, and then adjust your plans to utilize this new find. One has to be flexible, and Marilyn and I immediately thought this space would be perfect as a great built-in pantry, giving us much needed extra storage space. Plus, it lends a certain charm, when something old can be rediscovered and utilized anew. We thought, we could add louvered doors, and like magic, a pantry would be ours.

After all the hours, amid dust and drudgery, and sometimes narrowly ducking flying bits of construction shrapnel, we carted off the remnants of cabinets, countertops, sink, water heater, etc., etc., to the back courtyard outside, which was fast becoming an out-of-control heap of construction debris. A testimony to our efforts lie in the back courtyard…an awful looking pile of twisted debris, piled higher than the 8-ft. courtyard walls, leaving little room to maneuver our way in and out of the carriage house. What we would do to eliminate this awful mess was a matter for future resolution.

The next challenge was to remove the plaster wall surface, and expose the stud structure at the wall separating the screened porch from the kitchen. This is the wall that we wanted to remove to open the space from the future sunroom to the new kitchen. But, first, we had to go very carefully, because we did not know exactly what structure could be in that wall supporting the 2nd floor bath above. Likewise, unknown plumbing, heat ducts, and electrical were in that wall.

Gradually, and ever so carefully, we made our way knocking plaster away, bit-by-bit. It was just as expected. Very little support for the weight of the 2nd story, if any, was in that wall. The old construction methods were unlike today, in which a building's structure is built from the ground up, utilizing concrete footings, steel, etc. in the ground for a foundation. The old method relied, instead, on the wood framing of the wall itself to hold-up the structure, much like a pair of suspenders holds up a pair of pants.

We needed to invent a better way to support the upper level, because it would not be pleasant to find ourselves at one moment utilizing the bathroom facilities above, and the next moment find ourselves crashing thru the floor to greet our guests waiting in the sunroom below.

After some thought, and consultation with my friend and partner each day at work with CENTEX HOMES, Barry Rummel and I agreed on a solution and approach to our 'weighty' problem. The following weekend we were ready for action. We used a hydraulic jack to lift the second floor, ever so slightly, and with temporary wood bracing, remove all the weight from the partition wall that we wanted to remove. Fraction of inch-by-inch, the jack lifted the corner of the second floor structure. Each infinitesimal movement had to be followed with careful examination, because too much at any one time could crack the stucco exterior wall, and then we would have a major problem.

With care, however, the structure lifted and was un-weighted, and temporary wood bracing installed to hold everything in-place. A wood girder was constructed, and installed at the ceiling, from one end of the room to the other end of the room about 8 feet away. This would work well to keep the 2nd story in-place, and free from future sagging.

Likewise, with the jack available, Barry and I jacked one rear corner of the old screened porch, where it had sagged over the years to an out-of-level condition. Again, temporary bracing would hold the roof structure, until we could complete new framing for the future sunroom. All of this was completed over two weekends of hard work, but we were off to a good start.

Next, we removed the screening and structure of the screened porch. We were careful to save two original, well worn wood columns; the patina of years of coats of paint, and the density of their wood and weight, confirmed that these columns were more than likely original to the structure. It was fascinating to speculate just what these columns might have witnessed as they stood on-guard, holding the roof of this 150-year old home...home to so much humanity. The two columns just had to be saved. They would be perfect for use later, probably as a charming feature to ornament a gazebo that I wanted to design and build as part of the courtyard landscaping project to come. After several long weekends of work, and some late weekday nights, this first part of our demolition task was complete.

With the old screened porch now removed, we could start building our new sunroom. A concrete block sill was built, and mortared onto the old brick work that served as the floor to the original porch. These old bricks, and similar bricks of a narrow walkway to the porch entrance, would have to be preserved. Their markings told us that these bricks were made in kilns on the antebellum plantations surrounding Charleston. The manufacture of bricks was often undertaken on the plantations to utilize the labor pool that would otherwise be idle during months of the year when rice or indigo fields required little attention.

Once the footing system of concrete blocks was in place, Barry and I started framing the wall structure. The French door unit was set, and three sets of window units were installed into the wood framing. Already the new sunroom was taking shape, and we were ready for the next phase of construction.

The next phase of demolition was challenging. The bathroom on the second floor was very out-of-date, and needed major surgery. Our plan was to remove a nasty old cast iron tub, and replace it with a modern shower, and space for a built-in stacked washer/dryer. Removing the cast iron tub required a special solution; it could not be disassembled from the piping and carried down the stairs. First, it was much too heavy; second, it would not fit as we turned the corner of the narrow stairway. Our solution was pretty basic...smash the cast iron tub into pieces that could be carried away!

The following weekend, we had arranged for two macho plumbers to start our re-plumbing...the first step was the cast iron tub. Marilyn and I stood outside gazing to the second floor as Bruce and Robert wailed away with sledge hammers at that old tub. As we peered skyward, all hell seemed to break loose...not only was the noise shattering the neighbors' peaceful morning, but the walls of the house were literally and visibly shaking with each blow. We were concerned that the whole house would come down! There was no way we felt comfortable being that near the tremors of those walls, let alone being inside the house to observe the demolition first hand.

Within what seemed to be an hour of terror, but actually was mere minutes, Bruce appeared in our doorway with a sheepish smile of satisfaction, carrying remnants of that old tub; pieces of cast iron were tossed onto the growing pile of demolition devastation that was accumulating in our rear courtyard. Soon it was over. But, a new problem had to be solved.

The floor of the bathroom was ceramic tile that was cracked, ugly, and not level. The floor was out-of-level by nearly four inches over a 5-6 ft. distance. So, we definitely needed to replace the flooring and level the floor. Also we needed access for the plumbers to run new drain piping down to the new kitchen below on ground level. Our problem was that some years prior, at the time this bathroom structure had been added to the original building, concrete had been poured into the floor joists to serve as a base for the ceramic tile, but at a thickness of nearly six inches.

This concrete dilemma became evident as the cast iron tub was broken away and removed. All types of restoration projects reveal special unknown surprises to the builder...this was just one that we would uncover. The answer again required more sledge hammer work from our demolition gurus, Bruce and Robert. Almost to their glee, furious work began as hammers struck the seemingly unyielding concrete subfloor, but not before Marilyn and I escaped below to observe the ongoing devastation from a safer distance at ground level outside in the courtyard. Again, the walls literally and visibly shook, as the ferocity of the demolition rang out thru the neighborhood.

I watched carefully to see if structural tell-tale cracks would develop in the old stucco exterior walls; but, these walls had withstood blows over the many years…hurricanes, an earthquake, and the thunder of cannon bombarding the city under siege during the 'not so civil' war. After more than an hour of smashing torment, the old girl remained standing and steadfast. Our home had withstood yet another onslaught.

After all was complete, a gaping hole existed under what had been the flooring under the tub, and one could gaze down from our second floor to the entry door area of the soon-to-be sunroom on the ground floor. With that day's work complete, and our home still standing, I kidded Marilyn by sitting on the toilet on the second floor, and peering through the hole in flooring. I called to Marilyn who was sweeping debris at the first floor entry that we could "greet our visitors at the door" first-hand from our perch in the bathroom. We laughed heartily at such a silly thought; but these moments of mirth would serve us well over the long stretches of work that would follow.

You can well understand that one could quickly lose patience, and even sanity, during the course of a difficult project such as this, but a chuckle here and there seems to keep all things in perspective, and get one through the most trying of situations.

Over the next several weeks things went pretty smoothly. The plumbers, Bruce and Robert, ran new water and waste piping, and electricians started their work. One of the biggest challenges for the electricians was bringing our home up to most recent building codes requiring smoke detectors on all floors and within all bedrooms. Wiring had to be 'fished' between walls to key locations thru-out the house, and this required much destruction to the plastered walls. Most of the remaining wiring was checked for safety, and rewired if needed.

Meanwhile, I worked in the evenings after my day job, insulating our sunroom, installing flashing where needed, and covering the walls with wood sheating that would serve as the base for the new stucco treatment on the inside and outside walls of the sunroom. We wanted to stucco these surfaces in a manner that would most closely match the existing old, original stucco-over-brick surfaces, so that our 'restoration' when finished would look as if it had always been there.

TO THE GULF...TO THE GOLF!!: CHAPTER 7

It is important to take a break sometimes, and just get away to freshen mind and body. Marilyn and I decided that this was such a time. So, we planned a brief trip, packed our bags lightly, and jumped in our trusty Honda Accord for a drive to Florida's "gulf coast, for some golf", and relaxation.

We have owned a condominium apartment at the INNISBROOK RESORT & GOLF CLUB, Tarpon Springs, Fla., for some 25+ years. It is about 450 miles from Charleston, SC, that can be reached in about 8+ hours of driving. This is a perfect get away that is pretty accessible, and offers outstanding golf on four different 18-hole courses, all located within a 450-acre compound of breathtaking natural beauty and fine amenities.

Our apartment includes a panorama across five holes of the famous "Copperhead" golf course. The Copperhead course is rated in the top-50 courses in the U.S., and is host to a PGA tour tournament each year. With over 7,200 yards of length, interspersed among towering pine trees and rolling elevations, and with water lurking on many holes, the Copperhead course is a jewel of pristine beauty. Our balcony looks out over the 1st

fairway of Copperhead, and it's a joy to sit back and watch the golfers moving by, and often sputtering to themselves, as they tackle the monster.

We have sometimes visited Innisbrook accompanied by our friends, Barry and Gerri Blake, and Jim and Andrea Lowry. Both couples are 'golf fanatics', like Marilyn and I, so we thoroughly enjoy each other's company, and golf at Innisbrook.

This trip, we were joined by the Lowry's who drove separately from Charleston. My mother and father, Fern and Les Funk, live nearby, just a five-minute drive from our apartment in Innisbrook, so our trips to Innisbrook provide an opportunity to visit with Mom and Dad.

One of the joys of being at Innisbrook is walking around the 450-acre complex, experiencing the beautiful grounds and rolling terrain. Towering, majestic pine trees are everywhere, with shadowy pine straw beds beneath, littered with immense pine cones that have dropped from the boughs stretching high into the blue Florida sky. Wet areas of virgin cypress swamps are interspersed within the finely manicured grounds, providing a home to the bountiful wildlife we watch with keen interest.

A boardwalk bridge provides access to the innermost area of a natural pond and cypress swamp. The 'knees' of the cypress trees protrude above the water's surface...the 'black water' of the cypress swamp displays an endless dance of wildlife. The small, algae-like plant growth is alive with small spurts as oxygen bubbles rise to the surface, letting us know that so much infinitesimal life exists below the surface, that we cannot see.

Through the black waters, magnificent turtles swim effortlessly just below the surface, only occasionally popping their heads above water to feed on some unknowing insect.

Flocks of ducks swim toward us, ready to gather any crumbs of food we may toss their way. Large white egrits ply the pond's edge stalking their next meal, suspended in virtual in-animation, waiting with endless patience for just the right instant to strike-out at their prey.

Overhead, birds of countless varieties sail and glide through the air. Often perching on a branch, mostly for a brief moment, then the creatures dart off again caught up in their very own pattern of life…we can observe and marvel at this pattern we cannot fully understand.

Within the ponds, alligators still thrive. The alligator seems to be a relic of some ancient creature from the past, lying motionless warming in the sun on the pond's bank, simply oblivious to the passage of time, or the other birds and creatures that feed nearby.

Golf amidst this fairy-land of God's creatures, on a warm and sunny blue sky day, is an experience that is hard to duplicate.

This trip is like many others. Each day, Jim Lowry awakens before the rest of us, as he enjoys getting the coffee pots brewing…we need two pots, one for 'decaf' and one for 'high test'. It is a pleasure to awake to the aroma of freshly brewed coffee. All we have to do is stumble out of bed, and then enjoy good morning conversation with our guests…and, our coffee. After a breakfast of fruit, more often than not, picked fresh from the fruit trees which line the golf courses, we watch the morning news and weather on TV. Then, we begin to 'pysch' ourselves for our daily round of golf, generally with a tee-time about mid-day…not a bad way to go!!

Enjoying our passion...GOLF!!

This trip we have four rounds of golf scheduled. Each day, the 'guys' take on the 'girls' in a best-ball grudge match, mostly for 'honor', but certainly for the day's bragging rights. It is good fun, because often the matches are very close. On this trip, after the first three rounds, the 'guys' were leading the cumulative affair, but the 'girls' were still within striking distance. So, it all boiled down to the last day's round.

In fact, as we walked up to the eighteenth green, an undulating and wicked monster of a putting surface, the 'tournament' outcome still hinged on this last hole. Then, from nowhere, Marilyn made an 'impossible' putt from 25-feet away, and the 'girls' celebrated with 'high-fives' in a wild dance, while voicing jocular taunts to Jim and I to the effect that we were 'dead meat'!

But, I had moments earlier knocked a chip shot, miraculously from under a tree with tree limb protruding to interfere with a normal shot, to within 4-5 ft. of the hole. So, we had hope…but my putt was a side hill sliding putt, and no sure thing, and the 'girls' knew it, as they cranked up the pressure. But, first, Jim stood over a 20-foot putt, which had resulted from a good bunker shot out of the sand. As Jim eyed his putt, we could see 'concentration' in his demeanor, because Jim is a superb competitor. You can count upon him when the chips are on the line. Besides, there was no way I wanted to have to make my putt!

Jim provided the drama as he stroked his putt, and the little white sphere began its downhill, sidehill roll toward the hole… but it seemed to stop at rest just on the edge of the cup, and then gravity 'plopped' it into the cup! The 'guys' celebrated with unchecked jubilation, and high-fives, making sure the 'girls' knew what had just occurred. We had just snatched victory out of the jaws of defeat, and tied our match that day with the 'girls'. Now, we could all four celebrate, and reminisce over a great dinner, and camaraderie to follow that evening.

Then, it would be re-pack, and return home the next day. We were all reinvigorated, relaxed, and ready to resume our daily lives in Charleston.

THOUGHTS ON SPRING: CHAPTER 8

The end of February has arrived, and with each passing day, Springtime approaches Charleston as it has for more than three centuries. Today, the temperature reaches the high 70's, a perfect complement to the sunny, clear 'Carolina blue' skies. Spring is the earth's yearly gift to each of us, engendering a rebirth and reawakening in even the most callous of souls, and today in Charleston, the magnificence of the feeling reaches its zenith.

The whirl of activity around downtown's Colonial Lake is evidence that Spring fever has captured many hearts, each person wanting to escape into the sunshine and capture the moment, bathed in Spring's elixir for revitalization. Around the lake's sidewalks, skateboarders defy gravity with their daredevil moves; inline skaters glide by, some effortlessly, others a bit more awkwardly; joggers are everywhere, straining to gulp the sweet, fresh air.

Meanwhile, others are simply out walking, young and old, some by themselves while others chat with their companions. The numerous park benches are just as inviting for some. The feeling is unmistakable. Charleston is alive, and no more vibrant than on this gorgeous early Spring day. In a few months, early May usually, the massive plantings of Oleander bushes, which line the shoreside walkways of Colonial Lake, will burst into bloom giving further promise to the continuation of the color extravaganza throughout the city.

As I walked from lakeside, down Ashley Avenue toward the Battery, my senses went wild. Charleston cannot be more beautiful than in the Spring, with its profusion of flowers. Behind the brick walls, and iron gates, venerable green spaces of gardens are coming alive. Lightly scented Cherokee Rose vines tumble over the walls, under the canopies of giant live oaks that stand guard over centuries old walled-in gardens.

Bradford Pear trees have exploded with fine, white flowers, which are picture-framed in the backgrounds by the stately old homes, standing with such grandeur. Tulip Magnolias are early bloomers, with their "tulip-like" petals of soft lavender and white. Purple Wisteria blossoms, cascading over and softening the sharp spikes atop wrought iron fences, begin to shower the sidewalks with their delicate petals, and their perfume fills the air.

Camellias thrive in the cool Spring air, and are a staple of most gardens. Today the display of the pinks, whites, and reds of the flowering Camellias are at their peaks. Bowers of Lady Banks' Roses, not yet in bloom, crown the walkways of old, salvaged brick. Peering through the iron fences, the lushness of the new green growth is evident. Here and there Greek-inspired statues lend certain serenity to the scene.

When viewed in this manner, Charleston is a city set in a garden, caught between time, both yesterday and today, and pinched geographically by its rivers. As early as the sixteenth century, French explorers wrote, describing a wilderness abloom with cherry laurel, pink dogwood, magnolia, and jasmine.

The first settlers began building houses and planting gardens, right from the start. Houses were built close together, with their porches or piazzas positioned on high to capture what breezes could cool the day, and overlooking long sideyards enclosed by brick walls and entered through wrought iron gates.

Tantalizing garden views from the piazzas were important. Within these enclosed spaces, early Charlestonians reached into their European landscape tradition, and created formal plantings defined by geometric axes and raised planting beds. Later, Charleston gardeners would combine these European influences with plantings from Asia, including azaleas, gingko trees, and camellias. When combined with local flowering vines and trees native to the lowcountry, the lush gardens were created, and have since become a famous landmark for the city. The garden tradition endures. Each garden, now distinctive, reflects the personalities of their owner, some romantic, others formal, and some casual. Whether glimpsed from the street, or savored from within their flowery depths, each suggests a kind of paradise on earth.

Today, it is apparent from the looks and smiles of passersby that, even though Charlestonians have grown up surrounded by these loveliest of gardens, they have not lost their fascination. Residents are out on the streets, some walking their dogs, all basking in the sunshine, and clearly enjoying the freshness of the Spring air and the exquisite explosion of nature's new season. The moment is shared with the countless tourists, cameras in hand, who have come to experience Charleston's genteel, historic beauty.

As I walk the sidewalk along Murray Boulevard, the iron railing alone separates the passerby from craggy rocks ten feet below, which serve as banks for the Ashley River. Peering over the railing, my mind moves to ponder the relentless water slapping against the rocks, retreating, and then coming back again, as it has for so many years. The softened edges of the rocks, worn over time by this unending ritual of lapping water, and the green algae-covered barnacles clinging to the rocks, simply become a reminder of the rich history that these shores have shared.

To the west, the sun is just beginning to set over the James Island Connector bridge, a more recent addition to the Charleston skyline. The sun's beam of light glistens on moving rivulets of water as the Ashley River flows upstream, for the tide is coming in this early evening. Looking down the Ashley to the east I see Charleston harbor, and the silhouette of Fort Sumter seemingly still at guard at the mouth of the Atlantic Ocean not that far away. In the river, several sailboats are catching the gentle breezes of the day. A racing shell plies the waters, as the coxswain calls out the rhythm for the four oarsmen's strokes. The scent of seawater adds to the pleasure of the scene.

My walk resumes, and soon I approach White Point park, just around the corner from the imposing all-white structure of the Sumter Place residences at No. 1 King Street. From its highest stories, the rooftop view of the stately mansions along South Battery Street provides one of Charleston's most picturesque panoramas, so often photographed. The home at 8 South Battery is the only home on the Battery built pre-Revolution c.1768, and later acquired in 1785 by a young Revolutionary officer from Virginia, Col. William Washington, cousin of George Washington.

The house at 26 South Battery was built c.1853 by John Ashe, a wealthy planter, banker, and politician who had inherited the lot in 1828 and $10,000 for use in building the house.

To the west from King Street, along South Battery, the James English house at 49 South Battery was built c.1795 on a lot, which at the time, abutted the seawall along the shore of the Ashley River. The house at 64 South Battery, built c.1772, was home to William Gibbes one of Charleston's wealthiest pre-Revolution merchants, and was designed to be viewed not from the street, but from boats on the Ashley River approaching Mr. Gibbes' impressive 300-foot wharf.   Gibbes would enjoy his home only briefly, because following the British occupation of Charleston in 1780, Gibbes was arrested and sent to St. Augustine, his family evicted, and the house seized to be used as a British army hospital.

After the Revolutionary War, John Harth, a lumber mill owner and planter, purchased a lot next door at 68 South Battery, a lot subdivided from the land holdings of William Gibbes. At the time, Mr. Harth's property was the westernmost lot on what was then called "South Bay Street"; his home was built c.1800, and he operated a lumber mill from water's edge at this property.

About 1848, the city began buying land for a park..."White Point", or "Oyster Point" as it was known from the early days of settlement of Charles Towne, when oyster shells were piled high glistening white in the sunshine along the Ashley River shoreline. A bathing house served as a popular attraction through much of the nineteenth century, as well as serving as a site for forts and batteries during the Civil War. Only much later would the extensive land infill occur which would result in the present Murray Boulevard, site for the gorgeous residences now facing the Ashley River.

WORK CONTINUES ON 29 ½: CHAPTER 9

We turned our attention to the next major restoration task. The kitchen of '29 ½' was totally outdated, and not very functional. We wanted to open up the space, get more sunshine into the room, and make everything more contemporary and functional. The key was removing the wall which separated the previous screen porch, and entry, from the old kitchen on the other side of the wall.   Then we could take advantage of the huge increase in apparent space, and the new brightness that poured into the new open space.

Before our start of restoration, I spent hours working on a scale drawing of the kitchen space, including locations of existing windows and doors. With such a narrow, small space, the task of packaging appliances, new cabinetry, and the water heater (just another obstacle!) proved a major challenge. We wanted to relocate the sink to under the existing window, to provide a wonderful view out to the landscaped future courtyard, a major element of Marilyn's and my vision of what we wanted to accomplish.

Other considerations were: the existing window to the side looking onto our neighbor's rear deck of their home, known by the Charleston locals as '52 Smith Street'; the open entryway into our dining room; and, last but not least importantly, the existence and location of the electrical breaker box (it was certainly impractical to consider relocating this device, so we just had to work around it).

Painstakingly, my numerous drawings and sketches started to yield results. I would make modifications, then review them with Marilyn, utilize her input, and make more changes. Finally, we reached a plan that seemed to work for both of us! With a little luck, and some careful shoe-horning, and problem solving during construction, it just might work.

Work Gets Underway at 29 1/2

The debris pile begins to build.

Framing begins for the new Sunroom, after the old screened porch was demolished.

Windows are added to the new Sunroom.

With the new sunroom framing and new windows set in-place, I had completed insulating the walls, and placing plywood sheeting on the outside walls. A crew arrived, and within two days stucco had been installed on the outside and inside walls of our sunroom. We just stood back from outside in the courtyard, and marveled at the wonderful new visual impact now evident. The excitement is the reward, and the fuel, which drives one forward in such a task.

Next, an installer started work on placing the new all-white cabinets into position. Problems were resolved one-by-one as they cropped up, and decisions were made which provided needed direction for the installer to complete his work. What a difference the new cabinets made, both in the kitchen and upstairs in the master 2nd floor bath, and 3rd floor guest bath. Measurements were then taken for new countertops, and within a week the Corian granite-looking countertops were in-place. Again, the rewarding feeling of accomplishment gave Marilyn and I the energy we needed to keep going, with our vision becoming closer to reality.

A new shower in the 2nd floor master bath was constructed of marble panels, and custom-built marble shower pan to fit the tight space available for the shower. To its side we wanted to reserve space for a new stacked washer/dryer, which was a major "want" of Marilyn's. With cabinets, and shower installed, the plumbers could now complete their work. At the same time, electricians were working hard to solve their own sets of problems, and get everything buttoned back to an operable condition that would be acceptable to the City's building inspectors.

One of the time-consuming jobs, upon which we struggled, was getting the floors ready to accept our new flooring. The out-of-level floor in the master bath required special shimming to get the framing for the shower and compartment for washer/dryer fairly level; then, a complete float of a liquid material was applied to level the floor. In the kitchen, old layers of asbestos backed vinyl had been glued one layer on top of another over the many years. Trying to pry these layers off the concrete base brought my personal frustration to all new levels! What a mess! But at last persistence won out, the debris yielded to our tenacity, and what was left could be leveled off with epoxy filler. The kitchen, and two upper level baths were ready for new vinyl flooring.

The old brick surface in the former screened porch, and now sunroom, proved another matter. The bricks were so charming, and because they probably were constructed in one of Charleston's rice plantations and original to build of the carriage house c. 1850, they just had to be preserved. The problem was that they were simply imbedded in the dirt without any grout. This would not do for a new sunroom living space within our home. The only solution was to dig out the dirt between each brick, on hand and knee, one brick at a time; then, work concrete mortar painstakingly between each crevice on all sides of each brick, until the entire brick floor area in the sunroom was grouted and complete. My back and knees were sore, but pride in the job-completed made every minute of work worthwhile.

But, major tasks cannot be completed without some sort of minor 'disaster', and I was about to encounter just such a self-inflicted flirtation with 'disaster'. I had the idea (poor upon later reflection and hindsight) that the brick surface would look even better if I could make the brick surface glossy with a reflective appearance that I had much admired in magazine photos. I purchased a liquid product from our builder supply store, after standing some time in the aisle studying the instructions and labels on the cans of several alternative products. I found what seemed to fit the application just perfectly, and so, purchased it with great confidence (although lacking in both direct experience, and/or testimony/advice from other trusted users…ah, there is the lesson soon to be re-learned, once again!).

At the carriage house, I followed instructions on the label carefully. The label urged cleaning the bricks thoroughly with an acid wash. This I did, and with some noticeable trepidation. Marilyn, sensing this 'angst', and with a keen grasp of intuition (that, unfortunately for us males, resides more often with our female partners) sensed that something was about to be very wrong. Unfortunately, I drummed up a degree of bravado, and assured her "all would be well". On hands and knees, with mask in place over my mouth and plastic goggles over eyes, to protect me from fumes and possible splatter of the acid wash, I proceeded to scrub and wash each individual brick, one brick at a time. This task complete, and bricks dry, I applied the sticky, syrupy liquid that would hopefully bring the brick surface to its intended glossy luster. Always wanting the result to be even better than hoped, I applied the liquid just as thick as I could to each brick, and walked away basking in the glory of a job well done, as we left the carriage house and the bricks to dry over the evening.

But, alas, upon our return the next day, the brick surface was still tacky and sticky, and could not be walked upon. You have probably already guessed, but for the next several days the bricks became no drier. I had a sticky mess on my hands, much as if maple syrup had been spilled on the entire surface. This simply was not working, and what made matters worse, Marilyn was showing no reluctance in pointing out this 'disaster' to me. I completely lost it in frustration, and Marilyn was left to bail me out. She took the bull by the horns, decided this mess would never dry, and the only answer was to clean up the mess.

During the day, as I worked my day job, Marilyn worked ferociously on hand and knee scrubbing the sticky mess off each brick and the mortar grout between. As I came home that evening, she presented me with the problem solved...what a life savior she is!! To this day, we will never forget our agony, and through repeated chuckles we have had telling this story to friends, we now cherish our beautiful, charming brick floor even more.

CHARLES TOWN...COLONIAL FIELDS OF GOLD: CHAPTER 10

In addition to rice, indigo became an important influence on life in Charles Town. By 1740, rice production had enjoyed decades of doubling and tripling in quantities exported; but, in the decade of the 1740's, overproduction and shipping disruptions (resulting in higher costs) from the King George's War in Europe, sent the market price for rice tumbling downward by 70%. The amount of rice shipped from Charles Town dropped in half by the end of the decade.

These interim hard times, led the planters to experiment with raising indigo. The 1700's saw clothing died the color blue become the fashion rage of French nobility, and soon the English had to have it too. The indigo plant was the source for the blue die, and as demand in Europe soared, the English placed a bounty on it in 1748 to encourage attempts at growing indigo in the colonies. Attempts at growing indigo in the Carolinas were unsuccessful, until a woman named Eliza Lucas gave it a try.

Eliza managed operations at the Wappoo Plantation, one of three plantations owned by her family. The first planting of indigo fell victim to frost, the second to worms, and the third to sabotage by a hired foreman sent from Antigua by her father to help. But persistence paid off. As most of the plants went to seed, she also distributed the seeds to other nearby planters, such as Charles Pinckney, and soon production of indigo became widespread, supplementing rice production.

Charles Pinckney

Charles Pinckney's life, and its irony, exemplified the planter elite. Most everyone in Charles Town knew of his wealth; his seven plantations, his nearly 2,000 slaves, and his immense annual income exceeding $80,000. His was a lifestyle to be envied. His Snee Farm estate was luxurious, located just up the Wando River from Charles Town, on the site of the present Snee Farm golf club in what is now the city of Mt. Pleasant. Wine cellars, artificial lakes and ponds for fishing, fountains, and gardens all attested to his life of opulence.

His magnificent town home in downtown Charles Town was complete with elegant furnishings, paintings from the best artists in Europe, and a library of 20,000 books. The irony was that his life was not all that glorious.

He was deep in debt, and often missed payments to his creditors, and scandal surrounded him on occasion concerning his misuse of public funds. His personal life was a matter reported as local gossip of the day by the newspapers. After his first wife died, he married Eliza Lucas, but numerous affairs with other women were widely known. High levels of personal vanity and political ambition led many to despise him. Some in his family would not speak to him. And, despite the paradoxes, he was an example of gentility, wealth, education, and political influence, all attributes that characterized the Southern planter way of life.

Yet, despite much of life's advantages, he would succumb to malaria in 1758, like so many mere mortals. The planter way of life was held in the South to be superior to that of the industrial North, because it conserved and perpetuated the nobility of the individual, much as in the English nobility, which the Southern planter sought to emulate.

By the 1740's indigo had become a viable crop which could be grown on the high lands behind the lower level rice fields. By 1750, 60,000 pounds of indigo left Charles Town; by 1775, that amount would grow to 1,000,000 pounds. Indigo and rice production complemented each other nicely. As neither could be grown in England, the British mercantile system craved shipments of these crops to Europe. Rice could supplement European diets, and indigo was needed in the British textile industry.

With both rice and indigo in demand, the Charles Town planters flourished and became important links to the British economy. The planters grew the crops; but, the Charles Town merchants thrived on transport of these two crops as well.

The vast network of rivers, predominately the Cooper, Wando, Ashley, Stono, and Santee Rivers, made transport of these crops viable from the plantations to the port at Charles Town.

For a century, and until the railroad, these river systems would be the cog that kept the lucrative machine moving. Imagine the scene in the port of Charles Town in those days...as many as 100 sailing ships could be at anchor at one time, with a montage of smaller vessels passing by, running the gamut from plantation barges bulging with barrels of rice or indigo and black field hands rowing, to Native Americans or white trappers paddling their canoes laden with deerskins. It must have been an awe-inspiring sight.

Life in the Rice Fields

The plantations, and the rice fields, were situated on the fertile acres of the river deltas. The rice fields were at the edge of the rivers or large streams, each field relying upon the nearby water source to flood the field when needed, and each field constructed independent from other adjacent fields. Banks of earth, 3-5 ft. high and 7-10 ft. wide, separated each field from its adjacent field. The earth banks, ditches, and drains for each field were maintained by hand by slaves wielding hoes, often while wading and working in chest-high water, early in the Spring.

The tidal rivers and streams would flow new water into the fields with high tide, and conversely, drain the fields at low tide. Because rice does not grow well in salt water, the plantations and their fields were located upriver, beyond the so-called "salt point" of the tidal rivers and streams, so that the salty water from the ocean could not reach the rice crops. Fast flowing rivers like the Santee and Waccamaw were ideal because the brackish water was kept nearer the ocean; slower flowing rivers, like the Cooper and Ashley, simply required the rice fields to be further upriver.

Nature often wreaked havoc on the rice crops. Too little rain early in the growing season could stunt growth, while too much rain could delay the harvest or cause mold or decay to the plants. Hurricane season was a threat from June thru November. Alligators, snakes, moles, and rats also destroyed the fragile plants, and field hands were often given quotas of rats to be killed, with the rats often being eaten by the slaves after the rats were properly prepared and cooked.

Worms and grubs could also devastate a field, as well as great flocks of birds, like blackbirds and crows, who could darken the skies with their great numbers as they circled the fields overhead. But, the worst of all was the small bobolink, called "Rice Birds", who arrived in droves in May, so dense in their numbers that it was reported that large shadows would be cast on the fields beneath.

After harvest and during winter, the fields would be plowed under to loosen the soil, and allow the fields to be leveled perfectly so that water would not pool in low areas, because this pooling would cause the rice to grow unevenly, or even rot.

Seed would either be purchased each year, or prepared on the plantation. In early April, field hands constructed seed trenches, in rows about one foot apart. The seed, meanwhile, was being pressed into balls of wet clay, and allowed to dry. Innovatively, the clay seed balls could be placed in the seed trenches, without the need to cover the seed with soil. In this way, when the field was flooded, the seeds would not float to the surface and wash away.

After the seed balls were placed in the trenches, the field would immediately be flooded, and kept flooded by lowering a weir in a dam, until the seeds germinated within 3 days to two weeks, depending upon the weather.

The flooded fields also eliminated weeds from competing with the seeds, and choking out the fields.   After germination, the field would be drained.

By late Summer, the new rice plants would grow to about 15 inches in height, and their stalks would be sturdy enough to re-flood the field, so that the standing water would support the fragile stalks until harvest.   The field would then be drained again, several days before harvest. Harvest would start in late August, lasting 5-7 weeks, as all available manpower, both men and women, would be pressed to work grueling days in the sweltering heat and humidity of summer's worst time.   Work would start at dawn, and last late into night, often under torch lights to extend the working hours.

The rice stalks were cut with sickles, called "rice hooks", and the grain laid to dry for several days, upon the stubs of the stalks still in the ground. The dried and harvested rice stalks were then tied into sheaves, and stacked high in piles.   The harvested sheaves were then moved from the fields to the threshing location on mule-drawn carts, or flat bottom boats called "rice flats".   The mules were sometimes shod with devices similar to snow shoes, to help them traverse the often muddy fields, without bogging down.

Rice was milled at the plantation, by hand, using wooden mortars and pestles fashioned on the plantation by coopers, until the 1850's when steam powered threshers would become available. After milling, the rice was loaded into wooden barrels, again made on the plantation. Each barrel would hold about 600 pounds of rice. The rice was then ready to be transported down the tidal waterway system, to the port in Charleston, for export to world markets. The boats would depart when tides were going out to carry the boats to Charles Town; then return to the plantation when tides came in to help them.

The wealthy plantation "planter" oversaw the business operation of his plantation (often several plantations), but seldom actually directly supervised the labor. The rice culture depended upon slave labor, and the planter relied upon an overseer, or "slave driver" as he was called, and the field hands and household staff to run the plantation day-by-day. A social hierarchy existed among the slaves, valued by their age, sex, skiil, and productive capacity. The young, skilled (blacksmiths or coopers), and healthy were valued most highly.

The plantation operated as its own self-sufficient little kingdom, producing not only the cash crops, but enough food to feed the families, including as many as 300 slaves. Also, the planter would transport food and milk from the plantation to his city home to feed his family and staff while in the city.

In addition to food and supplies grown on the plantation, seafood was obtained easily from nearby sea and fresh water. Everyone on the plantation could enjoy sea trout, whiting, catfish, bass, clams, stone crabs, oysters, and shrimp. Also, fowl were raised on the plantation, including chickens, turkeys, guinea hens, and geese. In addition, wild fowl were attracted by the rice fields, including duck, wild turkey, partridge, doves, and "rice birds" or bobolinks which were considered a delicacy. Deer were usually plentiful in the pine and hardwood forests surrounding the rice fields.

Rice was also consumed in great quantities on the plantations, often being eaten 2-3 times each day, as an accompaniment or main course to each meal. Corn was grown, and converted into meal, grits, and flour. Irish potatoes, sweet potatoes, and yams were used in soups, puddings, or other delicious recipes. Jams, jellies, tarts, and pies were made from a wide variety of fruits and nuts that were abundant. All-in-all, everyone ate well on the plantation.

But, life, for the field hands especially, meant backbreaking labor, too often performed in the intense heat and humidity of summer, in muddy fields, sometimes in chest-high water, with critters a threat, and swarming horseflies and mosquitoes, which made the fields deadly places to toil.

In those days, no one knew the reason for the "sickly season" in Summer and Fall; only more recently, was it known that the mosquito was the primary carrier of malaria and yellow fever, and the water of the rice fields, in the breeding season, made the situation an ideal incubator for mosquitoes, until the first heavy frost killed them. The coming of the "sickly season" signaled the annual migration from the plantation by the wealthy planter, his family, and selected fortunate household staff; but, the majority of the slaves had only to hope for the best, as they were left behind to tend to the plantation, until the owner and his entourage returned again after first frost. And, the cycle would begin again.

With favorable geography, a natural transport system, and free slave labor, the strong market demand propelled both the planters and merchants to become rich and powerful. Charles Town became a trading center of the British Empire, and a crossroads of trade, during the golden age of sailing vessels that would last 100 years.

Its port was on the path of sailing vessels plying the trade winds from the West Indies and Barbados, and onto England and northern Europe. Then the ships would return after exchanging their goods for the finest commodities only available in England or Europe. Charles Town's population had grown to 6,800 residents by mid-century, and was the 4th largest city in the colonies, following only Boston, Philadelphia, and New York.

By 1740, eight immense wharves stretched far out into the Cooper River, serving up to 500 ships each year, and many smaller vessels. After the hurricane season, in the prime shipping period from November thru March, up to 100 vessels could be seen at one time riding at anchor in the harbor. Imagine looking into the harbor and seeing the glorious masts of the large sailing ships, bobbing at anchor in the harbor. Traffic around the wharves, warehouses, and markets bustled with humanity,

The town's growth pushed its boundaries. The walls and fortifications around the original 'walled city' were gone, as the city expanded and spread north to the present Market Street. New streets were built, and Queen, Broad, and Tradd Streets were extended westward to the marshes along the Ashley River. In the last ten years, Charles Town had nearly doubled its size to 150 acres. Property values soared by five-fold. Hundreds of new private and public structures were built.

But, all was not pretty. The streets became muddy quagmires, littered with the smelly testament to the horses, mules, dogs, and cattle that plied these busy thoroughfares. Adding to the stench was the fat discarded by the candlemakers, as well as remnants cast outside the butcher shops. Sanitation was unknown at the time.

And, as the merchants acquired wealth, they too followed the 18th century goal of becoming landed gentry, and invested their new wealth in land, and likewise became planters themselves. The early Charles Town traders were self-made men who worked hard to build their fortunes...men like Isaac Mazyck, a Huguenot; Gabriel Manigault; Joseph and Samuel Wragg; Arthur Middleton; and, Andrew Rutledge. The profits from trade went to buy land, and slaves to work the land. The slave trade flourished. Importation of slaves soared, in lock-step with the rising prosperity.

More than 40% of the blacks coming to North America as slaves passed thru Charles Town, and Sullivan's Island where they were quarantined. History has unfortunately dubbed Sullivan's Island "the Ellis Island of black Americans". By 1730, blacks would outnumber whites by a 2:1 margin.

The distinction between planters and merchants became more obscure through marriages of the affluent, as merchant and planter families were joined. The great merchants became planters, and vast rural plantations sprung along the river waterways, providing transportation to the port in Charles Town. The social model was the landed English country gentleman.

Groups serving the planters and merchants also benefited. Lawyers, shipbuilders, retailers, wholesalers, artisans, and craftsmen prospered.

Lawyers secured the credit needed for business, and were in abundance in Charles Town as this is where the courts were. Shipbuilding businesses were located near the harbor. Various trades were needed to support port activity, such as coopers, ropemakers, carpenters, bricklayers, cabinet makers, blacksmiths, painters, shoemakers, and tailors.

These artisans would start one-man businesses plying their trades, but often with success, would add apprentices and possibly slaves. Some would grow as entrepreneurs themselves or even become merchants themselves. White indentured servants would work elbow to elbow with black slaves as apprentices to their skilled artisans.

A diverse array of retail shops sprang up along Bay and Broad Streets. Prices were high, but if you had money or credit, Charles Town became "the place" to shop, with its reputation reaching all through the colonies. It became the wealthiest and most cosmopolitan city in the colonies. The latest fashions could be found in tailorshops on Broad Street. In January 1750, Benjamin Race advertised himself as a "tailor from London, giving notice to all gentlemen and others" that "they may depend on having their work done, after the newest and best fashions, and at reasonable prices"; but, the prices were high, yet people had money. Trowell's stores on Eliott and Tradd Streets advertised, "Gentlemen's Morning Gowns, Ladies Velvet Riding Caps, and Perriwigs".

Silversmiths and jewelers thrived. On lower Tradd Street, shops sold cider, rum, and sugar. On Elliott Street you could buy wine, rum, and lime juice.

The 'Pink House' c. 1712

An example of the city's early taverns and ale houses still stands at 17 Chalmers Street (formerly Chalmers Alley)..

The sailors and common laborers spent their time in the taverns and brothels that sprang up on Church and Tradd Streets. One surviving ale house from this period is the so-called "Pink House", built c.1712 of pink Bermuda stone with its distinctive tiled gambrel roof, it still stands at 17 Chalmers Street (or Chalmers Alley in those days), a sole testament to the bawdy colonial district within the bustling city. So-called "tippling houses" numbered over 100 in the city, with nearly half operated by women.

In January 1742, the *South Carolina Gazette* newspaper reported that "within the last six months, there has been imported here 1,219 hogheads, 188 tierces, and 58 barrels of rum, most of it lately". (A hogshead was a large cask or barrel containing from 63 to 140 gallons, while a tierce held 43 gallons, and a barrel probably 10-20 gallons.) Rum would flow as the rowdy crowds would pass idle time, and meals were served of salted fish, wild game, and rice puddings, while entertainment included cockfights and raffles.

The newspaper reported on an April day in 1735, that several "gentlemen" from the Christ Church parish met several "gentlemen" from Port Royal in a contest pitting their fighting roosters from one parish against the other parish. It was reported that in eight "battles" the Port Royal cocks won seven of eight contests. High stakes betting accompanied these contests, and it was reported "a considerable amount of money was won and lost" that day.

Public entertainment included occasional parades and bands which would march down Bay Street. Bonfires and candles would illuminate the streets for the revelers.

The more respectable clientele frequented taverns which catered to the planters, merchants, and artisans. Charles Shepherd's tavern located at the northeast corner of Church and Broad Streets became very popular. Meeting rooms upstairs would be used by the powerbrokers of the city to discuss political matters, or plot strategy, or simply just trade gossip; the so-called "long room" would even be used to launch the city's first theatrical production. Gentlemen's clubs would meet regularly at the other numerous taverns.

With immense fortunes being accumulated, the planters built spectacular houses in the city, many still standing, which allowed them and their families to flee their plantations during the season when the threat of yellow fever, malaria, and smallpox were greatest, escape the stifling heat of summer for the cooler breezes off the ocean, and to enjoy the cosmopolitan advantages of the good life in the city.

Disease's Deadly Scourge

Disease had been a deadly scourge for years. One of the worst of the "sickly seasons" occurred in 1712, with nearly ¼ of the population dying before its ravage ended. An Anglican minister wrote in 1715 about the decline in his church's members due to dreadful disease; he said, death seems to be in "constant attendance on God's alter".

A so-called "pest house" was established on Sullivan's Island, where patients were quarantined under penalty of fine or whipping until they were released by a newly appointed health commissioner. Slave carrying ships could not enter the port until the slaves were held in the Sullivan's Island pest house in quarantine for ten days. Even so, an epidemic of yellow fever struck in 1728, and again in 1732 and 1739.

During the epidemic of 1728, reports were that corpses were "so offensive and infectious" that even relatives refused to bury them, and food supplies into the city from the plantations were stopped for fear of spreading the disease.

In July 1732, the city was in the midst of a yellow fever epidemic. Many left the city. Business came to a halt. Funerals kept the bells of churches ringing constantly, depressing the city. Eventually, the city prohibited ringing the bells. By September, with cooler weather the epidemic ended, but not before 7% of the city's population was lost.

An article in the **South Carolina Gazette** newspaper suggested that citizens avoid coming into contact with those infected with smallpox. The newspaper suggested that citizens prepare themselves to fight the distemper "by vomiting, bleeding, or purging, and above all by keeping themselves in a temperate way of living".

Malaria and yellow fever were constantly present; but, it would be many years before medicine attributed spread of the disease to the mosquito, so prevalent near the marshy lowlands and rice fields on the plantations. By an ironic twist, however, immunity developed for those who were exposed to the disease but survived. As most families had been exposed over the years, the immunity spread through the families of longtime residents, and the threat of yellow fever diminished. But no such shield existed for the deadly smallpox.

In 1738, a cargo of slaves arrived by ship from Guinea, some infected with smallpox, and the epidemic spread like a raging fire. A Reverend Whitefield wrote at the time that the smallpox "spread so extensively that there were not a sufficient number of persons in health to attend to the sick, and many persons perished from neglect and want". In 1759 an even more deadly epidemic struck. The fear of disease and infection was so intense among the citizens, that rigorous quarantine regulations were developed over the years.

Smallpox ravaged Charles Town again in 1760, and again in 1762.

In January 1760, the newspaper reported the first incidence of smallpox in the city, at the home of Mr. Duvall, located at White Point; the newspaper went on to speculate the distemper was introduced by a boy brought from the pest house on Sullivan's Island before the "danger of communicating the infection was over"; with no other cases reported, and since White Point had been deserted of inhabitants, the newspaper reported that city officials hoped the disease could be prevented from spreading; but, such was not the case, and epidemic swept the city.

In March 1760, Eliza Lucas Pinckney wrote to one of her children how "a great cloud seems at present to hang over this province...a violent kind of smallpox rages in Charles Town that almost puts a stop to all business." At the same time, Robert Pringle wrote in his family bible that members of his family had just been inoculated, except himself, and later a number of his slaves were inoculated; all survived the inoculations, except for two female slaves.

The wealthy could escape the "sickly season" by trips back and forth from the city, or by trips to northern retreats, such as Newport, R.I.; families of the Mottes, Izards, Rutledges, and Middletons would return year after year to Newport. Meanwhile, those who could not afford travel, were left to battle the epidemics. The poor sought medical care and food from St. Philip's Church. Despite best precautions, Charles Town became known thru the colonies as the "sickly city".

Migration to and from the plantations, and back and forth by the seasons to their great houses in the city, became a ritual to the planters and their families.

The family would come to the plantation a month or so before Christmas, just after the first frost "had killed the fever". Christmas would become a year-end celebration, at its best in the country. Come January, many would pack up again and depart for the "gay season" in Charles Town. Family memories were recorded of the ritual of packing, unpacking, and riding for miles through the pine, live oak, cypress, and magnolia forests.

Imagine the thoughts of the children as they ride in their carriage, along pathways draped with overhanging magnificent live oak trees…it is a haunting, eerie feeling in the morning, with the fog not yet lifted, its silvery tendrils of mist rising from the black water swamps at trees edge, and mingling with the gray threads of Spanish moss dangling from the tree limbs, in a ghostly splendor, waving slowly in the gentle wind. The carriage passes a deserted graveyard, with its worn headstones rising into the morning mist. Suddenly, a bird cries out from the forest, and the children's fear reaches a crescendo; like all families on similar trips, they probably start repeatedly asking the same old question of their parents, "when are we going to get there??"

Spanish Moss

As an aside, so-called "Spanish Moss" is a mysterious plant that speaks of 'the South' like no other image. Pictures in our minds of Spanish Moss dangling from great live oak trees are easily conjured. But, the plant isn't really moss after all. It is a botanical relative of the pineapple, if you can believe that surprise. Spanish Moss, sometimes referred to as "tree hair", Spanish beard", or "graybeard", blooms and produces a seed pod.

Yellow-green flowers have petals about 3/8" long. The blossoms appear from April to July, when seed pods pop open to deposit seeds in the wind, finding homes in the crannies of live oak's rough textured bark. Spanish Moss feeds and drinks water from the air; it is not a parasite feeding on the trees. Although weighing almost nothing, this plant can absorb nearly ten times its weight in water from the air. The greener the plant, the more water it holds.

The Spanish Moss is also home to bugs and spiders, as well as an occasional bat. Often Spanish Moss was used in colonial times to stuff furniture, mattresses, and pillows. Tradition has it that the saying used when children went to sleep, "don't let the bed bugs bite", sprang from the bugs and spiders that could have remained lodged in the Spanish Moss stuffing the bed's mattress.

Birds carry bits of the moss to build their nests. So, the plant not only adds to the "southern mystique", but has its own role in the forest ecology.

The planter families could also travel by boat along the tidal rivers leading into the cities.   Boats could be used often, because when tides flowed inland one could time their return to the plantation, and when tides flowed out the trip could be made into the city.   For many, the family might return to the country in February or March, where the children could stay until May or June.   In between, the men might leave the women and children for trips to the city for business or political purpose.

With the rainy season in late Spring came the mosquitoes, and the "fever season", and the ritual trek to the city, where the family would stay until first frost, when the cycle would start again.

The "gay season" in Charles Town started with the arrival of the planters and their families in late January and lasted until Spring. Theatre, music, dance, politics, and good food were sought after elements of the social experience. The planters and successful merchants, always trying to emulate the British aristocracy, developed their own aristocracy in Charles Town, and soon their lavish lifestyle found no match anywhere in colonial America.   The barons were the elite and wielded immense power, and Charles Town was the center of their society.

Society balls, concerts, outdoor musical programs at the Orange Gardens, and the theatre season flourished during winter months. The St. Cecilia Ball, and the Jockey Club Ball which was dubbed the "most splendid of the season" became ritual "must attend" events.   Prominent families would feel obligated to give at least one lavish dance party in the season. A family might send their young 13 or 14 year old daughters to a boarding school in the city to be educated properly, and grow with refinement into a "proper lady", who could then take her place within Charles Town's society.

Theatre in Charles Town

The first theater started in the city on a Friday evening in January 1735, as the play "The Orphan" was performed in the upstairs so-called 'long room' of Shepherd's Tavern at the corner of Church and Broad Street. Soon crowded performances were a regular event for those who could afford a ticket for 40 shillings. A clamor arose for a permanent theater building, and construction started on Queen Street, just down the street from St. Philip's Church and around the corner from the Huguenot Church.

Queen Street had just been renamed from Dock Street, and out of habit the clientele dubbed it the "Dock Street Theater". The comedy play "The Recruiting Officer" opened the first season in 1736, with gentlemen and their ladies in box seats overhead, and lesser price ticket holders or servants below in the pit or on benches. Since the first plays were often risqué, the ladies frequently wore masks to conceal their blushes.

Society loved its music, dancing, and theater. The best musicians and actors were brought to Charles Town, even from Europe. The city became the "place to be" for theater in the colonies. This first theater building was destroyed in the Great Fire of 1740, to be rebuilt again some 200+ years later, in virtually the same location, and named again "Dock Street Theater". Today, the Dock Street Theatre continues the play-going tradition in the city.

Horse racing too became a regular social event, taking place in February. Not only the genteel planters and merchants and their families attended, but shopkeepers, artisans, and common folk eagerly attended as well. The race course was located to the north of the city, in what is now the location of Hampton Park and the Citadel military school. Throngs would pack the roadway to the race course, with people walking, and processions of magnificent carriages drawn by teams of two or four well groomed horses. The grandstand would be filled, offering the ladies and gentlemen the opportunity to show off their latest fashions.

By the mid-1700's, wigs had gone out of fashion, except for the elderly men. Hair was worn tied back with a ribbon, to provide much more comfort in the warmth of summers, and not many bothered to have it powdered these days. Excitement, anticipation, and merriment filled the air, as large sums were being wagered on each horse race. The races would last for three to four days, being viewed as the sporting event of the year. After the day at the races, the theatre, balls, and parties would occupy the elite for the evenings.

Cockfighting, though controversial even then, was frequented by those seeking to wager a few shillings. Hunting was a widely accepted gentlemen's sport, with organized hunting clubs, and the sounds of the hounds, horns, and horses echoing through the countryside during fox or deer hunts.

Families were important in the fabric of society and culture of Charles Town, and intermarriages would play an important role in shaping that society. First, alliances would occur only among the families of business partners or nearby planters. But, soon a melding of families took place, among the planters and merchants, drawn by the desirable social lifestyle of the city. An aristocracy of sorts was formed among the city's powerful families, much as in London with the English aristocracy. The families used the English gentry as their model, and remained more attached to the 'Mother Country' than their counterparts in the northern colonies.

The Arthur Middleton family is an example of how the aristocratic families became interrelated. The first Arthur Middleton was a merchant who arrived in Charles Town in 1679 from Barbados. By the Revolution, a descendant, also named Arthur, would sign the Declaration of Independence; the family tree would include a father, both grandfathers, a brother, father-in-law, and six brothers-in-law, each of whom had served important positions of influence as members of legislature. The family could claim relationships to at least 16 prominent families via marriage, including families Bull, Drayton, Manigault, and Rutledge, as well as British aristocratic families.

AN AFFLUENT COLONIAL CITY: CHAPTER 11

Charles Town on the eve of the Revolution flourished like no other city in the colonies. By the end of the colonial period, most of the city's prominent leaders owned plantations, including its lawyers and other professionals, and its merchants; and, every planter knew his economic well being depended on slave labor and the export trade.

It was a powerful center of wealth, trade, law, schooling, and culture, and an important gateway to Europe for the British. Trade out of colonial Charles Town was larger than New York City's, and its cost of living was higher. Port records showed that 360 vessels cleared the city's docks in 1765, with 100,000 barrels of rice going to 44 different ports of destination. By 1770, exports of indigo totaled 935,000 lbs., and rice export was a record 137,400 barrels (36,000 tons). All of this was grown on fewer than 2,000 plantations, with about 110,000 acres under cultivation, operated by about 37,000 "full hands" slaves in the fields, while another 38,000 slaves attended to household duties on the plantations or cared for the city houses of the planters.

The arithmetic means that one slave existed in the field for 3 acres of rice, or 2 acres of indigo. One acre of land under cultivation would yield 1,000 lbs. of rice, or 50 lbs. of indigo. It has been estimated that nearly 3,000 wagons annually would make their way onto what is now King Street with their goods.

Colonial Charles Town was the richest society in the colonies. At the time, 9 out of 10 of the wealthiest men in the colonies claimed Charles Town as their home, including Gabriel Manigault and Henry Laurens, two of the wealthiest. The wealthy planters, merchants, and professionals comprised just 20% of the city's residents, but controlled 75% of the city's wealth. This meant that most of the city's residents were not rich; and in fact, beggars and the poor overran the streets, giving stark contrast to the unparalleled opulence of the city's small, but prominent, band of elite families. A 'Poor House' was completed in 1771 at the corner of Mazyck Street (now Logan Street) and Magazine Street, to provide shelter for the indigent.

It is estimated that by 1750, the city's elite were comprised of 2,000 planters, 500 artisans, and 400 merchants.

A study has estimated that the currency of the day (pound sterling) would represent $50-$60 dollars U.S. today. The most successful planters could earn 2,500-3,000 pounds sterling each year, while professional physicians and attorneys earned 250-500 pounds sterling, and artisans could earn 100-150 pounds sterling.

On this basis, financial records of one of the entrepreneurial elite, Rawlins Lowndes, are interesting; he reported annual earnings of 1,500 pounds sterling from rice crops, 3,000 pounds sterling from property rentals in the city, and 8,000 pounds sterling from interest earned on loans he extended. This would place his income for the year at $75-90,000 from his rice production, but an additional nearly ten times that amount resulted from property holdings and personal loans.

Many public buildings were built during this time, which reflected the city's prosperity, and their designs were influenced by similar great edifices in England. St. Phillip's Church had been built on Church Street in the period from 1711-1723. An engraving from the **London Magazine** (1735) shows a magnificent edifice, reflecting English Baroque church design, including a triple Tuscan portico. The first congregation held services at the new St. Phillip's on Easter Sunday, 1723, and members

St. Philip's Church looking up Church Street.

carried their own chairs because the new sanctuary was not yet furnished. The father of the Methodist faith, John Wesley, preached there in 1737; George Whitefield, an evangelist who defied the Church of England in open-air meetings in Charles Town, was defrocked at St. Phillip's in 1740; and, years later, in 1791, George Washington worshiped there during his visit to Charles Town. The previous church had been built of cypress in 1682, on the exact site of today's St. Michael's Church.

St. Michael's Church, at the corner of Broad and Meeting Streets, was built over ten years to resemble St. Martin's in the Fields in London, and its bells were cast in England.

St. Michael's Church steeple...a target for British canons in the Revolution, and Federal gunners during the Civil War.

View up Broad Street toward the 'Four Corners of Law'.

The edifice was completed in 1761, with its steeple and bells and clock, topped by a gilded ball and weathervane, soaring 185 feet into the sky over the city's skyline. St. Michael's Church stands as an architectural monument to colonial times in Charles Town. Its visage could be seen from far offshore, an imposing view that would become a city landmark to this day. Over three centuries, its steeple would serve as lookout post during wars, and beacon for ships entering the harbor; its bells would toll for fires, curfews, funerals, and weddings; and, its bells would toll in celebration, time and again, as the city celebrated, first the new nation's independence, then the ends of enemy occupation, in both the Revolutionary War and later the Civil War.

The colonial Statehouse was built in the early 1750's, the "Exchange or Custom House" building in the late 1760's and early 1770's, each resembling their counterparts in London, Bristol, and Liverpool. No buildings in colonial America, even Philadelphia's Town Hall or Boston's Faneuil Hall, could surpass their grandeur.

Today's residents of the area can tour these buildings in the off-month of January with special passes. Marilyn and I have taken advantage over the past several years to purchase 'Tourist in Your Town' passbooks, which allow free access to these buildings, as well as plantations, historic mansion homes, Fort Sumter, and other tourist attractions in the area. The price for the passbooks is modest, so the program provides a great opportunity for locals to know their area even better.

Exchange Building

The "old Exchange Building" stands today, restored to the grand appearance it enjoyed when it was completed in 1771. It is exciting to tour that magnificent building today, and imagine what it was like in colonial times. Marilyn and I decided to do just that on a sunny, nippy cool day in January, as we walked for blocks along Broad Street, looking to the street's end at East Bay Street. The Exchange Building's striking Palladian architecture dominates the view, much as it dominated the view from the harbor in colonial times.

At that time, as Charles Town's bristling shipping activity grew, a larger and more impressive exchange and custom house was needed. Each merchant ship entering the harbor had to send a representative to the custom house to pay required duties. So, construction began in 1767 on the location of the original custom house on the "Half-Moon Battery", a semicircular fortification built in 1704, which projected out overlooking the harbor, above the seawall that was part of the original walled-city.

Today, you can visit the murky cellar area, and visualize the "Provost Dungeon" on the spot which was used to jail the pirate Stede Bonnet the 'Gentleman Pirate' and his crew, after their capture by Colonel William Rhett in 1718, prior to their hanging just a few blocks down Meeting Street at White Point Gardens.

The new Exchange Building faced toward the harbor, but over the centuries, the land has been filled, so that today the harbor is two blocks away; nonetheless, what was the rear of the building, still looks imposing today as it looks westward down Broad Street. As Marilyn and I entered the lobby area, our feet touched the very purbeck stone floor that the builders imported from England in their search for the finest materials. The exterior was built of Portland stone imported from England. The second story contained the city and custom offices, and the Great Hall, which would play such a prominent role in the upcoming Revolution, and a room that would later host ex-President Washington's gala receptions as he visited the city for a week in 1791. In this room, two banquets, a concert, and ball would be held in his honor.

Here in the damp, dark and cold ground level cellars of the Exchange Building, in 1773, citizens stored British tea they had seized in protest of the Tea Act, while their fellow colonists to the north were even more enraged, dumping tea into Boston Harbor at a "tea party". Later, the tea seized in Charles Town would be sold to help fund the patriot cause. In the Great Hall, South Carolina's delegates to the Continental Congress were elected in 1774; and in 1776, South Carolina announced independence from Great Britain from the steps of the Exchange Building.

Later, during British occupation of Charles Town from 1780-82, the British imprisoned patriot citizens in the dungeon, before forcing them to sign a loyalty oath to the King to gain their release. In 1788, 220 delegates crowded into the Great Hall to vote South Carolina's ratification of the United States Constitution.

We have a wonderful gift, being able to visit such a building today, and literally sense the very presence of our forefathers.

Colonial Statehouse/County Courthouse

At the corner of Broad and Meeting Streets, at the 'Four Corners of Law', stands the newly restored Charleston County Courthouse.

Some argue it is "one of the most important buildings in Charleston, South Carolina, and America". It dates back to 1753 when it served as the state's first and only statehouse, serving as the seat for the Royal British governors of the colony. Later, important discussions about the Declaration of Independence took place within its walls. Some of the present building's exterior and first floor walls date back to that original structure, although most of the building was destroyed by fire in 1788.

The building was reopened in 1792, but not completed for another twenty years. Some believe its graceful design influenced the design of the first White House in Washington, DC. In 1864, it was damaged by Union bombardment of the city during the Civil War, and then damaged again by the Earthquake of 1886.

But, Hurricane Hugo dealt it a fatal blow in 1989, tearing off a portion of its roof and causing severe water damage. For nearly 12 years, the 'Four Corners of Law' stood missing its crown jewel.

Now, a painstakingly, historically accurate restoration has been completed, preserving the building that stands today as the Charleston County Courthouse.

A new jail was also built at the farthest end of Broad Street, near the 'Poor House' and hospital, on what is today Franklin and Magazine Streets. No local college existed in the city until the College of Charleston was founded in 1790 after the Revolution, because the wealthy believed only an education in England itself was fitting and proper.

Magnificent residences were built as well, with adaptations of English influence. More than 200 homes were built during a ten-year building boom, many as part of the city's rebuilding following the Great Fire of 1740. With this boom, Charles Town's own version of traditional Georgian architecture evolved, which can still be seen today. Materials from yellow pine and cypress trees were cut, floated down rivers to mills, milled by hand or by wind-driven mills along the rivers, and then hauled downriver to Charles Town. By exposure to the salt in the tidal rivers, the wood became very hard and more impervious to rot or termites, which may help explain why so much of these magnificently built structures remain today.

Grand houses were of two basic styles: the so-called "double house" was designed symmetrically about a central foyer with elegant stairway; the "single house" was a single room wide, two rooms to each floor separated by a central stairway, two or more stories high, with a gable roof to the street and side porch entry through a false door off the street. Both could have multiple levels of side porches, or "piazzas", which offered maximum exposure to the cooling breezes from the water, and provided privacy from the street on minimum lot sizes which had been laid out originally based on English towns.

The designs also reflected many of their owner's West Indies' heritage, a look the city retains today. Nearly 300 of the city's most opulent homes were built between 1760-70. Many of the homes were furnished with furniture either imported from England, or built locally to pattern English designs. Mirrors, glass work, china, and art were imported from England. In the countryside, the grand Georgian style influenced the great plantation homes, an example being Drayton Hall, which stands today much as it did when it was built c.1742.

A Walk Along Church Street

Today, a walk along Church Street engenders an appreciation for the grandeur of these homes: 58 Church St., built c.1754 by James Veree, a French Huguenot carpenter, who later sold the house to Thomas Heyward, a signer of the Declaration of Independence; 59 Church St,, constructed c.1735 by Thomas Rose, a merchant; 69 Church St., built c.1750, and known as the Capers-Motte House; 71 Church St., Colonel Robert Brewton's house, built c.1721 and probably rebuilt c. 1741 after the Great Fire of 1740; 73 Church St., built c.1733, and given as a gift from Miles Brewton I upon his daughter, Mary Brewton's marriage to a physician, Dr. Thomas Dale; and, 87 Church St., the Heyward-Washington House, built c.1771 by Thomas Heyward, son of a successful rice planter, who used this as his in-town home, and offered it for lodging for President George Washington during his visit to Charles Town in 1791. Similar wonderful residences line Tradd Street.

Colonel John Stuart, a Scotsman who became superintendent of Indian affairs, was a merchant and trader who built a lavish home at 106 Tradd Street. He had become one of the wealthiest and most important officials in the city, earning 1,000 pounds sterling at his work (today, about $50,000-$60,000 annually), and owning 15,000 acres of land, worked by 200 slaves. His home was built for 2,350 pounds sterling ($120,000-$140,000 today) c. 1767-72, and stands today for us to admire. In 1775, John Stuart would flee the city and abandon his home in the face of British pressure; later, in 1782 the British would sell his home as confiscated property to a local merchant Alexander Gillon.

Nowhere else, but Charleston, can one find such an array of surviving pre-Revolutionary treasures.

Charles Town was bulging at its seams. By the 1760's, a new neighborhood was started in what is now Ansonborough. A young Captain in the British Navy, George Anson, owned land east of Meeting Street (between what is now Calhoun and Society Streets), land he reportedly won in a card game; later, streets were named George and Anson Streets, after him. Meeting and Church Streets were extended northward to George Street, and Boundary Street (later named Calhoun Street) became the northern limit of the extended city.

The 'Broad Path', or King Street at Boundary Street was the main road into the city from the country. Wagons with goods would enter from here, giving rise to the many small businesses and shops along King Street. Lt. Governor Bull wrote to Lord

Hillsborough in London in April 1770, reporting that more than 3,000 wagons a year arrive in Charles Town "loaded with indigo, flour, hemp and tobacco". Bay Street remained the hub for trade from its wharves.

Modern King Street Today

Marilyn and I enjoy taking our 'guests' on walks down King Street, letting the visitors browse the antique shops.

Today, modern Charleston's King Street harkens back to its historic past via a concentration of some 33 antique shops along a 1.2 mile stretch, each specializing in antique home furnishings, antique jewelry, or period clothing. Collectors from all over the world, year round, descend on this the heart of the city's antique district. No person interested in the search for old-fashioned treasures would miss a stroll down King Street.

Shops offer furnishings from the homes of the Revolutionary War, French and English furniture from the 18th and 19th centuries, or even furniture made in Charleston. When the district started in the 1940's and '50's, prices were more modest and pieces came from the homes of Charleston; but, now the shops are tony and upscale, reflecting high-end items often obtained throughout the world.

The shops rely on tourists and private collectors, but still retain their friendly mom-and-pop nature, and welcome all visitors that drop-in.

The city's limits were also pushed to the northwest by 1770, on land willed by John Harleston and plotted for residential lots. Its boundary was what is now Beaufain, Coming, Calhoun, and Ashley streets, and became known as Harleston Village. St. Philip's Church was also allowed by the Assembly to subdivide 17 acres granted by Mrs. Coming, bounded by George, Coming, St. Philip's and Beaufain Streets. (Harleston Village is the area in which our home at '29 ½ Montagu' is located.)

New streets were added in Harleston Village, such as: Wentworth, Montagu, Bull, Pitt, Smith, Rutledge, and Lynch (now Ashley) streets. The new streets were unpaved, as were other city streets, but some had foot paths beside the streets paved with brick and mortar.

NATURE WREAKS HAVOC ON COLONIAL CHARLES TOWN: CHAPTER 12

From its very beginning, Charles Town was threatened by nature, even more than the threats from the Spaniards and Indians (Yemassee and Creek tribes). The first large fire was recorded in 1698, and hurricanes hit the city in 1700, 1713, and 1728.

Like disease, fire would be one of the city's major problems. The Great Fire of 1740 proved to be the worst in America. On a Tuesday afternoon at about 2 pm, fire broke out at the corner of Broad and Church Street (near Shepherd's Tavern). A brisk northwest wind fanned the flames, and sparks blew skyward across the busy trading district. With dry weather for weeks proceeding, roofs of shops and warehouses ignited along Broad, Church, Elliott, Tradd, and Bay Streets. The fire reached most houses on the east side of Church Street, south to Vanderhorst Creek.

James Funk

The Streets Then and Now

As an aside, Vanderhorst Creek, is now Water Street. In walking Charleston today, one finds that many streets end abruptly, where someone's large property once stood, or where new land was made later by filling what was once creeks and marshes. Visitors to early Charles Town wrote in their letters that they were impressed with "broad, airy streets", giving pleasant views of the water. Today, these very same streets seem so very narrow.

Another interesting story involves a present-day street now called Philadelphia Alley. It is a mere one-block in length in the present French Quarter section of the city, extending as a narrow alley between Queen Street and Cumberland Street. In the days of the walled city, it was known as 'Cow Alley', because it was the path used to take cows out of the city and to pasture. From 1751, it was named 'Kinloch Court' after Francis Kinloch, a planter, who had purchased land in the area. Then, in 1810, an ex-Revolutionary War prisoner of war from Philadelphia emigrated to Charles Town, purchased the property, and re-named it 'Philadelphia Alley' in honor of his home city which he admired.

Explosions from the Great Fire of 1740 occurred from stores of deerskins, rum, pitch, turpentine, and gun powder. The crackling sounds of the fury of the roaring flames pierced the afternoon skies. People ran everywhere crying and shrieking for help, seeking safety, from the collapsing buildings. Life possessions and homes were destroyed as crowds watched helplessly.

By late afternoon, sailors from British warships in port came ashore, and began blowing up homes in an attempt to contain the spreading fire. In six hours the fire swept to Granville's Bastion, thru the west side of Church Street from Broad to Tradd Streets, and endangered the Miles Brewton house on Meeting Street. Fortunately, few lives, if any, were lost; but, 300 buildings were destroyed, including stores, some wharves, and the homes and life possessions of many.

Following the fire, an act was passed regulating rebuilding, and prohibiting houses built of wood.

Great fires also struck the city in 1778 and 1796. The fire of 1778 started in a bake house at Queen and Church Streets. A northerly wind fanned the flames from roof top to roof top. Houses were destroyed along Queen Street, then State Street to Broad Street, and then the fire burned along Elliott Street to Bedon's Alley and Stoll's Alley, consuming 250 houses in its path. Eyewitnesses reported "a sea of flames". It is reported that a visitor of Nathaniel Russell wrote: "many who, a few hours before, retired to their beds in affluence, were now reduced, by the all-devouring element, to indigence". The 1796 fire would burn from Broad and Meeting Streets to Cumberland and State Streets, destroying 500 homes.

Hurricanes also wreaked havoc on Charles Town. The city survived hurricanes in 1700, 1713, and 1728. The worst were yet to come.

The evening of September 14, 1752, was intensely hot, even hotter than the usual heat of the July/August summers. The usual southeasterly breeze suddenly turned to a northeasterly, and the winds increased, while the sky grew dark and threatening. As the winds increased, waves began to crash over the seawalls along the Battery, and were described as a "most violent and terrible hurricane". Soon a tidal wave hit bringing water 10 feet above high water mark. A small ship was literally washed up Vanderhorst's Creek, where Water Street stands today, and cast ashore at Meeting Street. Small vessels in port crashed against the wharves, and destroyed or badly damaged most wharves and bridges. Most vessels in the harbor were driven ashore. Roofs and chimneys came down, while tidal waves of seawater inundated White Point and the large homes nearby. Water crossed Queen, Broad, and Tradd Streets, and extended far up Church, King, and Meeting Streets. Residents fled their homes in panic for high ground. By 11 PM, much of the city was under as much as 9 feet of water, huge stands of pine trees were snapping everywhere, and 15 lives were lost. Then, suddenly, the winds calmed, and within minutes the flood waters receded.

A second hurricane struck 16 days later, on September 30th, 1752. In addition to the lives and possessions lost in the city, one half of the rice crop was lost, and exports of tar, pitch, and turpentine did not recover until years later when the woodlands reforested following the devastation from the hurricane's winds. The old seawall was destroyed, but a new one was built, which is today's Battery. In rebuilding, creeks and low-lying areas were filled, and east-west streets were extended river to river from the Cooper to the Ashley, while Church, Meeting, and King Streets were extended to South Battery Street.

On May 4th, 1761, a tornado hit the city and sank five ships at anchor in the harbor. Coming from the west, witnesses described the tornado as having such force that it "ploughed the Ashley River to the bottom and laid the channel bare".

The next worst storm would occur 228 years later, and be called "Hurricane Hugo"!

COOPER RIVER BRIDGE RUN...AND OTHER EVENTS: CHAPTER 13

It's the last Saturday in March, and Marilyn and I have set our alarm early for a Saturday morning. It's the weekend of the Cooper River Bridge Run...a 10K run that draws a massive group of runners, visitors to Charleston, and just local onlookers who have a great time. The Cooper River Bridge represents the challenge, which all runners must conquer, and picture-frames the event. The side-by-side pair of Cooper River Bridges has stood for many years as imposing landmarks in Charleston Harbor.

The first bridge, opened to traffic in 1929, and was named as a legacy to one of the city's most influential twentieth century mayors, John P. Grace; as it opened, it represented the first land linkage between Charleston, Mt. Pleasant, the Isle of Palms, Sullivan's Island, and north. The second bridge, the Silas Pearman Bridge, was completed in 1966.

We decided to take the day off from work on the carriage house, and walked east on Montagu Street for two blocks, then one block north on Coming Street along the College of Charleston's fraternity/sorority row, and east three blocks on

George Street through the heart of the College of Charleston campus. The early morning air was crisp, with the clear feel of approaching Spring, and the sun already promised to take the chill out of the day. We stood at the corner of George and King Streets, with crowds gathering, lining King Street, to catch the first glimpse of approaching runners in the Cooper River 10K Bridge Run.

This year marked the 22nd Annual run. The race has grown to be one of the premier 10K runs, and eighth largest in the world. Runners from all over the country, and some of the best in the world, come to Charleston for this race. The start gun went off at 8:00AM with 13,000+ runners beginning their sprint from Coleman Boulevard in neighboring Mt. Pleasant, with the Cooper River bridges looming in the distance. Almost immediately, the twin spans of the Silas Pearman bridges provide a severe test for the runners, with spans rising 164 ft. and 155 ft., requiring all the energy each runner can muster. Another 14,000+ entrants followed, to "walk" the 6.2 mile route into downtown Charleston.

The course poses breathtaking scenic views of Fort Sumter, the harbor, the Cooper and Wando Rivers, and then winds through Charleston's residential and shopping districts. This year the route followed King Street into downtown, then turned left onto Market Street, and then back up Meeting Street, to its culmination at the finish line at Marion Square.

Anxiously, we strained a look up King Street, trying to catch a first glimpse of the lead runners. Anticipation built in the crowd, with a good feeling of camaraderie and friendliness everywhere. The sun felt good curbside, as the morning's temperature lent crispness to the air. Then, suddenly, police cars appeared with lights flashing, and their sirens wailing in the morning air, as they came toward us along King Street to clear the path for the runners. Motorcycle police followed, and we could hear the whir of a helicopter overhead. Families were out; some had toddlers in tow, or even in strollers. One small guy next to us mirrored our excitement, but even more so, as he had no real clue as to what was happening; for him, it was just fun. Then, as we squinted into the morning sun, in the distance, the runners came. Preceded by a truck full of photographers and media, each leaning out to capture the lead runner's strain, the small pack of lead runners pushed their bodies to the limit.

The Kenyan runners led the pack of elite sprinters. With crowds lining the street waving and cheering, the eventual winner, Lazarus Nyakeraka, passed by, followed a few steps behind by second place finisher, William Kiptum, both of Kenya. The leg kick of these great athletes is amazing. Their stride is easy, but powerful, with leg kick almost touching their backs. Then, we glimpsed the first female runner, and simultaneous cheers erupted from the crowd.

A young mother next to us was there to cheer her husband to the finish. Soon he and thousands of other weekend athletes passed us by...some in agony, others seemingly in control and thoroughly enjoying the exhilarating experience. Still other runners were in costume...the crowd laughed as two younger men dressed as the "Blues Brothers" jogged before us. The winners finished in less than 30 minutes...the rest of the herd in an hour or more. Some couldn't run any further, pulled up, and then walked to the finish. For many, "to finish" was the real objective. Each has his or her own story. Some are recuperating from surgery, heart attacks, or the like; each had something to prove. Irregardless, all are winners.

And we too were winners, because Charleston had given Marilyn and I another unforgettable experience to cherish, and share with each other.

While the stragglers continued to pursue the finish line, we decided on a coffee and croissant, just down King Street, at

Starbucks. From the window table in the alcove on the second floor, we continued to watch runners pass by, as we munched on our roll and sipped our morning brew. The coffee tasted so good this particular morning. It was a special time.

As we left to walk back to our home that late-March day, the so-called "tulip trees" were in bloom; they begin to flower in late-February, their saucer-shape resembling tulips, with deep pink color at the tips of their petals, and white on the petal's underside. The stunning beauty of the tulip tree's display seems to call out that the spectacular yellow blooms of Carolina Jasmine, and Spring's flood of multi-colored Azaleas and the white bursts of Dogwood cannot be far behind.

The thought came to mind…just one weekend in Charleston, and the greatest distance runners in the world shared our town; and, at the same moment, the best amateur golfers in the U.S. were teeing off in their quest for the Azalea Invitational golf tournament title that weekend, an event held annually just across the Ashley River at the Country Club of Charleston's great course. What diversity! What choice!

BACK TO WORK ON 29 ½, AND MOVING DAY!!: CHAPTER 14

We were getting down to the last touches to make our carriage house livable, and we were so anxious to move in and begin enjoying all our hard work. Also, our lease on our apartment at "Palmetto Plantation" in Mt. Pleasant was about to end, so we were somewhat under the time pressure gun.

I wanted to add some trim carpentry detailing to the carriage house. First step, was adding moldings to detail four fireplaces. I purchased pieces of molding of various different looks and cross-sections, such as picture molding, dentil molding, and a grooved routed molding. Starting with each fireplace, I started to design ways to attach and build various combinations of these moldings to add a more finished detail to the surrounds and mantles of the fireplaces. One fireplace at a time, I attached the moldings, each fireplace unique and different in its look. As I stepped back from each, I was satisfied that each was improved, and would look quite elegant when painted.

The next challenge would prove more difficult, and yes, frustrating. In the living room I wanted to install crown molding at the tops of the four walls where the walls met the ceiling.

Now, anyone, who has even dabbled in carpentry, will tell you how difficult installing crown molding can be. This is a job to be left to trim carpentry experts…well, that inner sense of good judgment left me once again.

I decided I did not just want to install ordinary crown molding; I wanted to make it even more detailed than the pre-made moldings that can be purchased from the usual local lumber purveyor!

I visited the lumber store, and spent some time just 'playing' with pieces of moldings and crown, all the time trying to invent and visualize just the right look that I had in mind. After literally an hour or more of trial and error, I discovered the "right" combination. I would build a three-piece combination molding, using conventional base molding turned upside down; on top of this, a piece of saw-tooth dentil molding would be attached, exposing one inch or so of the curved section of the base molding on its bottom side; then, the finishing touch would be a piece of 4 ½" wide conventional crown molding, attached on top of the piece of dentil molding, now located in the center of the newly designed three-piece crown molding. It would be exquisite.

I hurried back to the carriage house to eagerly begin installation. Little did I know the journey in frustration I was about to take. You see, in an old house, particularly a 150+ year-old house, no wall is plumb, no corner is square, and no ceiling is flat! Working with this imperfection, installation of any piece of trim is difficult; but, even more so with crown moldings because every angle you try to fit and cut is different. No two are alike. The only way to make it fit is by trial and error. Take a measurement from the ladder, climb down, make a cut, climb back up and see how it fits…then, repeat the whole process, time and again. Often you simply must tack one end of the molding system in-place, then work your way along the molding, twisting and turning, and forcing the molding to fit the uncooperative walls and ceiling interfaces. Progress comes one foot at a time.

It took me two grueling weekends to complete the job, and it did not end without a few curses to the heavens (or Marilyn, who was the only human brave enough to be near me during this ordeal). But it all proved worthwhile. The visual effect of the new moldings was smashing. We just needed to caulk all the joints and surfaces where molding met plaster, and we were ready for painting.

Painting all the renovation work on '29 ½' Montagu was too large a task for us, and would take too long. So, we hired four painters. We wanted to repaint the exterior stucco which was a nondescript tan color, bleached ever so much over the years by the sun and weather. Marilyn and I found the colorful buildings of Charleston fascinating, like its famous 'Rainbow Row' of buildings along East Bay Street. The vivid colors could be found throughout the city, harkening back to the early Caribbean influence of its settlers, many of whom had arrived from Barbados. We decided to live a little dangerously, and select a bold, striking color for '29 ½'. This was so unlike us. We chose a vivid, pinkish, coral color from a palette of 'designer' paints at our local building supply store.

The painters were as eager as we were to see this splashy color on the tired, old walls. First, however, years and years of fig vine growth had spread its tiny tentacles over much of the front and entry side walls. The fig vine had to be pulled from the walls, and completely removed before painting could proceed. After this work was accomplished, painting began in earnest. In a matter of hours the building jumped out with a whole new look...Marilyn was sure we had made a terrible mistake, because neighbors and passersby stopped to gawk, and perhaps guffaw a bit, at our color selection. I tried to calm Marilyn, and asked her just to give it a chance, and perhaps time would make it more comfortable. We went away that evening not quite sure what we had done.

Then the rains came. We thought nothing of it until the next day upon our return to '29 ½'. To our dismay, the rain had washed the newly applied, and still not thoroughly dry, latex paint off the walls and onto the sidewalk below in puddles. Imagine pools of coral color on the sidewalk's surface! After a moment of horror, we simply looked at each other and laughed; we could have cried, but perhaps, this kind of moment is where some experience in restoration projects pays off. We knew it was not a big problem. We would simply have to repaint areas, and move on from here. I think the humorous moment served as some relief, because I was able to convince Marilyn that this color would be just fine, and she would like it in the end. And, this proved to be the case.

Painting of the interior of the house proved much less eventful and more routine. Within a few days, and several long nights, the painters were finished. The house looked great with that fresh, clean look only achieved by new paint.

Our next task was refinishing three stories of beat-up heart pine wood flooring. We turned again to an outside crew of experts for this task. Over a five-day period, they sanded all wood to its raw condition, applied a deep walnut stain, then a coat of sand sealer, followed by two coats of high gloss polyurethane. The result was unbelievable. These old floors had endured traffic through two centuries, and now they sprang back to a new, glistening look as if they were new pieces of wood. What a magical difference the refinished floors made, and what charm they added to our new home.

The last step before move-in was to complete wallpapering several areas. Marilyn and I had selected various papers and color schemes before, so materials were on-hand, and we decided to tackle this last task together. The dining room paper was vertical stripes of dark red and cream, and was installed without problems, with the help of our friend, Albert Spung. The living room paper was a soft yellow with cream stripe; this required a much slower, more careful process because the old plaster walls were much more fragile. Finally, we papered up the stairway with a blue-muted faux design, with the paper running just under a decorative chair rail molding I had installed up the staircase. After two weekends of work, we were ready to tackle the move-in.

I had made arrangements with Charles and two of his helpers to move us on a Saturday. Charles was a professional mover by trade, and I had built his home for him and his family in the Whitehall subdivision in North Charleston. I met the three moving men early on Saturday at the UHaul truck rental center on Coleman Boulevard in Mt. Pleasant. Here we rented a large enclosed moving truck for the day, and the three men drove the truck, following me to our apartment at Palmetto Plantation apartments in Mt. Pleasant. Loading went smoothly, and all was complete at the apartment by noon hour. Then, we drove to a nearby storage locker, where we had stored everything that wouldn't fit into our apartment from our move from Michigan. With the storage locker emptied (and just barely enough room for everything in the truck), we stopped for lunch, and everyone enjoyed the relaxed moments, as we braced ourselves for the challenge ahead.

You see, downtown Charleston's very narrow streets make navigation with a large truck difficult, and then parking the truck for unloading, next to impossible. Nonetheless, we made it. We cajoled our way into a tight parking space curbside in front of '29 ½ Montagu', and Charles managed to park the beast with minimum damage to the twin crepe myrtle trees which lined our curb between the street and sidewalk abutting our building. We breathed sighs of relief, and turned to the next obstacles.

The very narrow, old gate which was our entry posed a problem. Not only would its tightness make access for furniture difficult, but a single step also had to be traversed up to the narrow side entry pathway, with its old wall seemingly pinching us in and making the task even more difficult. But, Charles was game, and assured us we were in the best of hands. He even approached the doorways from the courtyard, into the new sunroom, through a narrow set of old French doors, to our small foyer and staircase up three floors, with a "no problem" attitude. And so, moving began.

Marilyn directed the movers where each item should be placed; while I tried to stay out of trouble. Everything went fairly smoothly, although we had just too much "darned stuff". Accumulation over the years, and a large home in Michigan, just resulted in too many "things", and agreeing amongst the two of us to throw anything away, was just too darn difficult. So, the mountain of boxes, furniture, accessories, tools, and "things" began to build quickly as the men made trip after trip from the truck, into the house, up the stairs, and then back for yet another load. Overflow began to accumulate in the courtyard outside, with packing boxes everywhere.

Then we faced a most difficult challenge. Everyone was tired by this time, and one always leaves the most difficult items to the end. Right?! A large, cumbersome, heavy armoire had to be carried to the second floor. But, stairways of carriage houses, built 150+ years ago, were not wide and turns were tight; they certainly were not built for our furniture. We would not quit, however, so the movers and I inched our way up the stairway with the awful burden, with Marilyn helping to guide and counsel us around the railings and turns. We made it.

The last item was our queen-size mattress and box springs. Its physical dimensions were larger than the space afforded by the turn in our stairway, and the ceiling overhead. The mattress was pliable, and could be bent and scrunched, though with no small difficulty. But, we had to deal with the unbendable box springs. As we tried every possible combination of angles and approaches, we met no success. Irregardless, the human spirit is simply amazing, and no one wanted to admit failure. We pushed, shoved, and forced until plaster on the ceiling and walls literally gave way, but all of a sudden, the box spring was free and the job accomplished. With sweat on every brow, we collectively collapsed down on the floor for rest, as everyone laughed that the only way that box spring would ever make it back down those stairs was if we took a chainsaw to it, and carried it out in little pieces.

With that last success, the men left, and Marilyn and I felt a sense of deep accomplishment, though exhausted, as we prepared to spend the first night in our new home at '29 ½ Montagu'.

REVOLUTIONARY CHARLES TOWN: CHAPTER 15

By 1763, Charles Town's political leaders were among the wealthy, and powerful. Henry Laurens owned numerous plantations, and was building a grand in-town home. Thomas Lynch was a successful rice planter. Christopher Gadsden was already wealthy, and began building the largest wharf in the colonies, as well as developing a new tract of property to the north of the city. John Rutledge, recently completed law school in London, and was already a prominent attorney in Charles Town. Unbeknownst to each, events were about to occur which would propel them into a conflict that no one could imagine, and as a group, they would soon become some of our country's greatest patriots.

The leaders of Charles Town had become proud of their community's success, and their "Carolina home". Though they honored England, and talked of her as "home", they increasingly referred to Carolina as "my country". Charles Town had grown to become an impressive city, which reminded them of their London or Bristol. They had patterned their new home in Charles Town after the great cities they admired in England, and with their success, loved both Charles Town and England.

In less than 100 years, they had built a wealthy and successful colony from "a dreary wilderness", and they expected plaudits from the British for their achievements. To the contrary, lucrative trade from the colonies made the colonies more important to Britain, and Charles Town's port was an important gateway. Instead of a British policy of laissez-faire toward the colonies, the last ten to fifteen years had witnessed changes in British policy, moving toward greater control, and a desire to capitalize on the new wealth via increasing taxation of the colonies.

By 1763, more than 1,700 British regular troops were stationed in Charles Town, and their presence alone brought resentment from many citizens. Britain decided to keep troops in America, and the need to support the cost of this occupation, contributed to the British resolve to tax the colonists even more.

Many in Charles Town, with its success and wealth, paid heavy taxes to Great Britain. The so-called Sugar Act of 1764 had some effect; however, the Stamp Act of 1765 levied taxes on various papers, including legal papers, newspaper advertisements, and even playing cards. Needless to say, the newspapers attacked via editorials the British right to tax the colonists "without representation", a long-standing tenet of British law.

The *South Carolina Gazette* newspaper took up the cry in its weekly publications in Charles Town. Public protests were organized. In October, 1765, the ship "Planters Adventure" carried dreaded stamps into Charles Town harbor, and remained at anchor under protection of the guns from Fort Johnson across the harbor. A group of spirited zealots in the city erected a 20-ft. high gallows in the center of town at the intersection of Broad and Church Streets, with a stamp distributor hung in effigy. A sign appeared at the front of the gallows, and read "Liberty and No Stamps" and carried a further warning "that if the effigy be removed, the guilty would be borne with a stone about his neck and cast into the sea".

The gallows stood all day that October 19th, accompanied by a muffled ringing of the bells of St. Michael's Church. With evening, a crowd of 2,000 citizens carried the figure along Broad Street, down to the harbor, where it was burned and the remains placed in a coffin, draped with a banner reading "American liberty".

A mob scene developed, and quickly deteriorated into a mad search of the houses of the men who were to distribute the stamps. An angry mob confronted Henry Laurens at his home in Ansonborough, looking for the dreaded stamps, rumored to be in his possession. He allowed a search of his home, and the mob departed only after he assured them that he opposed the Stamp Act. The group of so-called "Sons of Liberty" meant to assure that no stamps would be available as the law went into effect.

Sons of Liberty

Christopher Gadsden was the leader of the "Sons of Liberty". He was a powerful and effective speaker, who could work the crowds, particularly the less affluent labor class. Meetings were held at the "Liberty Tree", a huge live oak tree, which reportedly stood near present Market Street on land owned by Isaac Mazyck (others say it was located somewhere around present-day Alexander and Calhoun Streets). It is interesting to ponder.

School history classes teach of the importance of Revolutionary locations, such as Boston and its Tea Party, Paul Revere's ride to Lexington, and the signing of the Declaration of Independence in Philadelphia; but, what about the location of the "Liberty Tree" and the meetings of the "Sons of Liberty"...not many school children, or even adults for that matter, would answer "Charleston" when asked to name the location.

In February 1766, Christopher Gadsden wrote a column in the **_South Carolina Gazette_** newspaper in which he used the phrase "Aut Mors Aut Libertas", which roughly translates to "Give me Liberty, Give me Death", words that Patrick Henry would later make famous in 1775.

But not everyone shared the views of these upstarts, like Christopher Gadsden and his "Sons of Liberty". A faction of the wealthy and elite wanted to preserve the social, political, and racial system that had engendered their prosperity. William Wragg and William Henry Drayton (of Magnolia Plantation) wrote that their "freedom" could be lost if citizens followed the zealots and trouble makers.

For the next 3-4 months, port activity was in havoc, and this was the most important period for exporting the rice crop to Europe. Vessels were trapped at anchor in the harbor, because they were not permitted to depart without legal clearance requiring stamps. Meanwhile, more than 1,400 idle sailors were in port, causing a thriving pub and brothel business, but endangering the public's order and safety.

On January 27th, 1766, the city continued to suffer from the effects of the Stamp Act, as commerce had come to a standstill. No ships left port, and goods, especially rice, accumulated along the docks. Pressure mounted to open the port, but the citizen's Council voted 5-2 against it.

Then, Christopher Gadsden, and his "Sons of Liberty", reached a compromise with British Lt. Governor Bull, to avert the threat of violence from the sailors and allow the ships to clear port.

Eventually, unrest among the colonies and pressure from British merchants to restore unfettered trade, led to repeal of the Stamp Act in March 1766. The citizens of Charles Town celebrated in the streets, as the bells of St. Michael's Church tolled out in joy. A statute of William Pitt was commissioned as a tribute to his leadership in gaining repeal, and that statute stood at the center of Meeting and Broad Streets, until it was damaged by cannon shot in the impending Revolutionary War, and moved into the State House for safety.

Today, the statute, still showing the damage from cannon shot, can be seen in the new County Courthouse, at the corner of Meeting and Broad Streets.

The Stamp Act crisis tindered the fire of rebellion among citizen zealots of Charles Town. Moreover, it was the first time the colonists had resorted to violence, and it worked. This success would fuel the audacity of citizens to resist British authority in the future, and fan the first flicker of the flames of rebellion. From now on, both the British and the new-spirited "Americans" would be wary of each other.

In the Spring of 1767, British Parliament imposed the Townshend Duties on all glass, lead, paint, paper, and tea imported into the colonies. The tax was passed to fund Britain's cost for governing and defending the colonies. In the Fall, British troops moved into Boston to maintain order. At that same time in Charles Town, the city's elected representatives (called the Commons) met with their new British Governor, Lord Charles Montagu, to assure him that they did not intend to challenge Parliament. You see, most successful merchants in Charles Town did not favor disrupting the flow of imports via embargo, because trade built their fortunes.

The planters, in contrast, were exporters, and therefore hurt less by any embargo of imported goods. A meeting was held in July 1769 under the "Liberty Tree", where a compromise was fashioned. Nonetheless, anti-British sentiment was continuing to increase. In January 1770, "a general meeting of the inhabitants" was held at the "Liberty Tree" to discuss an item of enforcement of the boycott of British goods. A citizen, Alexander Gillion sought permission to import "100 pipes of wine", but by unanimous vote, the inhabitants voted to deny him permission.

British imports were cutback by 50%, and merchants lobbied for repeal of the Townshend Duties. British Lord North replaced Townshend as head of exchequer, and persuaded Parliament to make concessions, resulting in the removal of all duties, except for tea.

Step-by-step, with each struggle, a consensus was developing that the colonists would have to look out for their own welfare, because Britain was being influenced by her own financial self-interest and desire to reassert authority over the upstart colonists.

Meanwhile, trade was booming, a fact not overlooked by the British. By 1771, the price of rice had doubled over the prior two years. Planters invested their huge profits in even more land and slaves; slaves were made available to them via wealthy merchant traders. By the early part of the decade, annually more than 800 vessels exchanged cargo in Charles Town's port, and about 140 were British owned, plying the trade routes between Charles Town and England.

Tonnage through the port exceeded the volume in Boston, and even New York. Charles Town's population was 12,000 persons, though only roughly half of New York's; it was comprised of 6,000 blacks, 3,000 poor white, and 3,000 who owned property, including the roughly 1,000 elite and powerful who controlled about 75% of the city's wealth. As such, the city was important financially to the British, and many of the city's most influential citizens had longstanding ties to the motherland.

Several years passed, without major incident; then, the Tea Act was passed by Parliament to gain advantage over most American merchants for the British-controlled East India Tea Company, operating under consignment with a small group of favored importers in the colonies.

The Tea Act immediately rekindled radical fervor. In the Fall 1773, seven ships laden with East India tea pulled anchor from the Thames River in a group and headed for Boston, New York, Philadelphia, and Charles Town.

In the Atlantic, one ship, the "London", veered south toward Charles Town, and arrived at the mouth of Charles Town harbor seven weeks later in December 1773, bearing 257 chests of tea. The "Sons of Liberty", energized by Christopher Gadsden, took to the streets passing out notices along Broad Street, while urging anyone and everyone to a meeting at the Exchange Building. It may have been the heavens giving an ominous warning, because on December 5th it was reported that a "quantity of snow falls" and the streets were covered with snow, more than anyone could remember (any amount of snowfall is unusual in the city!).

At the meeting at the Exchange Building, sides were divided over whether or not to boycott. The planters favored boycott, as voiced by Charles Pinckney and his cousin, Charles Cotesworth Pinckney; the artisans were the most vocal for boycott, led by Christopher Gadsden himself. This coalition tried to enlist support of the leading merchants, including Miles Brewton, but the merchants generally opposed a boycott of the tea. The arguments were heated, but a message was sent to the captain of the ship "London", urging him to leave the harbor or risk his ship being set aflame. Before mob action took over, Lt. Governor Bull and British custom officials seized the tea from the ship, and under British guard, stored the tea in the basement of the Exchange Building. The tea remained there, until later during the Revolution when it was sold to help fund the patriot war effort.

In Boston, events were more violent, and citizens dressed as Indians staged their own "tea party". In June 1774, the British King and Parliament retaliated by closing the port of Boston. Christopher Gadsden was furious, viewing this as a hostile act against Boston. He swung into action, organizing a meeting in July that would last over three days in Charles Town, attended by over 100 of the city's most influential citizens, and at times with spectators numbering nearly 400 persons.

Again, differences existed, with one side a coalition of planters and artisans, while the other side was mainly comprised of merchants. They did agree on one compromise, reportedly as proposed by the brothers John and Edward Rutledge; a Charles Town delegation would represent the city in Philadelphia in September.

It was hoped that the so-called 'Continental Congress' could develop a unified response plan for the 13 colonies, rather than each colony acting on its own. At a general meeting at the Exchange Building over 1,500 persons voted for South Carolina's delegates. The delegation selected included: Henry Middleton (planter), John and Edward Rutledge (attorneys), Thomas Lynch (planter), and Christopher Gadsden. The merchants' slate had included, Charles Pinckney, Rawlins

Lowndes, and Miles Brewton; but these men did not make the final delegation.

Images of Revolutionary Days

Today, Marilyn and I walked along present Broad Street, because Broad Street today still invokes the feel of what it must have been like in pre-Revolutionary days. We stood in front of 116 Broad Street and gazed up at the home built c.1763 by John Rutledge for his bride Elizabeth Grimke. The original building had a Georgian façade, and underwent major renovation in 1853 which gave it the intricate cast-ironwork and Greek Revival look it has today.

Looking just across the street, at 117 Broad Street stands the home of Edward Rutledge, younger brother of John Rutledge. This home was built in the Georgian style c.1760 by James Laurens, brother of Henry Laurens. In 1788, Edward Rutledge purchased the home, to live across the street from his brother. Although the home has been changed greatly over the years, it still stokes one's imagination to think of the brothers Rutledge, and what their lives must have been like in those times.

Who were the Rutledges? John Rutledge was the oldest of seven children, born to Dr. John Rutledge and wife Sarah who had emigrated to Charles Town from Ireland in 1735. His father was a successful doctor with a practice on Broad Street, and became a planter. The Rutledge children were raised in a family of newly acquired wealth, status, and political influence. Eldest son

John was trained as an attorney in London, and quickly developed a successful practice in Charles Town. His new bride, Elizabeth Grimke, was from a prominent family who had come from Germany in 1733. With John's early legal success, he began to invest in land.

Two of John's brothers became merchants, and one married the daughter of Christopher Gadsden. Brother Edward married a daughter of Henry Middleton, an extremely wealthy planter who was one of the richest men in the colonies. Brother Hugh married Ann Smith, daughter of Thomas Smith of Broad Street, and the couple moved to a home at 19 Queen Street. Hugh Rutledge served as a vestry at St. Philip's Church, and later a trustee of the new College of Charleston in 1785.

Such were the times in colonial Charles Town, as alliances of great families developed interconnections which assured them great social and political influence and power. The Rutledges, Draytons, Pinckneys, and Middletons were all families interconnected. Many families were like the Rutledges, who grew to maturity as British gentlemen and colonists, who were reluctant to break political and economic ties with Britain, or forsake their British heritage.

But, the movement toward independence would forge a new nationalism, and an even stronger allegiance to the state of South Carolina.

John Rutledge was elected to the Commons House of Assembly in 1761, at age 22 years. Four years later he represented his colony at the

Stamp Act Congress, with Thomas Lynch and Christopher Gadsden. In 1767, John was named to a commission overseeing construction of the new Exchange and Custom House. In 1773, Edward Rutledge was thrust into public life as the crisis initiated by the Tea Act unfolded.

In October 1774, the Continental Congress met in Philadelphia. Patrick Henry reportedly called John Rutledge a most eloquent orator at the Congress, and wrote, "he shone with superior luster". South Carolina's delegates generally "accepted the necessity for independence, but still felt affection for Britain, and remembered their prosperity within the empire". The Congress departed Philadelphia resolved to resist until favorable relations between the colonies and Britain could be re-established.

Another ship carrying tea consigned to local Charles Town merchants arrived in Charles Town harbor in November. In an attempt to avoid mob violence, the city's leaders convinced the merchants to dump the tea into the Cooper River. Hesitant resistance was making way toward a general consensus of all-out resistance.

In April 1775, the British decided to send more troops to the colonies to enforce their policies and re-establish order. When Charles Town's leaders heard of this, they moved in a night raid on April 20th to seize arms and powder stored in the public magazines, and hid the cache in homes throughout the city. Then, gunfire erupted in Lexington and Concord between Massachusetts colonials and British regulars. In Charles Town, fear swept the city…fear of attack by the British, or Indians, or slave insurrection. At this point, there were few thoughts of 'independence', just fear of what would happen next.

A "Council of Safety" was formed in Charles Town. But, in June 1775, two merchants passed a rumor that the British would arm slaves and Indians, thereby inciting an angry mob who stripped the two men naked, tarred and feathered them, and carried them on a cart through the city's streets for all to see and jeer. Mob sentiment was beginning to replace law and order. Out of fear, many citizens loyal to Britain prepared to flee the city.

In September, the British Royal Governor William Campbell left the city for safe refuge on a British warship in the harbor. On the same day, the city's leaders acting via the Council of Safety ordered Colonel William Moultrie to occupy Fort Johnson to protect that approach to the city. In mid-November, hulks of old vessels were sunk in the Cooper River to prevent entry by British warships. In response, British ships fired on William Henry Drayton's ship, and Drayton returned the fire. Nothing was hit, but the first shots of the Revolution had been heard in Charles Town...it was November 11th, 1775.

Now loyalists, and some of the wealthy who could afford to leave, fled the city. Others hurriedly started work to fortify the city for its defense. On the northern side of Charleston harbor, stretching for nearly four miles is Sullivan's Island, and across the harbor to the south is Morris Island, both serving as natural fortifications to the city and harbor entrance.

Further to the north of Sullivan's Island, is the Isle of Palms (then known as Long Island), with Dewees Island at its northern tip. A 20 ft. high walled escarpment was built hastily of palmetto tree logs on Sullivan's Island to protect the harbor entrance. Events were rapidly getting out of hand, and emotions were at a ragged edge.

A 2nd Continental Congress met again in Philadelphia in early 1776. Those in attendance were shocked when South

Carolina's volatile Gadsden and Drayton proposed independence from Britain; Henry Laurens called the idea "indecent", while John Rutledge called the idea "treasonable". That brash idea was tossed aside, for the time, and a more cautious approach was followed.

But efforts at reconciliation did not work. By Spring, reports were reaching Charles Town that British General Sir Henry Clinton was organizing 2,000 British regulars for an assault on the city. Meanwhile, more than 4,000 colonial militia and volunteers were rushing into the city to defend her under command of Major General Charles Lee. Col. William Moultrie and his infantry were dispatched to the palmetto fortress on Sullivan's Island, while 800 men under Col. William, Thomson were sent to the north of the island to protect Moultrie's men from a landed assault. A militia soldier wrote to his brother in England about his experience on Sullivan's Island, "...encamped on this island for this month past, and have lived upon nothing but salt pork and peas, we sleep upon the seashore, nothing to shelter us from the rains, but our coats, or a miserable blanket. Nothing grows upon this island, it being a mere seabank, and a few bushes, which harbor millions of musketoes (sic), a greater plague than can be hell itself".

In early June 1776, dispatches reached John Rutledge, who was serving as President of the South Carolina colonial government, that Sir Henry Clinton was about to land his British-regular troops on Long Island (now Isle of Palms), while the British Caribbean fleet was sighted off Dewees Island, consisting of some fifty vessels including the flagship of Sir Peter Parker, Admiral of the Royal Navy. The presence of such vast military and naval forces just twenty miles north of Charles Town left little doubt that the British objective was to deal a mighty blow to the upstart colonists, and 'upon South Carolina was the blow to fall'.

On June 28th, 1776, the British tried to cross the tidal creek from what is now Isle of Palms, across Breech Inlet, onto Sullivan's Island. The patriotic defenders numbered 1,175 men, facing a mighty trained fighting force of 2,900 British regulars and 262 guns. But, the creek and its treacherous currents proved impossible to cross for Sir Henry Clinton's forces in the face of Col. Thomson's defense. The patriot casualties were 12 dead and two wounded, while the British lost 219 men.

At the same time, the British navy opened fire on Moultrie's position on Sullivan's Island. While the fort's spongy palmetto logs absorbed the British navy's best shots like sand bags, Moultrie's guns pounded the British fleet, because three ships came too close to shore and ran aground, and could not escape the pounding from cannon. As the British succeeded in pulling back, nightfall fell, and it was over. After 11 hours of battle, the once proud British fleet limped away, picked up Clinton's disheartened regulars from Breech Inlet, and sailed back to New York. Moultrie and Thomson's men sustained less than 40 casualties, and most importantly, claimed the first victory for the colonials against the mighty British Empire. The fledgling nation had asserted itself, rebuffed a far superior force, but most importantly, gained an important moral victory. Days later, the welcome news reached Philadelphia where the Continental Congress was preparing to sign the Declaration of Independence.

Sergeant. William Jasper

There were a number of heroes that June 28th, but none more of a hero than an enlisted man, Sergeant William Jasper. During the battle, a canon shot destroyed the flagpole which flew the militia flag (indigo blue with white crescent moon in the upper left corner). Sergeant Jasper grabbed a nearby gun sponger pole, attached the fallen flag to it, and re-raised the flag on its makeshift pole, to fly over the bastion in the face of enemy fire.

Later, a palmetto tree was added to the flag to commemorate the heroic defense of Fort Sullivan, and that flag became the present-day South Carolina state flag.

It would be an additional hard-fought six years before the British would be driven from America finally, and another nine years before the new nation's Constitution would be ratified, but on this special 28th day of June 1776, a vision was etched of men and women standing tall in the face of their enemies, ready to sacrifice to decide their own fate. This vision would become the concept of liberty which we cherish to this day. While the battle at Lexington and Concord would start the war officially, and the battle of Yorktown would end it, this first colonial victory in Charles Town would provide a most valuable boost to the growing patriot cause.

Word spread quickly through the thirteen colonies, and it became a rallying cry for the more radical patriots, while quieting those who favored reconciliation. Henry Laurens wept at the thought of independence, and wrote that he felt like a dutiful son driven "by the hand of violence" from his father's home.

And, driven they were. News arrived in Charles Town, that the Declaration of Independence had been adopted in Philadelphia, and signed by Charles Town's Arthur Middleton, Edward Rutledge, Thomas Lynch, and Thomas Heyward. It took nearly a month for news to trickle down from Philadelphia. The August 2nd-14th, 1776, issue of the *South Carolina Gazette* newspaper in Charles Town was one of the few newspapers in the colonies to publish the full text of the Declaration of Independence for the city's citizens.

But, the ensuing Revolutionary War would not touch Charles Town directly for the next four years, until 1780. Following their failure in the attack on Sullivan's Island, the British war effort was directed toward the northeast quadrant of America. In so doing, the ports in Boston, New York, and Philadelphia were effectively bottled up, so that port activity in Charles Town was even more active. Wartime trade, though sometimes illegal, was extremely profitable, and increased the wealth of the city's merchants even more.

With a robust port activity, the city was jammed with sailors and military. The brothels and tippling houses near the wharfs on the Cooper River were jam- packed, spilling out into the streets with drunken and rowdy sailors and soldiers. Rumor spread that the devastating fire of 1778 which burned 250 houses was arson perpetrated by British Loyalists or Tories, or perhaps by sailors, who slipped into the city at night from a British man-of-war anchored off the harbor.

By 1779, the British decided an offensive thrust into the South was needed, a response in part to less than decisive forays against George Washington's army in the north. Also, France entered the war as an ally to the patriots. By May 1779, Savannah and most of Georgia were overrun by the British, under the command of Sir Henry Clinton...the same Clinton who had been vanquished nearly four years earlier by the colonists at Charles Town's first encounter of the war. On May 7th, when patriot General Moultrie returned to Charles Town, after being pursued by the British, he found the citizens of the city "frightened out of their wits".

Now, the British and Sir Henry Clinton moved in earnest toward Charles Town. Clinton landed this time to the south on John's Island, and his forces advanced just short of the Stono River.

With enemy British forces poised just outside the city, the siege began. Marauders looted and pillaged plantations along the Ashley River. Patriot defender General Benjamin Lincoln ordered General Moultrie "to proceed immediately to Bacon's Bridge" to organize the militia; and, if he had to retreat, "effectually destroy the bridge".

General Moultrie reported back that he was keeping a "detachment of horse constantly waiting on the enemy, to observe their motions". But, General Benjamin Lincoln and his men were running short of food and supplies. In December, George Washington dispatched 1,400 additional troops, supplies, and four naval frigates to assist in the patriot defense of the city.

Slave labor was used to dig trenches and build cannon positions at the peninsula city's exposed northern landed entry, at the very intersection of King Street and Boundary Street (now Calhoun Street). This main defensive position, or redoubt, became known as the Citadel. The city's defenders numbered about 5,000 in February 1780, all ensconced on the peninsula. From St. Michael's Church steeple, British fires could be seen across the Ashley River, while British reinforcements were reportedly approaching by sea. Then, in April, the British crossed the Ashley River, though both sides traded cannon fire each day. Two hundred British cannon began to pound the city.

Imagine yourself, a citizen of the city, cowering in some corner of a street, seeking whatever protection a doorway or building arch could provide. Virtually no one was safe in the streets now. Only soldiers walked the streets. Dogs were left to roam the streets. The smell of gunpowder was thick in the Spring air, not the usual sweet aromas of Jasmine and other sweet scents from the Spring flowers bursting forth throughout the city.

As the British inched further and further around the outskirts of the city, the stranglehold strengthened. No escape routes were left. Meanwhile, the incessant bombardment continued, cannonballs whizzing overhead, shells hissing, explosions deafening, and powder magazines every now and then exploding with a savage fury.

A cannonball crashed into St. Michael's Church, and rebounded to tear the arm off the statute of William Pitt, which had been erected at the intersection of Meeting and Broad Streets in recognition of his support as Prime Minister of England in repealing the divisive Stamp Act.

William Pitt's Statute

Today, you can see that same statute of William Pitt, one of the oldest statutes in America dedicated to a public figure, less the arm torn off by the British cannonball. The statute resides not far from its original location. The statute had arrived in Charles Town in 1770, to honor England's greatest supporter of the colonists, as the colonists argued to Parliament against the insidious Stamp Act. The statute was originally displayed in the street at the intersection of Meeting and Broad Streets.

After William Pitt fell into disfavor with the American revolutionaries, or because the statute was playing havoc with traffic in the street, it was moved by the city fathers; first, to an obscure location at the grounds of the nearby city arsenal; then, in 1808 it was moved again to the grounds of the City Orphan House (built c.1792), located between Boundary Street (now Calhoun Street) and Vanderhorst Street; then, in 1881 it was relocated to the then newly renovated Washington Park, behind City Hall, and nearby its original street location; in 1885, it was moved indoors, and displayed in the city offices at the corner of Meeting and Broad Streets, where it would reside for more than a century, stirring emotions for all who gazed upon it, imagining those revolutionary days in Charles Town, while the empty pedestal still stood in Washington Park.

Just recently, the statute has been relocated one more time; now it stands proudly overlooking the lobby of the new Charleston County Courthouse, at Meeting and Broad Streets, at the 'Four Corners of Law'. Above the statute, carved into the limestone walls, reads one of William Pitt's best-known sayings: "Where Law Ends, Tyranny Begins".

General Lincoln soon acknowledged that the situation was hopeless, and negotiations with the British for surrender of the city began. When complete, on May 12th, 1780, after 42 days of siege and bombardment, Charles Town fell to the British. The surrender included 5,500 men, arms, and supplies. With this, the British controlled all four major American ports; and, the British began to celebrate what would be their greatest victory of the war. Charles Town would remain an occupied city for the remainder of the war…another 2 ½ years.

CHARLES TOWN: AN OCCUPIED CITY: CHAPTER 16

With the British holding Charles Town, her citizens were forced to take sides. Many of the city's most influential citizens signed a required "Oath of Allegiance", pledging allegiance to the British, and swearing not to take up arms against the Crown. Some of those signing the oath included: Henry Middleton, Charles Pinckney, Rawlins Lowndes, and Gabriel Manigault. Some signed the oath to protect their vast wealth and lands; others signed, simply supporting the British cause.

Patriot soldiers captured by the British were held prisoner at Charles Pinckney's Snee Farm.

Meanwhile, Charles Town's Tories fraternized heavily with the British. The British officers moved into wealthy Tory homes, drank their finest brandy and wines, and partied deep into the nights with their ladies at gala receptions, balls, and concerts. The British often invited black slave women to these elegant affairs.

Still other citizens continued to support the patriot's cause, often at great expense to their personal freedom and their fortunes.

John Rutledge left the city in exile upon British occupation. British officer Lt. Colonel Moncrief used Rutledge's home on Broad Street as his quarters, while the Loyalists seized Rutledge's lands and his 180 slaves. Rutledge's brothers, who stayed, Edward and Hugh Rutledge, were among the 37 patriots taken by the British as prisoners, and placed in the dreaded dungeon of the Exchange Building; later, they were among those exiled to St. Augustine, Florida. Thomas Heyward, a signer of the Declaration of Independence, was also among the exiled to St. Augustine; and, his home at 87 Church Street was stormed by an unruly mob.

Thomas Heyward Home (87 Church Street)

Later, in 1791, George Washington stayed in Thomas Heyward's home when the ex-President visited Charleston following his presidency. The home can be toured today, offering the visitor a chance to relive those historic Revolutionary days.

British General Henry Clinton commandeered the Miles Brewton house at 27 King Street as his headquarters. For the next 31 months, this home would serve as the center for British control of the city.

Miles Brewton House as British Headquarters

The Miles Brewton house is like none other in Charleston today. The house and its occupants have lived the ups and downs of the city's rich history, like no other family.

Miles Brewton's father emigrated with his parents to Charles Towne from Barbados in 1684. He practiced a trade as a goldsmith, and fathered six children. His son, Miles, became a wealthy merchant; daughter, Frances, married Charles Pinckney; daughter, Rebecca, married Jacob Motte, Jr.; son, Robert became a goldsmith, like his father, and succeeded his father as the city's Powder Receiver.

Son, Miles Brewton, was born in 1731, and worked as a young man in the mercantile business, and by 25 years of age was a successful trader. He married Mary Izard, daughter of Joseph Izard, a French Huguenot rice planter. He invested in rice plantations, and became one of the largest traders in slaves. Miles Brewton was said to invest his wealth in "ships, land, and conspicuous consumption". By linkage with his wife's wealthy family, and his own skills, he owned interests in 8 ocean-going trading ships and a number of plantations.

In 1765, at 34 years of age, work started on his exquisite city home at 27 King Street, which was completed c.1769. He inherited the land for his home from his prosperous grandfather and father. He patterned his home from Italian villas of the Renaissance period. Interior and exterior wood carvings were done by master carvers who emigrated from London. The primary structure is cypress wood, explaining why it has stood impervious to termites and rot for so long. Its floors were heart pine. Reportedly, the balcony floor was originally covered with lead, which nearly 100 years later, would be removed, melted down, and cast for Confederate bullets.

In 1773, Josiah Quincy of Boston visited at the Miles Brewton home, and wrote in his diary: "dined with considerable company at Miles Brewton, Esqr's, a gentleman of very large fortune: a most superb house said to have cost him 8,000 pounds of sterling. The grandest hall I ever beheld…". The outbuildings included a kitchen, laundry, and carriage house.

Miles Brewton, when forced to take sides, favored the patriot cause although his fortune was closely tied to the Mother Country. But, tragedy would strike him and his family before the first shots of the Revolution. In August 1775, the Brewton's and their three children were lost in a storm at sea as they sailed to Philadelphia. His wealthy estate and home at 27 King Street were inherited by his two sisters, Rebecca Brewton Motte and Francis Brewton Pinckney. Rebecca Motte and her family took residency at 27 King Street. In 1780, following her husband, Jacob's, death, Rebecca Brewton Motte and her three daughters were left alone at 27 King Street, as the British occupation of Charles Town began.

Rebecca Brewton Motte's bravery is a shining example of the undaunted courage evidenced by many of the city's citizens. When confronted by British commanders, about to takeover her home as headquarters for Sir Henry Clinton himself, she refused to give up her home. And, although the British showed great courtesy and respect, as 'her guests', she and her daughters were prisoners of the British and at their mercy.

Out of fear, and for their protection, she kept her three daughters locked in isolation in a third floor garret of their home, constantly guarded by her servant. Effectively, the three daughters were held in their "prison" room throughout the 2 ½ years of British occupation.

Isaac Hayne's Sacrifice

The sad and tragic story of Isaac Hayne is another example of the sacrifices many were asked to pay as this young country, and the citizens of Charles Town, struggled for their freedom.

Isaac Hayne was 35 years old, and already a successful rice planter, partner in a company that produced cannons and gunshot, and member of the Provincial Congress, as well as loving husband and devoted father of seven children. Two of his children had died in early childhood, and by 1780, five children remained ranging from four to fourteen years of age.

In addition to the family plantation, "Hayne Hall", he owned two other plantations, with landholdings totaling nearly 10,000 acres. He was a gentleman, and known to be a man of principle.

As the British approached Charles Town, a smallpox epidemic raged and Isaac's wife and several children became gravely ill with the disease, while at their plantation in the country.

Isaac Hayne left the plantation and rode some twenty miles on horseback to obtain medical help in Charles Town.

On his journey, he was detained by the British, and giving little thought to the consequences, he decided to sign the "Oath of Allegiance" to gain his release, so he could return to his family with the desperately needed medicines. But, his efforts were to no avail, and his wife Elizabeth and daughter Mary succumbed to the disease.

Distraught by their deaths, Isaac Hayne accepted a commission in the South Carolina Militia fighting for the Patriot cause. But, on July 26, 1781, he was captured by the British, and immediately transported to the Exchange Building at the corner of East Bay and Broad Streets, where he was imprisoned in the infamous and dreaded Provost Prison.

The following day a British court of inquiry was quickly assembled to determine the fate of Isaac Hayne. The so-called inquiry quickly turned to a lynch mentality. Two ranking British commandants, Colonel Nesbit Balfour, British Commandant of Charles Town, and Lord Rawdon, British Commandant of Forces in South Carolina, decided to make an example for any Patriots who reneged on the "Oath of Allegiance". On July 29th, they decided that Isaac Hayne would be executed on July 31st at six o'clock, and a proclamation was so issued.

The proclamation backfired on the British. Both loyalist Tories and Patriots, alike, united in their condemnation and outrage at the proclamation.

146

The entire proceeding, they argued, flew in the face of accepted English Common Law. There was no counsel, and there was no trial. In fact, they argued, only proven spies were "hanged from the nearest tree". And, Isaac Hayne was certainly no spy.

Petitions were circulated calling for clemency. Even the Governor of South Carolina, appointed by the British Crown, pleaded that Hayne's life be spared. Crowds gathered in the streets.

Under intense pressure, British Colonel Balfour and Lord Rawdon agreed to a stay of execution, but only to August 4th, so Hayne's surviving four children could be brought to town to visit their father for the last time.

Upon the children's visit, Isaac Hayne was led from the dungeon prison to an upstairs room off the Great Hall of the Exchange Building, where a black cloth-draped coffin already stood, and armed soldiers guarded the door. Imagine the fear and anguish as the children viewed their father in this fashion. Isaac asked his eldest fifteen year-old son to accompany him to the place of execution, and asked of him, "when I am dead, bury me beside your mother".

In a last ditch effort to plead for compassion, the children's aunt took them to British headquarters at the Miles Brewton house at 27 King Street. In the drawing room, they were received by Lord Rawdon. Tearfully, the children knelt before Lord Rawdon to beg for their father's life. Unmoved, Lord Rawdon reportedly snorted, turned away, and dismissed them. The execution would take place as planned.

Then, at mid-day on a Saturday, August 4th, 1781, a procession led Isaac Hayne out from the Exchange. He walked along Broad Street to his place of execution, the streets crowded with hushed and saddened spectators. Imagine being streetside to witness such an event. Isaac Hayne walked past dressed in brown breeches with white stockings, wearing a wig braided into a short ponytail. His gait evoked resolute firmness, composure, and dignity, his grief stricken son by his side, accompanied by an escort of British soldiers in their scarlet and white dress uniforms. An eerie, and tragic, majesty would forever be the scene etched in the mind of each onlooker.

Hayne arrived at the place of execution, and shook hands with the three gentlemen he had named in his will to care for his children. Serenity fell over the crowd, as he ascended the execution cart. The executioner struggled to pull the cap over his eyes, so Hayne responded: "I will save you that trouble", and pulled the cap over his head. His final words were, "I will only take leave of my friends, and be ready". With that, he gave the signal for the cart to move away.

The gruesome sight was witnessed by his son, Isaac Hayne, Jr., who then had to accompany his father's body on the long trip home to "Hayne Hall", and his final resting place. It was reported that his son, years later, could repeatedly be heard calling out to his dead father. The son died insane at age 35 years.

The British officers dealt harshly with the Patriots, whom they considered 'traitors' to Britain. On October 16th, 1780, General William Moultrie complained to British Lt. Colonel Balfour about the conditions of imprisonment of some of his "Continental soldiers" aboard British prison ships in the harbor. Lt. Colonel Balfour replied that, "he would do as he pleased with the prisoners for the good of His Majesty's service, and not as Gen. Moultrie pleases".

'The Patriot' Movie Evokes Revolutionary Images

The imagery of Revolutionary Charles Town came back to Marilyn and me for several weeks in the Spring. It seemed so strange to watch crowds of men in tricorn hats, greatcoats, vests, and stockings, accompanied by women in long lacy dresses and hats, all boarding city buses to ease the traffic snarl they had caused downtown. The explanation...the cast and extras from a movie being made in Charleston were breaking from a day of filming.

You see, many movies are shot in Charleston and the surrounding area. This particular 'shoot' was part of an elaborate 2 ½ days of filming, in which some of Charleston's most historic streets served as the backdrop for the Revolutionary War epic movie, "The Patriot", by Columbia Pictures. Parts of Meeting Street and Tradd Street were closed off to everyone, unless you were the movie's star, Mel Gibson, a horse, or dressed in period costume wearing a tricorn hat as one of the hundreds of movie extras.

All modern vestiges, such as traffic signals, had been removed from the streets for authenticity. The pavement was covered with wood mulch to simulate the dirt streets of that time. Even the sounds of the horses, and their unmistakable smells, lent a certain authenticity that made it easy for the mind to drift back in time to those colonial days. The week's filming was primarily along Tradd Street, at the South Carolina Society Hall, and at a home at 69 Meeting Street. The 69 Meeting Street home is a 3 ½ story, stucco-covered brick building, designed in the Federal style so popular in colonial times.

Extensive filming had already taken place at the College of Charleston's Randolph Hall in the courtyard called the 'Cistern', as well as in the surrounding countryside, including at the black cypress lagoons of Cypress Gardens. On a crisp but sunny afternoon, Marilyn and I took a guided boat trip through the lagoons. From a flat bottom boat, we observed alligators gliding through the swamp, or just basking in the sun. Wood ducks, hawks, osprey, herons, and egrits inhabited the majestic cypress trees, which tower above the swamp waters. The call of warblers and Carolina wrens pierced the silence.

Then, we toured Cypress Gardens via 4 ½ miles of walking paths, and crossed the stone bridge and campsite building which had been built to stage scenes from the movie 'The Patriot'. We experienced the ink-black waters, amid towering cypress trees and dense foliage, much as encountered by the patriot General Francis Marion, known as the "Swamp Fox", and his gutsy group of marauders.

Francis Marion, the "Swamp Fox"

In August, 1782, General Marion and his men ambushed a group of British regulars, just north of Moncks Corner at Wadboo Creek. His band of men emerged from a tangle of cypress trees and surprised the British with a guerrilla warfare tactic he seemed to pioneer.

Francis Marion was able to create havoc for the British from the swamps, and become famous as the "Swamp Fox", because of an earlier quirk of events on March 19th, 1780. A dinner party was given that night in Charles Town at the home of Captain McQueen, at the corner of Orange Street and Tradd Street. Following custom, host McQueen locked his home's doors so no one would leave, and encouraged his guests to drink heavily, by giving repeated toasts to 'victory and liberty'.

One guest was not inclined to heavy drinking, and instead chose to leave the house via a 2nd-story window. In climbing out the window, he fell, and the gentleman broke his ankle. This turned out to be his good fortune, and the good fortune of the Patriot cause. Because of his injury, he departed the city to his plantation to recover, and in so doing, escaped capture by the British when they entered the city on May 12th. The gentleman's name was Francis Marion.

Another skirmish had taken place earlier in the war at Wadboo Creek Bridge. This land was once part of the 12,000 acre Wadboo Barony granted to James Colleton in 1683. The land remained in the family until it was confiscated by the British during the Revolution.

Today, Wadboo Creek can still be enjoyed, much the same as it was over +200 years earlier, meandering its way to the headwaters of the Cooper River. It bends and winds its way through a pristine mix of bottomland and pine forests, and into the cypress swamps. So near to civilization, yet civilization seems so far removed. A 7-mile canoe and kayak trail allows passage and spectacular close-up views of the dark glass-like waters, which mirror the towering centuries-old cypress and gum trees.

Hikers can reach the area from the Palmetto Trail access, where Swamp Fox Passage crosses. Alligators peer over floating water lilies, turtles are perched on decayed driftwood logs as they sun themselves. Wood ducks fly overhead, and a white ibis darts from tree to tree. An osprey guards its nest, and the eerie solitude of the swamp is broken only by the squawks of a lone osprey as he calls out from time to time to onlookers below.

For weeks, Marilyn and I had watched with much fascination and interest as the movie set people from 'The Patriot' constructed a façade onto the entry of Randolph Hall, within the center quadrangle of the College of Charleston's downtown campus. A new set of massive steps was built, looking so old and real, that we both would regularly walk up and touch it to realize it was just a movie prop. From these steps, the movie would show a young boy emerging from the building to shout to an assembled crowd outside that the delegates had voted for independence.

Once, Marilyn and I were returning from a walk into town, walking along George Street across the street from Randolph Hall. At the same time, we both looked to our left, and remarked, "I don't remember that beautiful old house" we were seeing. Then, as we walked a few steps further, we broke into chuckles and laughter, as we realized "that old house" was merely a movie façade that had been built to conceal from the movie camera's eye the College of Charleston cafeteria behind it.

A wonderful story occurred on the day of filming at Randolph Hall. Marilyn, interest piqued to a feverish level, left our home at 29 ½ Montagu and walked four blocks to watch the movie's filming. She positioned herself at an iron gate, accompanied only by a security guard on-duty to restrict entry. Much to her amazement, the movie's star, Mel Gibson, walked out of a door within twenty feet of her. She waved, and he returned her wave. This was a moment she will cherish forever!

But, Marilyn is fearless, and tenacious. She was not through yet. She found a nearby bench, and climbed up upon it, to peer over the courtyard wall to see the filming action. As she was feeling pretty good about deftly procuring such a favorable viewing location, one of the movie's staff tugged at her back. She would have to get down, because the filming and camera's eye could find her countenance peering over the wall in the background of the movie. I still get a kick each time I let my mind picture that happening.

The British occupation of Charles Town would last 2 ½ years. During 1781, General Nathaniel Greene's forces of Patriots would fight their way through victories in the South Carolina countryside, until they were within 15 miles of Charles Town, and threatening to encircle the British within the city.

General Greene waited on the western banks of the Stono and Ashley Rivers. Meanwhile, General George Washington stunned British General Lord Cornwallis, and the British surrendered at Yorktown on October 19th, 1781. With Cornwallis' defeat, the British Parliament decided to end the war as soon as possible.

The British commander of Charles Town received orders to negotiate evacuation of his troops from the city. After controversial agreements were reached regarding confiscated property, debts, and disposition of the city's Tories and commandeered slaves, the British evacuated the city on October 27th. The British took everything they could haul away. As the Continental army slowly moved into town, the British fled off Gadsden's Wharf. The townspeople lined the city's streets greeting the victorious 'Americans' with cries of "God bless you, gentlemen! You are welcome here, gentlemen".

Meanwhile, the massive British fleet lay at anchor in the harbor, poised to depart. And, depart they did on December 14, 1782.

In a convoy of 40 ships, the British left with 3,700 Tories (or Loyalists), 5,000 slaves, booty of indigo, silver, fine china, wine, and even the bells of St. Michael's Church.

> (On November 30th, 1782, the new country and Great Britain signed the preliminary Treaty of Paris that unofficially ended the Revolutionary War. The following year, Britain, France, Spain, and Holland officially recognized the independence of the thirteen colonies that would become the United States.)

The city of Charles Town lay in ruins, as well as its outlying plantations. For the next two years, riots, demonstrations, violence, and vengeance were directed against Tories who had remained in the city. A new City Council form of government was established in 1783, to reclaim law and order within the city, and the city's name was shortened to "CHARLESTON".

Rebuilding from the city's ruin, and rebuilding for a new nation were needed. It would not be the last time Charleston would have to rebuild.

What happened to the 56 men who signed the Declaration of Independence? Five men were captured by the British as traitors, and were tortured before they died; twelve men had their homes ransacked and burned; two men lost sons who died as soldiers fighting for the Revolutionary Army; two men had sons captured; and, 9 of the 56 men fought and died from wounds or hardships resulting from the Revolution. All these men had pledged 'their lives, their fortunes, and their sacred honor'.

In December 1783, John Rutledge returned to Charleston. Edward Rutledge returned to practice law, and purchased in 1788 the two-story Georgian style double house of James Laurens (brother of Henry Laurens) at 117 Broad Street, across the street from the house of his brother, John. The brothers found a city thoroughly devastated by war and the British occupation. Property had not been maintained; and, many citizens faced homes in ruin. Small farmers, as well as the wealthy, had fewer slaves because nearly 5,000 had left with the British, some slaves leaving voluntarily and others under duress by the British.

Rice exports fell to market bottom at a mere 20% of their pre-war level, and at the same time that volume collapsed, profits fell even further as the British levied new taxes on imports. Then, in 1784 and 1785, bad weather further compounded the plight of the rice planters.

The market for indigo never recovered from the loss of British subsidies. Combined with this, the East Indies became a larger producer of indigo. Soon, indigo would be abandoned as a viable crop in America.

With these market difficulties, the high interest rates on credit, if available, made debt very expensive for the planters. And, cash was simply not available. The large planters, like the Rutledges, found themselves deep in debt.

Framers of the Constitution

John Rutledge, along with Charles Pinckney, Charles Cotesworth Pinckney, and Pierce Butler, attended the convention in Philadelphia in 1787, and helped draft the new Constitution of the United States. Prior to leaving for Philadelphia, Charles Pinckney dined at the home of John Rutledge at 116 Broad Street, to discuss the upcoming convention. Both men proved highly influential in shaping many aspects of the new form of government. John Rutledge chaired the committee assigned to draft the Constitution, and many believe, he had the largest role in drafting the document.

Charles Pinckney would be nominated for Vice President with Presidential nominee John Adams, and later be nominated by the Federalist Party for President in 1804 and 1808, although losing those elections.

Despite John Rutledge's impressive political accomplishment, he found himself in growing financial difficulties during the 1780's, and attempted to restore his fortune through heavy land speculation, but only succeeded in getting more and more in debt. In 1790, he was forced to mortgage his home at 116 Broad Street to provide adequate security for his obligations. By 1794, he had to rely on financial assistance from his son and brothers, especially Edward. Large tracts of his property had to be sold to fend off the creditors.

His long time friend, President George Washington, nominated John Rutledge for Chief Justice of the Supreme Court, but difficulties developed in securing his nomination. This political setback, coupled with overwhelming financial burdens, led to failing health. A true southern "gentleman" had lost his pride and his dignity; depression and despair became too much to handle. On a December morning in 1795, it all became too much. He left his house at 116 Broad Street, and walked west to the Ashley River, where he walked into the river fully clothed and tried to end his life. He was rescued by a passerby, but he never recovered from the humiliation, and his public life was over. Both he, and his brother Edward, died in 1800. John is buried in St. Michael's Church graveyard; Edward is buried at St. Phillip's churchyard.

A GARDEN COURTYARD IS PLANNED FOR 29 ½: CHAPTER 17

Marilyn and I have been living in our newly restored carriage house for a number of months, and with another Spring approaching, we have to get back to work because our backyard walled courtyard is in shambles from the construction. We have to finalize plans for a beautiful garden courtyard, and get ourselves motivated to start the arduous task. But, first, we decide to explore some of downtown Charleston on foot.

We leave the carriage house, and walk about 4-5 blocks east, and find ourselves ambling along the numerous shops along King Street. Turning left from King Street onto Queen Street, we wonder past the great restaurant called "82 Queen Street", and soon find ourselves upon the fountain at Waterfront Park. Children, from small toddlers to young teenagers, are frolicking in the cool sprays of the fountain, while others wade in and out of the pool glimmering in the sunshine, as the fountain spray cascades below. The children are screaming from the cool blasts of water, and having fun as only children can do, while parents and fun-seeking onlookers watch the merriment.

James Funk

Past the early Spring flowers, just now in bloom, past the grassy park area where a group plays pass and catch with a football, past families picnicking on blankets, we come to the boardwalk pier jutting toward Charleston harbor. Wonderful benches are constructed as swings for kids, lovers, and just single bodies relaxing to catch a few glorious winks of afternoon sleep. The pluff mud under the pier and at water's edge lets us know of its presence via its unique pungent smell, revealing that low tide has exposed the mud, and its decaying ecosystem of life within, only to be covered over and hidden once again when high tide completes its never ending cycle. The fiddler crabs are evident from the ooze visible from their diggings on the un-dredged mud flats.

We enjoy our time here on the pier, gazing across the harbor's glistening water to see the ship USS YORKTOWN moored at rest on the opposite shore, a lasting testimony to one era in Charleston's long military history. Another historic site can be seen in the distance, once guarding the mouth of the harbor, Fort Sumter. It is said that while bombardment of Fort Sumter was underway starting the Civil War in 1860, Charleston residents watched and enjoyed cocktails from the rooftops of their homes along the Battery. Never let it be said that the Charlestonians would stop a good party simply for a little skirmish.

Egrits and pigeons fly overhead, as we look to our left at the imposing silhouettes of the Cooper River bridges arching over the horizon, connecting peninsular Charleston to neighboring Mt. Pleasant. Under the bridges pass a constant stream of massive container ships, which make the port of Charleston the 4th busiest in the country. The buoys bob with the currents, marking the channel for the cargo ships' safe passage. It never seems routine to watch one of these mighty vessels ease its way into or from the deep water ocean just beyond.

If we are fortunate this day, we will be able to watch playful dolphins in a carefree swim not far away. And the breeze, the ever present breeze, feels so wonderful. Living in a port city, with the rivers and ocean so near, is truly a treasure.

But back to work is a must. After a wonderful Saturday morning's walk, we head back to the carriage house. Planning must continue on the garden we want to develop in our rear courtyard at 29 ½ Montagu.

As with the start of any project like this, I find it absolutely necessary to work the design out on paper first. I started with measurements of the space we had available in the courtyard; it was quite small, and compact, so every square foot of space needed to be planned and used efficiently. Our entire lot size was 37 ft. wide in front, by 48 ft. deep, and 39 ft. wide at the rear courtyard wall. Half or so of this minuscule lot space of roughly 1,825 sq. ft., or less than 1/20th of an acre, was taken by the house footprint; therefore our courtyard was about 20x40 ft., or 800 sq. ft. The trick was to design as much garden as possible in the limited space; we wanted it to feel cozy and intimate, a quiet haven removed from the hustle and bustle of the nearby city street out front; yet, we wanted to avoid a crunched and crowded feeling.

I started with pencil and paper, constructing a scaled drawing of the courtyard. A circular planting area, just outside and centered on the double-French door entry to our sunroom, would be a perfect spot to feature a statute which would create a focal point of interest as guests approached our rear entry. Massive, beautiful banana trees were growing at the courtyard wall just off the kitchen, and they would certainly need to stay.

The narrow brick pathway leading from the old black entry gate at streetside was perfect, but a visual feature of interest was needed as one walked through the gate. I thought an answer would be an arbor, featuring the old columns from our original screened porch which had been saved; this would lend some historical continuity, and the arbor could be draped with overhanging vine, with a concrete bench under its shade, offering the visitor a refreshing spot to sit and ponder the peace, beauty, and tranquillity of the garden.

Nearby I reserved space for construction of a water garden, envisioning the beauty of water lilies floating on the water's surface, as a fountain, and waterfall feature provided the peaceful entrancing sounds of cascading water. We also needed space for an umbrella table and chairs for outdoor dining. Likewise, cozy small seating and conversation areas were needed, where we could utilize the outdoor wrought iron furniture which had come with our purchase of the home from David Kludt. Lastly, our planning had to provide a visual and noise buffer for the air conditioning equipment located in the back right hand corner of the courtyard. A paved, curving, and graceful pathway would then link all of these design elements.

With these design objectives in mind, it became just a matter of trial and error, transporting a visualization of the final product to paper, and getting all the space and sizing elements to fit in scale. After a number of attempts on paper, as well as refinements and fine-tuning after discussions with Marilyn, we arrived on a final plan. A final design on paper could also be used to calculate the quantities of materials needed for construction.

But, before new construction could begin, a few cleanup items faced us big-time. Literally a mountain of construction debris had been piled in the courtyard from the months of restoration work inside the carriage house. This was a mess, major challenge, and dilemma; and, the 'palmetto bugs' (Charleston's 'polite' word for cockroaches) were finding the piles perfect for their homes. Likewise, two large loquat trees were messy and maintenance problems for the courtyard, and their foliage provided too dense a cover for anything to grow well in the courtyard.

Our answer was to call on a friend named Joe Keating, who hauled debris from my construction site at work, and Joe could also trim trees and knew something about landscaping. We recruited Joe, and on a Saturday morning he knocked on our gate, with a helper, both eager to get started.

While the helper hauled debris from our courtyard, piece-by-piece, to a dilapidated trailer parked at our curb, Joe studied our tree situation and donned his cleated boots and readied himself to climb the trees. Marilyn and I stood and watched in awe, and sometimes with apprehension. Joe worked, perched high above us, with cleats dug into the tree's bark, while wielding a buzzing chainsaw. A rope was tied to each major limb before cutting began. Then, after the chainsaw completed its work, producing a mighty roar that seemed to shake the neighborhood, Joe would lower the rope holding the severed limb to the ground. Bit-by-bit the tree began to disappear, with Joe deftly maneuvering each limb to the ground safely, in such a tiny courtyard space, and with absolutely no damage to our courtyard walls.

As the limbs and branches accumulated on the ground, they would be cut into pieces small enough for his helper to cart away to the street, and pile curbside. Soon, the first tree was down, and then the second tree. Finally, Joe tackled pruning of a giant Ligustrum that had grown over the many years from its common shrub form into a gigantic tree which draped its massive branches so artistically over our new sunroom. Joe told us that this was surely the largest Ligustrum tree he had ever seen. We wanted to keep this tree, because it was a showpiece, and offered a wonderful visual framework for the rear view of the carriage house, standing just off the entry to the house, a mere two feet or so from the wall and windows of the sunroom. After Joe completed his artistic pruning, it looked even more magnificent.

In one day of hard work, Joe and his helper had rid us of the massive, ugly piles of construction debris. With the two trees removed and pruning of the giant Ligustrum, the sunshine could find its way into the courtyard so plants could grow. With the job complete, we gathered in our sunroom to celebrate and enjoy several cold beers. Before long, we were all laughing raucously as Joe held us entranced with stories of his youth, and growing up in Charleston. As the day ended, and Joe pulled away from the house with his trailer overflowing with our debris, Marilyn and I were content and pleased as we looked forward to the next phase of our courtyard project.

ANTEBELLUM CHARLESTON, AND "KING COTTON": CHAPTER 18

The period between the end of the Revolutionary War and the start of the Civil War would comprise about 75 years, and witness great swings between highs and lows, particularly for the economy in Charleston. 'Antebellum' Charleston would be called pretentiously by some "the capital of Southern Civilization". Charleston would become unique because of: its geographic isolation, which helped in its defense; its plantation culture; its intellectual and family ties to Europe and the mother country of England; and, its intimate society, built on close networks of families, with diverse ethnic heritage.

Although the influential families maintained close ties and friends in Boston, New York, and Philadelphia, the people of Charleston developed a homogenous way of thinking and outlook upon their life...it became their very own "Southern way of life".

By 1790, the first census reported a population in Charleston of 12,000 whites and 35,000 blacks, both slaves and free blacks. A greater number of black Americans lived in Charleston than in Boston, New York, and Philadelphia combined. At the start of the Revolution, the Continental Congress stopped foreign slave trade. While large numbers of slaves had been imported into South Carolina in the 1770's, Charleston's leaders did not disagree with this temporary ban, perhaps because the influential planters were amenable to reducing further additions to their already high debt. Henry Laurens even advocated freeing the slaves, but Southerners led by John Rutledge blocked any statement concerning slavery from the Declaration of Independence.

Any impulse to take progressive steps toward emancipation came to an end in the 1790's. The great slave insurrection in Santo Domingo sent waves of fear through the southern slaveholders, both blacks and whites. As refugees from Santo Domingo poured into Charleston, fear grew rampant. A fire in 1796 was thought to have been started by a black West Indian refugee. In 1798 a mass meeting of the citizens was held in St. Michael's Church to discuss the fear of threatened attack. A city ordinance was passed in 1806 forbidding the assembly of more than seven "free persons of color", unless attended by a white person. Furthermore, free persons of color could not assemble for dancing or "other merriment" without receiving prior written permission.

The rice planters, with much to lose, never supported emancipation of their labor force. But, with the advent of a new crop, cotton, the rice planter's voice would soon be joined by the upcountry cotton growers, who also needed slaves. Thinking became more rigid, and polarized, in both Charleston and the upcountry of South Carolina. A "Southern way of life" made the slave question non-negotiable.

Cotton would change lives in Charleston. The first ship sailing from an American port with cotton departed from Charleston's wharves in 1784. But, the invention of the cotton gin by Eli Whitney in 1793 had the most marked effect on Charleston. While rice trade was increasing, a new market for cotton was developing. So-called "sea-island cotton" was grown near the coast, and it was a very fine, strong cotton that was easy to weave, and its cloth had a luxurious feel, that commanded a much higher price than the more inferior "upland cotton".

However, Eli Whitney's new machine would change all of that...with his cotton gin, "short staple" cotton could be harvested efficiently, and this variety of cotton could be grown productively in more diverse backcountry regions. With the availability of slave labor, the agricultural revolution exploded the market for cotton. Cotton became king.

While Charleston's economy would continue to depend upon rice, as well as slave trading, shipping, and retailing, its major export would become cotton. For years, upland cotton would be planted in the Spring, harvested in September thru October, converted in the gins in October and November, and transported by boats down the rivers to the port in Charleston for export to English and European manufacturing centers.

Whereas the Lowcountry elite had always been located in Charleston, now the upland cotton growers were eager to rise to the levels of prosperity and power previously enjoyed only by the elite in Charleston. Soon the upcountry was challenging the power base held exclusively by Charleston.

Furthermore, great gains were being made in the North which would erode Charleston's power. In New England a shift was occurring toward the start of an industrial economy, and New York City began to gain importance at the expense of Charleston.

While Charleston had been the center of commerce along the Atlantic coast, the new age of industry changed that dominance. And, the change from sailing ships to steam-powered vessels left Charleston behind.

But changes were masked for a time by the exploding boom in prices and demand for sea island cotton. In 1791, South Carolina grew 1,500,000 pounds of cotton; in a mere ten years, that grew to 20 million pounds, and then doubled again in the next ten years. From early 1800, increasing demand for both cotton and rice, coupled with rising market prices, fueled Charleston's longest economic boom. By 1818, the price of raw cotton reached $.35 per pound, which would be its peak price during the antebellum period.

Slave labor became even more essential to the economy. The city that grew wealthy and powerful from slavery, would ultimately become its staunchest defender, and ultimately suffer the most from it…but, that was years to come.

Fueled by prospects for immense profits from cotton and rice, the slave trade was resumed in 1803, after being stopped for the years following the Revolution. Over the next several years, 40,000 slaves entered the country via Charleston. While opposition to slavery was increasing in Europe, and just starting in the North, Charleston turned a deaf ear.

Commercial life boomed along the city's wharves, and shoppers crowded King Street's stores. The streets and wharves were crowded, and the sounds of the throngs echoed with the speech of varying foreign tongues of traders and sailors. The docks bulged with cargoes of bananas, coconuts, and coffee being unloaded from the ships, before the ships were reloaded with rice and cotton for the journey to Europe's eagerly waiting markets.

The fury of port activity lasted through April, when the last ships would leave port headed for Europe. By June, the harbor was nearly empty, and the wealthy would flee the city's hot summer.

Fashions in clothes had changed, and became simpler, as the century turned to the 1800's. The men cut their hair short to let the wind blow their bobs, and knee-breeches were replaced by tight fitting "panta loons". Women changed from hoop skirts and heavy silks, to high-waisted dresses of soft silk and muslins in the Empire-style, and the dress lengths dared to stop just short of the ankles. When the lady went out, she donned a long coat of soft muslin or satin, and carried an embroidered handbag displaying beautiful and painstakingly intricate needlework. Sometimes the lady wore a stylish soft silk turban on her head, as shown in some of the portraits of the time painted by Thomas Sully.

Thomas Sully was a renowned portrait painter, born in England, but raised and educated in Charleston. He painted some 2,600 portraits, including portraits of four Presidents, and some of his portraits are displayed in Charleston today at the Gibbes Art Museum on Meeting Street.

A women's fad, at the time of the French Revolution, was to cut their hair in a "crew cut" as an expression of sympathy for the French victims of the guillotine; the closely cropped hair was covered by a wig when out in public. The irony of the story goes that the wigs were reportedly made from the actual human hair gathered from the victims of the guillotine.

Dueling

Dueling, though controversial, was still in vogue. A local newspaper reported that in the early morning hours of October 21st, 1786, a Dr. Ladd reluctantly met a Mr. Isaacs on the field of honor. With some 20-feet between them, the two men faced each other. Dr. Ladd had a change of heart, and fired into the air; but, Mr. Isaacs fired at his adversary, wounding him in the knees. Dr. Ladd died two days later, at the age of 22 years.

Earlier, in October 1775, a less tragic duel occurred between two of the city's most prominent citizens. It seems Henry Laurens and John F. Grimke reached a heated disagreement over the opening of 'private letters' by someone other than its recipient. A challenge was issued, and the two men met at the 'field of honor' to resolve their differences in a duel. But, Henry Laurens thought better and refused to fire, because he was opposed to dueling; John Grimke tried to fire, but his pistol malfunctioned. The two men were spared, and somehow, patched up their differences in a gentler way.

Fortunes were made, and new mansions built in Charleston. Planters and merchants alike prospered, and continued to build in-town houses, which became more spacious, larger and grander. Charleston grew to the north and west. Ansonborough, Wraggborough, Mazyckborough, Radcliffeborough, and Elliottborough were established to the north of Market Street; Harleston Village and Cannonborough grew to the west of Meeting and King Streets.

Planter families became wealthy with the production of both cotton and rice...families like: Alston, Heyward, Izard, Legare, Lowndes, Manigault, Middleton, Pinckney, and Vanderhorst.

The power and aristocracy in the city were in the hands of the planters, but its composition was ever changing. The sons of wealthy planters could become lawyers, which would serve as a stepping stone to politics. Likewise, a newcomer could make a large fortune as a merchant, but then he might invest his wealth in plantations, and education for his children.

These children, then, could marry into more established planter families. In this way, the social fabric was being interwoven among both planter and merchant families, each enjoying the phenomenal success wrought from the bustling activity of this port city. Yet, the four cornerstones of the social pecking order remained constant: ancestral family name, material possessions, occupation, and education.

Families of Intermarriage

The prominent families became more and more intertwined through marriages within the families. One of the grand homes stands today at 14 George Street, in what is now Ansonborough, but in the area called Middlesex when it was built in 1797. The house is known to locals as the Middleton-Pinckney house.

When built, the house sat upon a bluff, overlooking marshy vistas to the northeast, and a creek ran to its north in what is now the Calhoun Street area.

A woman by the lengthy name of Frances Motte Middleton Pinckney started building the house for herself and her son John Middleton. Her lineage speaks volumes of the societal structure and linkage of the prominent families within the city. Frances Motte was the daughter of Rebecca Brewton Motte; Rebecca Brewton Motte's father built the magnificent home at 71 Church Street, and her brother, Miles Brewton built the Georgian mansion at 27 King Street.

Rebecca inherited the Miles Brewton mansion when the Brewton family perished at sea while traveling to England. In that house, Rebecca locked Frances and her two sisters away in the attic, to hide from the young British staff officers of Sir Henry Clinton, who had commandeered the home as his headquarters during the British occupation of Charleston during the Revolution.

After the Revolution, Frances married John Middleton, who had fought in the war, and she moved to his home at Crowfield Plantation. John Middleton's father was Henry Middleton, who had created the beautiful formal gardens that can still be enjoyed to this day at "Middleton Place Plantation", off Highway 61 along the Ashley River. John and Frances fathered a son, but John died soon after. The widow Frances started construction on her George Street town home in 1796, and shortly thereafter, Frances married Thomas Pinckney.

Thomas Pinckney's previous wife was the elder sister of Frances, but she had died while Thomas was serving his country as minister to the Court of Saint James in England, leaving him with a family of young children. So, widow and widower, Frances and Thomas wed, joined families, and joined together to continue work on the George Street town home. In their wills, it was revealed that Francis Middleton Pinckney contributed $14,000, while her new husband contributed $35,000 to the construction of her dream home.

Middleton Place Gardens/Ashley River Plantations

Today, Henry Middleton's "Middleton Place Plantation" is well worth the 20-mile trip up the Ashley River corridor from downtown Charleston. A drive along Highway 61 offers a breathtaking glimpse of the 'Old South', and its serene beauty. Canopies of majestic live oak trees, draped in Spanish moss, overhang the roadway. The Ashley River corridor has been dubbed "one of the most important river corridors in America" by preservationists. It offers a rich historic trove, as nearly 40 plantations once lined both sides of the Ashley River, although many were destroyed by Union troops during the Civil War. Its broad marshes, live oaks, and cypress swamps remain undeveloped examples of pristine riverscape beauty.

Middleton Place Plantation can be toured today. Spectacular views can be seen from the property, perched high on bluffs, overlooking the Ashley River as it winds its way through remnants of the old-time rice fields which lined its shores. From 1741, when Henry Middleton first acquired the property through marriage, it was home to four generations of Middleton's. Henry Middleton was President of the Continental Congress; Arthur Middleton signed the Declaration of Independence; a second Henry Middleton was Governor of South Carolina; and, William Middleton signed the Ordinance of Secession at the Civil War's beginning.

The main house was burned by Union troops in 1865, and its gutted walls finally fell to the Earthquake of 1886; but, the ruins can still be seen by visitors. The formal gardens, surrounding the house, have been restored and offer the visitor a magnificent glimpse of nature's treasure. Camellia groves, Crepe Myrtle, Tea Olive, China and Tea Roses are revealed in the formal gardens and lawns. A cypress lake can be circled via pathways laced with Daphne Odora, lilies, and other indigenous plants. A walk in the woods showcases native Azaleas, partridge berry, trillium, and wood violets which cover the forest floor. Woodpeckers rat-a-tat-tat on hollow spots of trees, while geese, swans, wood ducks, and mallards swim beneath the arching cypress bridge, which reflects in its picturesque beauty in the black water beneath.

Nathaniel Russell House

Another example within Charleston is the Nathaniel Russell house, built in 1811, at 51 Meeting Street. It stands today, an example of immense wealth and the Adams-style architecture so prevalent in its day.

But, the house still standing today is remarkable, because a few months after the house was completed, a tornado tore off the roof, broke windows, and ruined furnishings. Later, the house was damaged by Union shells bombarding Charleston in the Civil War. With his fortune lost by war, its owner Governor Robert Alston could have lost the house to ruin. But, a contractor offered to repair the house without immediate payment, because he had worked extensively for Governor Alston during good times. Mrs. Alston offered to repay him from money she could make by opening a boarding school within her home to make ends meet. By this agreement, and the future work by preservationists, the house was preserved for later generations to admire as a lasting edifice to the grandeur of those times.

Today, it is a magical experience to be able to walk the streets of Charleston and gaze upon so many of these magnificent mansions and public buildings, virtual treasures, which remain essentially unchanged from that bygone era some 200 years ago. You can close your eyes and imagine seeing the ladies of 1800's Charleston passing by dressed in lace and new crinoline, with low cut gowns, and full sweeping skirts covering their ankles. They held in their gloved hands folding parasols, which were new, and the latest fashion.

As one's imagination deepens, the clip-clop sounds of carriages drawn by horses, lumbering in the heat and humidity of Charleston in July or August, intensifies the vivid picture in your mind. Even the unseemly smells, from occasional droppings from the horses onto the street, make the sensation more real (although the City now requires horses to wear diapers!). Then, you are sharply drawn back to reality by the whirring sounds of automobile traffic, often speeding by in too much of a hurry, and you realize that the carriage passing by is loaded with tourists gathering their glimpses of the wonders of present-day Charleston.

And, the sidewalks are actually filled with streams of tourists, often with children in tow, stopping now and again to gaze through the iron gates of these stately mansions, to enjoy the beautiful gardens partially hidden behind the centuries-old walls.

In antebellum Charleston, beautiful gardens were cultivated, such as Magnolia Gardens along the Ashley River, laid out in 1843 by the Reverend John Grimke Drayton, and filled with imported Camellias and Azaleas from the Orient.

Charleston became the undisputed aristocratic, intellectual, and literary capital of the antebellum South. Writers, painters, silversmiths, and poets flocked to the city. Theatres flourished.

Great architects, like Gabriel Manigault and Robert Mills, designed a number of the city's great buildings. The most renowned novelist of the time, William Gillmore Sims, called Charleston home.

Decorative wrought iron on balconies, and garden gates and fences, became a way to distinguish the great homes of the wealthy. German blacksmith artisans arrived in the 1800's, and their designs were often patterned from British art, particularly from London's fine ironwork. The ornate artwork of these skilled ironwork craftsmen can still be found today throughout the city, such as the gates of St. Michael's Church cemetery (c. 1840), and the so-called "Sword Gate" (c.1848) at the mansion on 32 Legare Street fashioned by a young German, Christopher Werner, who began his renowned career in Charleston. The gates at City Hall's Washington Park off Broad Street, and at St. Philip's Church on Church Street, are further examples of the ornate ironwork of early 19th century local craftsmen.

Jewish Congregation in Charleston

Between 1790 and 1820 Charleston had the largest Jewish population of any city in America. Jewish immigrants were among the first settlers, arriving as early as 1695, but worshiped informally until 1749.

In 1749, the Kahal Kadosh Beth Elohim congregation was organized, as the 4th Jewish congregation to form in the colonies.

In 1792, construction began on a Georgian-style synagogue at 86-90 Hasell Street, the largest synagogue in America. The edifice was destroyed by the Great Fire of 1838, although the present wrought iron gate on Hasell Street dates to that original building.

The present structure in the Greek Revival-style was started in 1840, and dedicated in 1841. It is now the second oldest synagogue in the country, and oldest in continuous use (it was designated a National Historic Landmark in 1980). Beth Elohim's cemetery on Coming Street is the oldest Jewish cemetery in the South.

City Hall

One of the great public buildings of the time is the present City Hall at 80 Broad Street, one of the four buildings at the corners of Broad and Meeting Streets, known as the "Four Corners of Law". The other corners include: the U.S. Post Office (Federal government); the Charleston County Courthouse building (County government); and, St. Michael's Church (Secular government). The City Hall (City government) sits with its imposing double staircase so close to Broad Street. The building was designed by Gabriel Manigault in 1801 as a branch of the First Bank of the United States. The bank lost its charter in 1811, and was purchased by the city of Charleston in 1818, and has served as City Hall ever since.

City Hall has withstood, though damaged, the ravages of cannon shells during the Civil War, the Earthquake of 1886, and the tornado of 1938. The chambers, where City Council has met for more than 160 years, and its overhead visitors' gallery, echo with the sounds of the city's history. Its 27 black walnut desks were made for council members in 1818. Its walls are lined with portraits of mayors, as well as original oil paintings of figures important to state and national history, including U.S. presidents: Andrew Jackson, Zachary Taylor, James Monroe, and George Washington.

The oil portrait in City Hall of George Washington, commissioned by the city and painted by John Trumbull, carries an interesting story. The story goes that Trumbull's first painting was rejected by the city, because it depicted a younger Washington at the Battle of Trenton. The council preferred an older Washington with Charleston in the background, to honor the week that Washington spent in Charleston in 1791. The present portrait depicts Washington, with Charleston Harbor and the spire of St. Michael's Church steeple in the background. Historians believe that after city council accepted the second portrait, artist Trumbull told officials he needed to add some finishing touches. He did so, adding a horse, with its posterior end most prominent and legs spread above the city skyline, as an untoward gesture to the city fathers. The painting has since been referred to as "Trumbull's Revenge".

Old City Jail

Another more ominous example of the public buildings built in the 1800's was the Old City Jail. The structure stands today, its four-stories peering out and over the old stucco walls which enclose its imposing presence from the streets and sidewalks below. Worn bricks on its walls peer out from beneath areas of decayed and chipped stucco, as if partially revealing its very heart, and the deep dark secrets concealed within. Barred windows, decayed parapets, massive yawning archways, and locked wrought iron gates, all add to the aura and chilling mystery as one peers at this hulking structure. The building has been purchased from the City for $1 and is being restored, to be used as a Trade School.

On a Saturday in November, Marilyn and I walked several blocks to visit the Old City Jail. The "Hat Ladies of Charleston" were sponsoring an Art Fair, with local artists and craftsmen displaying their works within the eerie confines of the jail's rooms, where prisoners were held en masse. As part of the Art Fair, we toured the Old City Jail and peered out its barred windows, much as the prisoners must have done. Outside in the courtyard, stood the horse drawn iron-barred caged cart that was used to transport prisoners, often to their hanging. This sight added to the day's spooky feelings.

You see, the story goes that the Old City Jail is, to this day, Charleston's most haunted place. Today, it sits eerily neglected and unoccupied at the corner of Magazine and Franklin Streets, much as it was when built in 1802, atop a plot of ground that was once a potter's field before the Revolution...a community cemetery for the city's indigents and criminals.

179

As the British occupied Charleston in 1780, the story continues that the Redcoats forced captured Continental soldiers to file past the powder magazine that had replaced the cemetery, tossing their muskets inside the gunpowder storage area. Disaster struck, when a musket discharged, igniting the gunpowder. A horrific explosion occurred, and sixty-two lives were lost, and, according to witnesses, "body parts rained down on the city", some landing as far as five blocks away on the steeple of St. Philip's Church.

Then, the jail was commissioned to be built in 1802, and it came to house some of the city's most notorious villains. The last of Charleston's pirates stayed there, before they met the hangman. Denmark Vesey, a freed slave accused of planning a slave revolt, was held there before he was hanged.

Denmark Vesey

Denmark Vesey's story is worth recall, because it speaks volumes of the fear of slave insurrection that was prevalent among the city's citizens in the early 1800's. In 1800, Denmark Vesey was a slave of ship's Captain Joseph Vesey, whose ship sailed and traded between the ports of Charleston and the Caribbean. Denmark's intelligence, and self-education, were such that he could read, write, and speak several languages...skills virtually impossible to acquire by slaves.

Lotteries were frequently used in those days to raise funds for charities and public works, so Denmark bought a lottery chance, and won

$1,500, an unheard sum in those days. With his winnings, he bought his freedom for $600, started a carpentry business as a "free man of colour", and soon became prosperous, while living for two decades in the city. He acquired various properties (including several wives) and a home at 20 Bull Street in the newly developing Harleston Village.

He was a thinker with broad views, and articulate. His reputation grew among the city's slaves, even reaching slaves on the plantations. Then, in 1822 a slave insurrection occurred briefly, and was stamped out quickly after a boastful co-conspirator was overheard talking of the plot. Denmark Vesey was accused of being its organizer, and jailed. It was said that Vesey's ambitious plan was to incite riot, travel south recruiting slaves to his cause along the way, and then join rebels against the French in Haiti, presumably to create a "new world order". But, fear swept the city upon his incarceration, and shook the very fabric of aristocratic Charleston society, because slaves and free blacks outnumbered the white population. Despite controversy regarding his guilt, he was convicted, and later executed, along with 36 slaves. His execution was meant to send a warning to both slave and free black alike. No longer would the places of free blacks or slaves be secure in Charleston.

Ghosts at the Old City Jail

But, let's go back to the story of the Old City Jail. Despite all the notorious characters it housed, none is more fascinating than the story of Lavinia Fisher, and her ghost who is said to haunt the Old City Jail to this day.

In 1819, Charleston was plagued by bandits who were robbing travelers and their wagons as they brought goods toward the city, and a few even disappeared never to be heard from again. Finally, the city fathers had enough, and the sheriff, a Colonel Nathaniel Cleary, was dispatched to rid the city of this problem. The sheriff headed out of town with his posse, along the Old Kings Highway (now King Street).

Inns of all types dotted the route, many with names that marked their distance from town. It was thought that the bandits were using some of the inns as their headquarters.

The sheriff and posse encountered a bandit group at the Five-Mile House, and when the bandits refused to surrender from within, the posse burned the inn to the ground, as the bandit group fled. The posse continued onward, and encountered another bandit group at the Six-Mile House, but the bandits fled into the woods as the posse was just arriving. Sheriff Cleary thought his job was done, and returned to Charleston to boast of his accomplishments, leaving just a single member of the posse to guard the Six-Mile House.

But, alas, the bandits returned at night, surprised the lone guard, and beat him badly. As he was being beaten, a woman's voice called out for the attackers to stop. As he looked up through blood streaming down his face, he gazed into the eyes of a beautiful woman, and thought he was saved. He relaxed, leaned against the window behind him, but the woman wound up her arm and delivered such a mighty blow to his face that his head was driven through the window's glass.

The woman was Lavinia Fisher; and, she and her husband, John, were the ringleaders of the bandits.

Fortunately, the lone guard, though dazed and badly beaten, managed to escape, and return to town for the sheriff. Sheriff Cleary, with posse in tow, headed back to Six-Mile House, and this time captured the Fishers and their bandit gang. With the bandits in custody, the sheriff investigated the scene for bandit loot, but instead found bodies buried in shallow graves behind the inn.

Now, Lavinia Fisher's macabre story began to grow to mystical proportions.

Newspapers reported a few bodies found, but rumor among the city's citizens had the number of bodies growing each day. It was said that Lavinia posed as an innkeeper to lure victims, poisoned them with oleander tea, stole their belongings, and buried them in the yard behind the inn. As the town's story of her exploits mushroomed, Lavinia sat in the Old City Jail awaiting her trial.

Lavinia's trial, and that of the gang members, was a circus followed day-by-day by the newspapers and public. The Fishers were found guilty, and sentenced to hang. The Fishers attempted to escape jail by sliding out a window and down a rope made of blankets. Some of the gang escaped, including husband John, but Lavinia was left behind. Shortly thereafter the escapees were recaptured within the city.

Lavinia spent her time in jail, pacing her cell, shouting profanities that made men blush, and hoping for a pardon from the governor because she was a white woman who should not die by public execution. A pardon never came. On February 18, 1820, at 2PM, the Fishers donned white robes which they requested for their execution.

Lavinia stood at the arched doorway of the jail, and screamed, as they led her out past the throng of onlookers outside. Nearly the entire town turned out to witness their execution, as they were conveyed by wagon through town to the gallows at Meeting and Lee Streets. It is a chilling thought to ponder whether the prisoner's cart that stands today in the Old City Jail's courtyard was the same cart that hauled the Fishers to their unseemly fate.

At the gallows, it took two guards to drag the screaming Lavinia up its steps. She stretched out her arms to the crowd, and pleaded for mercy. Then, seeing no mercy forthcoming, her mood changed violently. She stomped her foot, and cursed at the top of her lungs, calling for the governor to be dammed. As the nooses were lowered over the heads of the Fishers, Lavinia spoke with anger, "if you have any messages for the devil, give them to me and I will deliver them". Their bodies were buried in a potter's field, but their story never died.

During the Civil War, a Union soldier imprisoned in the Old City Jail swore he saw a woman dressed in white walking down a basement hallway. Later, a captured Union soldier of the black 54th Massachusetts Regiment reported a similar sighting. Until the jail closed its doors finally in 1939, dozens of guards and prisoners claimed to have seen the same white clothed woman pacing the jail floor; some reported seeing her through the jail's windows.

Just a couple of years ago, a College of Charleston student by the name of Andrea Fisher peered into a window of the vacant jail, and saw a beautiful woman in long white robe, pacing. Knowing nothing of the story of ghosts, or Lavinia Fisher, the student tapped on the window to get the lady's attention, and called out to see if the lady would let her inside.

But, the figure seemed oblivious. Then, as if awakened, the figure turned to the window, locked eyes with the student for an instant, and the student reported a chill running down her spine.

The figure held her gaze for a moment, then turned away, continuing her walk until her form disappeared into the hallway's darkness. It wasn't until a year later that the college student heard the ghost story on a Charleston ghost tour, and thought 'Oh, my God'. Hurriedly, she called her father, because she shared the last name 'Fisher' with the ghost; they researched, and found a 'John Fisher' in their family tree, and he had supposedly come to the Charleston area; with a gasp, they realized that this would have made the notorious Lavinia Fisher her great-great-great-great aunt! Who doubts that ghosts haunt Charleston?

Though the antebellum years in Charleston are viewed broadly by most people as a time of unparalleled prosperity, the truth is that the economy suffered its ups and downs, and the city was comprised of striking contrasts.

The city's planters were dependent upon the weather to grow their crops, the availability of debt to finance their extensive operations, and the strength of the market price and demand for their crops; and, the success of the city's port activity and foreign trade were directly tied to the market demand for rice and cotton as well. Thus, dependent upon a two-crop economy, and foreign market to boot, Charleston was vulnerable to economic vagaries.

The national currency collapse of 1819-1822 caused rice and cotton prices to freefall downward; then, overproduction softened the market from 1822-1829, as competitors expanded outside the state. While Charleston had been the country's most important rice port, she could never command such dominance as a cotton port. The rich soils of Alabama and Mississippi proved to be stiff competition for the world cotton trade, and the New Orleans port would overtake Charleston as an exporter of cotton.

The *Charleston Courier* newspaper reported that during that eight-year period, land prices fell in half, while talented persons left the city and sought employment elsewhere. The newspaper reported of the city that "many of her houses are tenant less, and the grasses grow uninterrupted in some of her chief business streets". Many of the antebellum planters were deeply in debt from living beyond their means.

Compounding the predicament of economic recession, and national business panics in 1837 and again in 1857, the city's citizens continued to be constantly threatened by disease, and fire. Malaria, typhoid, and yellow fever were constant threats. Nearly two dozen outbreaks of yellow fever occurred, and after 1832, several cholera epidemics. Women in their pregnancies were in constant danger; if not disease itself, the drugs used by the medical profession were often even more dangerous; and, medical techniques were primitive, such as the use of purging, leeches, blisters, and bleeding the patient. While the "remedies" were administered by well-intentioned physicians, if disease didn't get you, medical treatment itself could be almost as deadly a threat, and life-spans were short for many.

Furthermore, the city was struck by at least five major fires. On October 9, 1810, a fire ravaged downtown Charleston, destroying 250 colonial and antebellum homes. The fire started in the late evening in a small, wooden house on Church Street, near St. Philip's Church. It was a windy evening, and it had not rained for nearly a month. The fire raged down Church Street, engulfing wooden structures as if they were dry kindling. For 24 hours, firefighters and citizen brigades battled the ferocious flames, as the inferno moved toward the Battery. Queen Street was devastated, and nearly a dozen homes were lost on Broad Street.

Helplessly, onlookers watched in horror as glowing ashes were swept high into the wind, lighting on roofs of homes on East Bay Street, and even a home on Tradd Street. The city lost a large portion of its colonial stock of homes that awful day; 10 homes on Church Street, 44 on Union Street, 14 on East Bay Street, 26 on Queen Street, and 11 on Broad Street.

The Great Fire of 1838 destroyed nearly a quarter of the city. From King Street east to the Cooper River, between Market and Society Streets, some 1,000 buildings were lost, and 5,000 people left homeless. The fire was so severe that an ordinance was passed to ban further construction of wood buildings.

Life in the city had such striking contrasts. Though wealthy families experienced immense prosperity, it was most often achieved by the back-breaking labor of hundreds of slaves.

> (What would appear to be tragic stories, happened with regularity at that time. An August 16th, 1810, article in the newspaper reported that Maurice Brown, a 'free black' man, had negotiated to buy his wife and children from Hannah Lesesne for 650 pounds sterling.)

Though the city took pride in its stately public buildings and private mansions, vultures circled overhead feeding from the stench of offal from the nearby slaughter houses on the outskirts of town, and garbage cast into the streets outside the markets. Though gorgeous carriages plied the city's streets, the streets were filled with mud, and the unmistakable aroma and remnants of the horse-drawn society of the day. Though the residences were beautiful, and lush gardens offered wonderful vistas, the wealthy families would flee in summers to cooler seaside or northern pine forested resorts, northern spas, or Europe, leaving behind, both black and white, to sweat out the oppressive heat and humidity of Charleston's July and August, while hoping against hope that the diseases of the "sickly season" would pass them by.

Such were the events in the 1800's that influenced daily life in Charleston.

A GARDEN BEGINS TO GROW AT 29 ½: CHAPTER 19

Our carriage house is located in the city borough known as Harleston Village. Harleston Village stands on land originally granted to Henry Hughes and John Coming, who was the first mate on the ship "Carolina" which first sailed up the Ashley River with the first settlers of "Charles Towne". The marsh land and mud flats, first witnessed by those settlers, included a narrow tongue of peninsula of white sand and oyster shells, blazing white in the sun's glare; it would be named "White Point", and later, today's White Point Garden at the Battery.

Years later, a first seawall was constructed of palmetto logs, with an adjacent walkway of wood planking. The wooden structures were destroyed by a hurricane's gale force winds and crashing seas in 1804. It was rebuilt, this time with the ballast rocks carried in the hulls of trading ships. During the War of 1812, 15 large guns were mounted on the rock seawall as a shore battery, leading to its name the "Battery".

By 1852, the seawall was turned west toward King Street, and the marsh filled. The East Battery seawall received great damage from the gale of 1854, but was repaired. From 1909 to 1911, nearly 50 acres of the so-called "Ashley Embankment" marsh were filled, and became Murray Boulevard, extending west along the Ashley River to Tradd Street.

Tidal creeks and marshes were not conducive to housing, but the water power of the tides was utilized in the late-1700's to establish lumber mills, and later rice mills. By the 1840's, steam-powered mills were concentrated just to the western edge of Harleston Village along the banks of the Ashley River. Chisolm's Mill and West Point Mill along the Ashley River, and Bennett's Mill on the Cooper River were the grandest. Nearly 40% of the rough rice grown at the plantations surrounding Charleston was processed in these mills.

The last and largest mill was the West Point Mill, built in 1860. Much of the structure stands today, and you can gaze across its docks, toward the green shore of James Island, squinting into the dazzling sunset across the mirror-like images dancing red in reflections off the Ashley's water, while imagining what life was like during that era of planters and seaport merchants, and large ships laden with white gold…rice, or cotton!

John Harleston, a nephew of Mrs. John Coming, inherited much of the land in 1770 that would become known as Harleston Village. He divided the land into lots, and streets named for the important men of his day: William Pitt, John Rutledge, Christopher Gadsden, Lt. William Bull, and our street named after the Royal Governor, Sir Charles Greville Montagu.

In the 1840's and 1850's, our neighborhood of Harleston Village boomed, with an explosion of growth, and many large homes were built. The neighborhood attracted many of antebellum Charleston's best, including professionals, authors, essayists, and city leaders. Coming Street became the most popular area for the city's free blacks, and Denmark Vesey is believed to have lived nearby on Bull Street.

Our home at 29 ½ Montagu Street was built in 1850, a part of that glorious past, and Marilyn and I were determined to preserve as much of its authenticity as possible. To that end, we had learned that a thriving plantation-based brick industry had existed for 120 years in Charleston from the 1740's to 1860's, and the bricks on the walkway of our carriage house were authentic and made in Charleston. You can tell 'Charleston bricks' from others, because the 'Charleston bricks' have visible tiny black flecks of coal-like material.

Charleston Brick Industry:

Along the shores of the Wando River, a once thriving brick industry existed. Remnants of this can still be seen along parts of the river's shoreline at low tide; exposed brick fragments and long-abandoned clay pits serve as reminders of this aspect of Charleston's past.

Local brickmaking dates back to the late 1600's, but the practice received a boost when the Assembly required in 1713 that all buildings in the city be made of brick, as a response to a series of devastating fires which easily consumed the all-

191

wooden structures. Although the act was repealed in 1715 because too few bricks were available, the requirement was reintroduced in 1740 following the fire which destroyed much of the city, and still again following the Great Fire of 1838.

Over 120 years, and until the end of the Civil War, more than 50 brick makers operated in the area, nearly half located along the Wando River and its tributaries. Slave labor could be utilized to make bricks during the times of year when rice crops did not require their attention. In many cases, the sale of bricks could provide one-third of a plantation's income. The Wando area was perfect for brick production because it had the right clay, wood was abundant to fuel the kilns, slave labor could be utilized in the off-season on the plantation, and the river provided easy transportation to take the bricks to market in the city.

Both English and French brick makers came to America and brought their skills with them. Plantation bricks were made entirely by hand. Carefully blended clay, sand, and water was placed in single or double molds, which were then thoroughly dried in the sun, and removed from their molds, before being fired at high temperature for several days in wood-heated brick kilns. The bricks were brown in color, although they were referred to as "Carolina Grey" bricks.

Several prominent families dominated the industry. The Horlbecks, who owned Boone Hall plantation, became famous for their bricks. By the 1800's, John Horlbeck's Wampancheone

Brick Mill, located on what is now a subdivision of homes known as 'Brickyard Plantation' in Mt. Pleasant, was making more than one million bricks per year. Brick making at Boone Hall continued, after the Civil War until the end of the 19th century, but it was the only brick maker to operate after the war. When slavery went away, most of the brick making skill disappeared, and free slave labor was no longer available, so times changed.

We wanted to preserve, and reuse the historic old bricks in our new courtyard. Furthermore, a premium was placed on these bricks, as salvaged "Charleston brick" is currently selling for about $1,500 per thousand, compared to today's new brick at about $260 per thousand.

The first step was to remove a good portion of the bricks on the walkway at the rear of the carriage house, though the brick walkway through the entry gate and along the side of the house could stay. Each brick had to be removed one brick at a time. As each was pried out of the soil that had retained it for so many years, we scrubbed each brick with a brush and water, and some required old excess mortar to be chiseled off. As each brick was thoroughly cleaned, it was stacked off to the side so it could be used later. This tedious process required most of one weekend of work. But, the next step was even more tedious, and backbreaking.

The terrain was too low in the backyard, causing rainwater to stand and even drain toward the house. This had to be corrected. The only choice was to bring in additional fill to raise the level near the house, and slope the soil back and away from the house, so that storm water would runoff rearward on the lot toward the garden wall and away from our house.

The problem was how to transport the fill material from the street to our rear yard. The entry gate was very narrow, a step-up existed from just within the gate, and the brick walkway to the rear of the house was also very narrow. No motorized equipment could be used; in fact, it was not even practical to use a wheelbarrow, as it could not fit readily through the entry gate. The only alternative required me to haul the fill material by toting it from the street one 5 gallon bucket at a time! This was a down-right tiring thought. If I would have really known the sweat, torment, and agony of the job, I probably would not have been able to convince myself to get started.

But, start I did! I decided that the best approach was to order a light gravel material to use as a good leveling base for the brick and paver stone pathway areas. I could then place paving stones, outlined with our precious historical bricks, on the gravel material which would serve as a good, solid base. Five tons of gravel was ordered, and dumped in one massive heap at the front of our house at curbside. That's right…5 tons! All of it had to be transported by hand to the rear courtyard, bucket-by-bucket. Five gallons at a time, each bucket weighing perhaps 20 lbs., the task computed to about 550 round trips!

Also, the entire process needed to be completed with quickly, because I was sure the City fathers would not want a pile of material blocking Montagu Street for any lengthy period of time.

And so the tedious process started. After returning home from work, I would spend the next week or two of evenings loading and lugging the gravel material to its destination in our rear courtyard, dumping my buckets, and trudging back streetside for yet another load. I joked with Marilyn that I felt like a 'human backhoe'.

What made matters worse was that motorists driving by would call out some derisive phrase, like "that ain't no way to move gravel", or, something less civilized and endearing.

When I get into a mode of concentration, however, things do seem to get done. Either I was going to finish this task, or my back would give out. Sooner or later one of those two outcomes was going to happen. Somehow, though, the awful pile seemed to get smaller and smaller, and finally disappeared. The tedious task was complete, and my back had not given out!

Now we were ready to have our paving stones delivered. Marilyn and I decided on 12"x12" precast concrete stones with a top layer of imbedded pea gravel. We thought this look would go well, particularly with the old brick being laid to surround each paver stone for an "older look". The pallets of paver stones were delivered streetside, and also had to be carried two pavers at a time to the awaiting courtyard project, but this was nothing compared to the previous 'human backhoe' job.

Next we had to build a pedestal on which we could mount the five-foot high masonry statute that would be a focal point for the rear courtyard. Oh, yes, we had located and purchased a lovely statute, called the "Rose Lady". She was a beautiful figure, standing seductively with a drape modestly clinging to a discreet portion of her body, while she clung to a bouquet of roses. The "Rose Lady" was a perfect addition to the courtyard, which would attract immediate interest as any visitor rounded the corner of the walkway from the street and entered the courtyard, and add charm to the whole visual experience.

I constructed a 2'x2'x2' high pedestal for the "Rose Lady", mortaring some of the old bricks in place to form a base that looked old and original, and then capped the brick base with four of the paver stones. Both Marilyn and I thought the finished product was just great, looking tired and aged, as if it had always been there.

Now we had to mount the statute into position on its pedestal. I had placed a steel rod in the center of the pedestal and mortared it into place. A concrete bit was used to drill a hole through the bottom of the statute, so that the statute could be slipped over the rod, and the rod would serve to secure the statute in its place on the pedestal. But, the statute probably weighed about 100 lbs., so it would not be easy to lift the statute into position, and drop it down over the steel rod. Marilyn and I called over to our neighbor, George, who was in his usual position, studiously reading what seemed to him to be important material, on his massive porch overlooking our courtyard.

By the way, throughout our restoration work, George was a curious, interested observer. He would call out questions, as he was observing our work, or often come around his house and through our gate, to observe what was happening first hand. It was nice having George so interested, and he would always offer encouraging words. So, gladly, George came over to give us a hand with the "Rose Lady"; and, the three of us, with much effort and straining, were able to lift the statute into just the right position and lower the statute onto the rod and a bed of wet concrete mud that was waiting. I finished troweling the concrete neatly around the base of the statute, and one more job was complete.

The "Rose Lady" had a permanent home, and great vantage point from which to oversee our glorious courtyard.

A view from the streetside entry gate, and along the narrow walkway to our rear courtyard.

The 'Rose Lady' statute stands in all her glory, guarding our courtyard.

A GREAT STORM IS BREWING: CHAPTER 20

In 1829 the U.S. government decided that a fortified position should be established at the mouth of Charleston harbor just 3 ½ miles from the peninsula of Charleston and insight from the seawall at East Battery. The strategic value of a shoal of sand bar, a mere 2 ½ acres in size and located halfway between Sullivan's Island and Morris Island, was unquestioned; the historical significance of what was to be called 'Fort Sumter' could never be anticipated. Crowds would gather along the Battery to watch construction of the fort...the walls were pentagon-shaped, about 40 ft. in height, and built of oyster shell enforced cement and gray Carolina bricks manufactured at one of the local plantation brickyards. No one could ever imagine what was to happen at this site some 40 years later.

Things were changing. The first half of the 19th century saw steam replace sails on the great ocean-going vessels, and no longer would the trade winds favor the port of Charleston. Competition increased. The new South Carolina Railroad opened in 1833, linking Charleston to Augusta, Georgia, with the 136 mile stretch of rail being the longest in the world at its opening. The locomotive could travel at over 20 mph, pulling two cars. Opening of the railroad was a boost to the Charleston economy, because upcountry cotton crops could again be transported through Charleston, recapturing business lost to steamboats using the rivers to ports other than Charleston.

Machines, likewise, were beginning to do work previously done by skilled craftsmen for centuries. For example, iron fences, gates, and balcony railings, previously "wrought" by skilled hands, could now be made in molds by "casting" the iron. The present balcony railing at the Dock Street Theatre and the fence and gate of today's John Rutledge house at 116 Broad Street are examples of cast iron workmanship.

Fashions too were changing, and becoming more elaborate. Ladies replaced their sheer high-waisted silk and cotton dresses for the new full-skirts of rustling taffeta topped by tight fitting bodices. Men donned brightly colored trousers, plumed coats, and tall beaver hats.

But, the biggest change of all was social and economic, and for many of the wealthy and elite, they could only watch frustrated and helpless as their once cherished "Southern way of life" would come to an end. A social struggle would result in an awful war that would rip families apart, free their slaves, and thus destroy their ability to maintain the lifestyle to which they had become accustomed; and eventually, it would render their social class extinct.

The changes, however, took time and were subtle. Prosperity and the economy were based upon two crops...rice and cotton, and both relied upon slave labor for their economic viability. But, slave labor was growing increasingly more contentious and unpopular, particularly in the North where it was not an economic linchpin.

Meanwhile, during the 1840's, prosperity shone on Charleston's wealthy like before the Revolution. But, instead of looking to expand their horizons as in the golden age of the late 18th century, the powerful Charlestonians of the 19th century became more protective, and inward looking, particularly with respect to the growing debate on slavery, which was a bedrock of their economic survival. Wealthy planters and merchants indulged in luxuries and traveled extensively, often to Europe. New wealth was also being generated from cotton, as it was all over the South. A great Irish migration to Charleston occurred in the 1840's, when Irish workers traveled in work gangs to refurbish and re-dig through arduous labor the ditches, canals, and banks on the rice plantations.

By 1850, the city's population was about 27,000 people, made up of 14,000 whites, 11,000 slaves, and 2,000 free blacks.

By 1860, South Carolina was producing over 60% of the nation's rice, grown by only 500-600 planter families. Nearly half of that rice production (56 million pounds per year) was grown in the Georgetown District (just north of Charleston) by less than 90 planter families. One of these families was the Pringles who produced about 1 million pounds per year, with about 100 slaves. Their story provides an interesting snapshot into the lives of the successful planters of the day.

Lifestyle of the Pringles

In 1822, Mary Motte Alston married William Bull Pringle in the drawing room of her father's home, the so-called 'Miles Brewton House' at 27 King Street, under the dazzling lights from the immense crystal chandelier, which made the room sparkle as if from dancing diamonds. The young bride of 19 years of age, Mary, and her 22-

year old husband, moved into the mansion at 27 King Street to live with her parents, the Alston's.

Mary Motte Alston's father was Colonel William Alston, who at 35 years of age, had married in 1791 Mary Brewton Motte, the then 23-year old daughter of Rebecca and Jacob Motte. (You will remember that it was Rebecca Brewton Motte who stood up to the British officers, who occupied this very same home as their headquarters, during the British occupation of Charles Town during the Revolution.) Colonel Alston had served under the 'Swamp Fox', General Francis Marion, during the Revolutionary War.

Colonel William Alston had acquired the 'Miles Brewton House' for his bride, purchasing the home from his bride's mother and her aunt, Francis Pinckney, for 7,000 pounds sterling. Just two weeks after their wedding, the newlyweds entertained first-President George Washington as he visited Charleston in 1791, following his term in office.

Colonel Alston had a passion for horse racing, and breeding race horses. The Alston's could be counted upon to attend Race Week at Washington Race Course (now Hampton Park), as it was the social event of the season. Colonel Alston also became friends and confidant to Presidents Monroe and Jefferson, frequently meeting them at the spas of Warm Springs, Virginia.

William Bull Pringle, Mary Motte Alston's new husband, was a son of Judge John Pringle, one of his ten children. Judge John Pringle was one of three sons of Robert Pringle, a very successful merchant who built a mansion at 70 Tradd Street. John Pringle had clerked for then Chief Justice John Rutledge, before inheriting his father's home at 70 Tradd Street. John's law practice soon flourished, and became very lucrative. In 1795, he purchased a nearly 1,500 acre estate, called Runnymede, a two hour horseback ride from Charleston along the Ashley River, which added to the rice plantations he already owned on the Black and PeeDee Rivers.

Despite sharing the mansion with parents and in-laws, life for the newlywed Pringles was luxurious, beyond the foreboding iron fence, gate, and walls topped with menacing spears of ironwork, within the stately mansion at 27 King Street. Mary and William Bull Pringle enjoyed all the trappings of wealth. Passing thru the entry gate, a lavish formal garden, patterned after English gardens, was outlined by walkways lined with crushed oyster shells. Mockingbirds, cardinals, and other birds enjoyed the lush garden, and shady trees.

Guests climbed the stone steps up two flights from King Street, and entered the residence through a massive cypress door, opening to a magnificent entrance hall with two chandeliers overhead and a floor of stone imported from England. Stunning ornate woodwork and paneling added to the richness in the foyer and other rooms. Off the foyer was a parlor for greeting guests, or to be used on special occasions, such as funerals. Beyond, was the family dining room; across from it, a library contained more than 5,000 books collected by the family over generations.

'Miles Brewton House', 27 King Street, home to the Alston-Pringle families.

Ocupied by the British as headquarters during the Revolution, and by Federal forces following occupation of Charleston in the Civil War.

A massive stairway led from the foyer to the second floor, which contained two bedrooms and a drawing room that served as a ballroom for dancing. The drawing room was lavishly appointed and included a magnificent chandelier of English origin c.1790, under which several

203

generations of brides stood for their weddings, including Mary and William Bull Pringle. An exquisitely furnished withdrawing or card room served several purposes, sometimes as bridal suite, and sometimes as maternity room where most of the children were born.

Throughout the home fine artwork adorned the walls. Artwork, you see, was important to the wealthy, antebellum families, like the Alston's and Pringle's, because it provided a display of status which reflected the British system where occupation, wealth, and family ties meant everything. Portraits were important, as they conveyed family ties and demonstrated wealth. Likewise, art treasures acquired through a family's travels, especially to Europe, were displayed prominently in the home to further the family's image with their society peers.

From the second floor, a circular corkscrew stairway led to the third floor garret, and the two rooms Rebecca Brewton Motte used to hide her two daughters from the British officers who confiscated the house as their headquarters during British occupation of the city in the Revolution. The garret also served to house large stocks of wine, Madeira, and brandy.

The family loved Madeira, and consumed great quantities of the white wine fortified with brandy. The Madeira was imported by the "pipe" (126 gallons) into the city from the Caribbean islands where it was made. A specially built area in the garret at 27 King Street held 1,200 bottles of Madeira, left to age until it was consumed. Saturday night formal dinners were held regularly at the home, where Madeira flowed freely, and it was said, "the doors were locked, and no one left until the sun began to shine the next morning". (For, you see, it was polite custom in those days to lock the door of the home after party guests arrived, and then encourage them to drink heavily, as toast upon toast were offered to the party guests.)

At street level, rooms in the main residence house served as an office for plantation business and record-keeping, a sewing room, and a storeroom for meat, game, fruits, and vegetables.

Outbuildings within the estate's walls included a kitchen house, with large cistern for storing water, and huge baking oven/fireplace. A twin-bay coach house included stalls for coach horses, riding horses, and space for the livery of overnight guests, as well as space for cows and fowl; two tack rooms, and a harness room were part of the stable. A privy, and living quarters for the servants completed the outbuildings.

Family servants at this city estate grew to number 32 persons, including 19 adults and 13 children, all serving just 6 Pringle/Alston family members, and their horses and livestock. Each slave was dressed in a handsome uniform, the male servants wearing a dark green broadcloth coat, vest trimmed in silver braid, and red and green trousers. Clothing was issued to each servant twice each year. Summer clothing would be issued in May, when the family returned to the city from the plantation, or traveled to the seashore, mountains, a northern spa, or Europe; winter clothing was passed out in late November before the family returned to the plantation. The Pringles would leave four servants behind to tend 27 King Street until their return, while the other servants would travel with the family on their migrations.

The Alston and Pringle family regularly attended church at St. Michael's, where they sat in pew No.2 in the middle aisle, north side of the church. Colonel Alston had purchased this pew in 1832. Likewise, William Bull Pringle's father, Judge Pringle, was a founding member of St. Michael's Church, and had purchased pew No.29. The Pringle's and Alston's were not unlike most of the wealthy planter or merchant families, in attending church regularly when they were in the city, either at St. Michael's or St. Philip's churches.

On the plantation, the Pringle/Alston men would hike, fish, crab, or hunt, leading the opulent life of English gentlemen. The ladies' life, on the other hand, was drudgery, isolation, and boredom on the plantation, far away from the exciting social life of the city. Mary Pringle also spent much of her time pregnant, as the Pringle's delivered 13 children, averaging a delivery for Mary every twenty months.

Mary's duty, like other antebellum women head's of household, was to manage the large household, including family, servants, and guests, requiring much skill in discipline, organization, and record keeping.

Runnymede plantation was a favorite destination point for the Pringle's and Alston's. Located on the Ashley River, between present Middleton Place plantation and Magnolia Gardens, it was a two hour ride by horse back from Charleston. Judge Pringle had purchased the property in 1795 after a fire consumed the original house, which dated back to the early 1700's; he rebuilt the house on its original foundation, and renamed the plantation. Runnymede was nearly 1,500 acres, comprised of about 400 acres improved, and about 1,060 acres of gorgeous virgin Lowcountry rolling terrain, which sat perched above the rice fields, bordering the banks of the Ashley River.

The Victorian plantation house of Runnymede was about 5,000 sq. ft. in size, and referred to as an "artist's dream", with a gable roof over the front entry, and a porch that wrapped around its eastern, southern, and western sides. Its back faced the river, and rice fields. Two large hallways stretched from front to back of the house on the first and second floors. Two rooms were off each side of the hallway on each floor. A third floor was only partially finished. The doors were hewn of black walnut, and two massive 10-ft. high pocket doors closed the main room off the entry hall. The detailing was the work of fine craftsmen, including mantles for the fireplaces fashioned from Italian marble; wood trim was cherry, walnut, and ash; its glass was etched. All in all, it made for a truly elegant country retreat.

An inventory in 1850 listed the following among Runnymede's assets: 4 horses, 3 mules, 40 milk cows, 70 cattle, 70 sheep, and 40 pigs...all stock, in total, valued at $1,000, along with $800 of farm implements and machinery. In total, Runnymede was valued at $10,000.

Runnymede would produce 80,000 pounds of rice each year, along with food for the family and slaves, consisting of 900 bushels of corn, 150 bushels of peas and beans, 800 bushels of sweet potatoes, and 200 pounds of butter. Its sheep would provide 300 pounds of wool to be spun for clothing.

Mary Brewton Motte Alston, Mary's mother died in 1838; and in 1839, at age 82 years, Colonel William Alston died one of the richest planters in South Carolina, with an estate valued at over $1 million. He held plantations with over 700 slaves, valued at $350,000, or about $500 per slave. His 21 slaves at the 'Miles Brewton House' at 27 King Street were valued at just $8,000, or a mere $400 per person. His real and personal property, cash, and other holdings totaled nearly $575,000. His sons inherited plantations, while his daughter, Mary Alston Pringle, inherited the family home at 27 King Street, along with various personal property and securities.

William Bull Pringle's father, Judge Pringle, died in 1843 at age 87 years. His estate, though not nearly as large as Colonel Alston's, was still quite substantial at $250,000. His sons inherited interests in his plantations and Tradd Street home, including his son, William Bull Pringle.

In a short four year period, William Bull Pringle and wife, Mary Alston Pringle, had inherited sizeable holdings from two immense family fortunes. Through marriage and inheritance, he acquired a home at 27 King Street, and control over plantations, slaves, and property that made him a wealthy 'Southern gentleman'. He was handed all the tools he needed to succeed in the booming antebellum rice culture around Charleston.

William Bull Pringle continued to oversee the Runnymede plantation, and grow it, to the point where it produced over 1 million pounds of rice in 1859 (more than a ten-fold increase from the 1850 inventory). In the strong rice market of the 1850's, rice commanded from $0.03 to $0.04 per pound, making his gross profit from rice production a little over $30,000 per year. Each plantation was pretty much self-sufficient, growing most of the food needed, and making other supplies, like barrels needed for the rice, rope, candles, blacksmith items, etc.

So, much of the gross $ proceeds from rice production would find its way into the family coffers as profit. But, the lifestyles of the Southern planter gentleman and his family required great outflows of cash to keep up socially with the likes of even-richer families, like the Middleton's and Manigault's. Often, the profits from production of their crops were not enough to finance their lavish lifestyles; by the 1850's, the Pringles, as well as other planter families, were getting deeper and deeper into debt.

Expenses mounted up fast for gala entertaining, dining, dances, horse races, and expensive clothing needed to mingle with the elite. And, then there was extensive travel, to northern spas and summer retreats, and often Europe. And, education also drained finances, as sons needed to be sent to the finest schools, often in Europe, while daughters were sent to expensive finishing schools in the city.

The Southern planter with this opulent lifestyle, and the influential and wealthy merchants and professional people who profited and shared in this lifestyle, had so much to lose from any threat to their "Southern way of life". As the great debate over slavery gained momentum, led by abolitionists in the North, the staunchest foes of abolition were in the South, and particularly among the powerful in Charleston and South Carolina.

Over the next five years, the Pringle's, like so many other families, would experience chaos and devastation so horrible, that their lifestyle would be changed forever, never to return. Everything would be in shambles. Family members would be in their graves. Their beloved city would lie in ruins, their family would be destitute and in exile. Their plantations would be devastated by neglect, and pillaged of whatever was left of value.

Runnymede Epilogue

Even the Pringle's beloved Runnymede plantation would fall victim to the fury of a "not-so-civil" war; the mansion house was set afire by Union troops in 1865. It would be rebuilt for a third time in 1882, on its same foundation again, by Charles C. Pinckney who had purchased the property after the war. For a time, Pinckney mined phosphate on the property, as phosphate mining in that area along the Ashley River had become a new industry which fostered economic recovery after the war's devastation.

The final death blow to Runnymede, however, would be spared for another 142 years, for fire would deal its last blow on an evening in September, 2002. Near the ruins of the fire, a bell lay in the ashes to the north of this once proud house. The bell, one of the few recognizable objects that survived, bore the date "1704" cast in its side, near a large crack caused by the heat of the fire. The bell had been mounted at the top of a large live oak tree, just north of the house. In grander days, this great plantation bell had echoed over the sprawling rice fields and through the lush woods, beckoning the head of the plantation to come immediately for he was needed at the house.

COMPLETING THE GARDEN: CHAPTER 21

With the "Rose Lady" statute in place, standing proud as if overseeing our in-progress courtyard garden at '29 ½', we were ready for the next phase of restoration.

One of the design features of our garden would be a pergola, or arbor, with an open roof of cross rafters or latticework, supported by four posts or columns. The arbor was to be positioned at the end of the walkway to the side of our house, to serve as an inviting focal point, drawing visitors as they entered through our streetside gate. The arbor would be covered with the vines of Carolina Jasmine, presenting beautiful, delicate yellow flowers in the Spring. The arbor would also provide a shady spot, with a small concrete bench placed underneath its center, for a person to sit, reflect, and peer into a garden water feature to be built at its side.

Building the arbor took several weekends. I had been saving two original old columns that were used to support the roof over the screen porch, before we converted it to a sunroom. Marilyn thought these columns would be perfect, facing the walkway entry…visually, providing intricate aesthetic detail, and secondly, preserving an important historical element of the old carriage house. Just imagine the sights which these columns had witnessed over a century and a half.

The other two posts to the rear of the arbor were 12 ft. 4x4 treated lumber, which I set into the ground in concrete. The arbor was to be about 5'x5' in size, and about 8' high. But, Marilyn had an idea for another extension of vine-covered latticework that would extend back from the arbor, above the courtyard wall, and overlook the long backside of the water pond. This required setting another 12 ft. post in the ground. With posts and columns in-place and secure, I could start work fashioning a cross-lattice roof over the arbor, using 2x6 lumber placed on end with lumber wedges placed between each piece to give it a regular and uniform appearance.

The arbor has been completed, and we seem to be happy and satisfied with our work..

The last step was to construct the criss-cross lattice pattern, which would enclose two sides of the arbor. I decided to use 2x2 strips of lumber for the design. As all of this came together, I was thankful for the power tools we have today…a miter saw, circular saw, and air nail gun made the job fairly easy. Just imagine what a task this would be for a craftsman working only with crude hand tools in days gone by.

The arbor was completed, and looked just right to Marilyn and me. Now, Marilyn made a giant mistake. She volunteered to paint the arbor. This proved to be the most arduous and time-consuming task…painting lattice is not easy! But, Marilyn persisted, and our arbor was complete.

Next, we had to tackle our most ambitious project…building the water pond. We wanted a kidney-shaped pond that would be about 16 ft. in length by 8 ft. wide, and tuck nicely into the back left hand corner wall area, adjacent to the new arbor and observation bench, and alongside the side courtyard wall. Above the pond was the lattice overhead extension of the arbor, that would be perfect with Carolina Jasmine vine entailing itself over and under the latticework, with inviting looks of lush vine and a delicate profusion of yellow flowers.

After all, the first step in any design task is to visualize how the finished product will look. Next, one's mind should be allowed to run as free as possible, unbounded by conventional thinking, which only serves to constrain creativity. Marilyn and I generally found ourselves good at doing just that…thinking unconstrained. In fact, Marilyn was so good at coming up with new ideas, that I often joked with our friends, that "my job in our partnership was to sort out Marilyn's ten new ideas, discard the nine that made no practical sense, and then have the courage and audacity to attempt putting the really good idea into action".

With that in mind, we (or maybe I) decided to do a really ambitious waterfall feature at one end of the water garden. With a water pond design in place, we assembled the materials.

Instead of purchasing rocks or boulders for the walls, I economized by deciding to use discarded broken-up concrete, gathered from a construction site where a 4" thick driveway had to be crushed and removed. The 'debris' pieces of broken concrete look just like rocks and boulders, as if they are placed carefully with their uneven bottom sides facing up. A rubber-like mat material was purchased to serve as the water-tight liner for the pond, and waterfall feature.

Next, we spray-painted the shape of the pond on the ground, and began digging to excavate the varying depths of the pond. Different depths are needed, because certain water or bog plants like shallow water, others like 6"-8" of water just over their root balls, while others like water lilies can be fully submerged in 12"-20" of water. Digging did not take too long, and the soil from the dig was used to enhance the plant bed areas in other garden locations.

With the hole in place, we spread the rubber-like liner material with enough excess material so it could extend up the sides of the pond, and be retained by the wall rock structure. Next, rocks were placed carefully, to interlock with each other, and form an artistic, interesting random look. The waterfall feature was trickier. After much patience, I was able build the rocks into a cascading spiral that would allow the water to flow down a constructed waterslide, into two staged small holding ponds, and then empty into the main pond. The waterfall required a pump in the center of the pond, which would not only pump water to the top of the waterfall, but would lift the water through a fountain attachment. The fountain not only provides special visual, as well as audible, value to the water pond, but also acts to circulate oxygen through the pond to enhance growth and vigor of the plant life.

Our last step was to purchase a wide variety of plants for the pond. Water lilies were a primary plant, because their flowers floating at the surface of the pond, with various colors and shapes, provide an extraordinary visual experience which is so restful, and yet, breathtaking. Other plants included purple water iris, the large pointed leaves of the 'arrowhead' plant which grow gracefully skyward and sway with the wind, bog grasses, and small floating algae-like plants. You see, the plants have to be selected, and carefully inter-mixed, otherwise one variety can overrun the pond. Instead, what is needed is a carefully planned eco-balance among the plants. To this end, Marilyn was aghast when I purchased a quantity of snails for the pond; the snails would serve as a natural 'vacuum cleaner', consuming murky algae and other unwanted plant life that could make it impossible to keep the water clean and clear.

With the three main structural elements in place (the "Rose Lady" statute, arbor, and water garden), we needed to install the paving stone and brick pathway surface. An intricate curving pathway had been designed, which included a circular walk around the "Rose Lady", featured prominently in the center of the courtyard, in front of our set of French entry doors to our sunroom, overlooking the courtyard. The paver pathways would weave their way around the contoured plant bed areas to provide a visual extravaganza. A paver area was also included for an umbrella table with four chairs for dining, and an intimate casual seating area for wrought iron chairs and small end tables, where we could gather for coffee in the morning, or a glass of wine before dinner, or just a casual hang-out place to enjoy the garden experience.

The 12"x12" pea-gravel covered paver stones had to be placed one-by-one, on hands and knees, and leveled into their proper position for proper walkway contour (and drainage); then, one-by-one, our old 'Charleston bricks' were positioned again on hand and knee (somewhat worn and aching by this time!) to surround each paver stone, and achieve the desired pattern. About 500 sq. ft. of paving area had to be laid in this painstaking fashion over a several week period.

After all the paver stones and brick surrounds were installed, and adjusted where corrections had to be made, we were ready for the final step for the walkways. Concrete mortar was mixed a batch at a time, and then on hands and knees, worked (or pointed) into each of the crevices between the paver stones and bricks.

By carefully packing the mortar down into the depths of the joints, the mortar would bind the paver surface together, and also add an 'aged' visual effect. Just before the mortar set, a special tool was used to finish the grout, and then the surface was brushed to give a broom finish.

When finished, the walkways blended beautifully, and we were more than pleased and proud of the effect we had achieved. Not only did it look great, but it looked tired, and worn, like it had been there for years...sort of like we were beginning to feel! But, this was just the design look we had hoped to achieve utilizing the old, historic 'Charleston bricks'.

Now we were ready for the plant material. Magnificent old banana trees were already in place off the kitchen door, a special novelty feature for us 'Northerners'. Two 'Natchez' Crepe Myrtle trees stood at the back courtyard wall, and they were trimmed back, and reshaped. We had also been nurturing a small, young Sega Palm we had purchased while in our apartment...this was planted in a prominent corner off our breakfast gathering patio. English Ivy was growing, and well established on the north courtyard wall, so we transplanted a number of sprigs to the circular planting area surrounding the "Rose Lady" statute. Other plants that already existed in the

217

courtyard, or streetside, were divided and transplanted to new locations.

Our plan was to create a mosaic of plants that were positioned carefully to achieve visual appeal via differing heights, textures, colors, and leaf shapes. Likewise, we wanted the flowers to not only provide maximum variety, but also bloom at different times of the year, to give anticipation and excitement to all seasons in the garden. The last ingredient was aroma; both Marilyn and I wanted to savor the exquisite fragrances of so many plants and vines that can only be grown in this semi-tropical climate.

The last groupings of plants were purchased from various nurseries with these objectives in mind. A wonderful, deep pink Azalea was perfect for the space just outside our French door entry to the sunroom. Confederate Jasmine would present beautiful white flowers, as its vine matured and climbed along our entry walkway, but more importantly, its unmistakable sweet perfume would be a continuing treat.

The water garden begins to grow, with tender-loving care.

Other fantastic aromas would come from Mock-Orange and Daphne Odora. Carolina Jasmine's delicate yellow flowers on its vine would fill in the spaces on the sides and overhead on the arbor. Canna Lily provided different texture, and interesting leaf shape and color variation. A variety of grasses also added to the visual backdrop and mosaic, particularly as motion was added to the garden experience as their delicate tufts would

219

seemingly dance in the winds. Groupings of Daylilies, Siberian Iris, and Black-eyed Susans were a must. Most of our plantings were perennials, that just seem to get better and better as they become established; but, we also saved room at the walkway's edges for annuals, because they add so much variety in texture and color.

All of these glorious plants were purchased over a several week period, and planted. So quickly, all the hard work that Marilyn and I had endured was paying off, as we stood proudly and gazed at our completed courtyard garden. It was Fall, and now, we just had to water and watch, eagerly looking forward to the explosions of color and excitement as the Spring growing season comes to Charleston.

CHARLESTON BECOMES A TINDERBOX: CHAPTER 22

The 1800's had seen sectional differences between the North and the South become more and more distinct. Money and industry grew in the North. The South, though economically successful, remained agrarian; and, its crops required a large labor force. For a time, the increasing costs of maintaining slaves just for rice production almost eliminated slavery as an institution. But, then came 'King Cotton'. Short staple, or "green cotton" was too expensive to harvest, and not a viable crop for many years...until, Eli Whitney (a Northerner) invented the cotton gin, which automated the separation of cotton fibers from the seeds. It was then that cotton became profitable. And, as growing cotton utilized slave labor, slavery again became economically feasible, and even a necessity in the South. As cotton became 'King Cotton', slavery expanded with it.

Southerners defended slavery only as it was practiced in the South, and only rarely argued that slavery would last forever. As the voice of abolitionists, mainly in the North, grew louder, their attack on slavery was based on Christian principles that slavery was "historically evil". Meanwhile, proslavery advocates defended slavery from ample passages in the Bible. The debate became an increasingly secular religious battle, and interestingly, within same religions. Protestants, Methodists, and Baptists preached different interpretations from their pulpits, whether in the South or in the North.

The debates heated up beginning in the 1830's, as radical abolitionists preached their ideology in the North. Southern ideology, though left unexpressed for years since the debates concerning slavery around the Revolution, came under assault once again. This forced Southerners to rally to their own defense, leading to a growing homogeneity of thought regarding slavery, and an intense defense of the institution.

Southerners, lead by their ministers from their pulpits, mounted a defense of the morality of slavery. They argued that slavery, as it was practiced in the South, was in harmony with freedom, and their free operating economy was successful and demonstrated the "genius of the age". The Southerner believed in "personal freedom", but saw no inconsistency with slavery. It was said: "you are free to contain yourselves within the roles society (or Providence) has set for you, and in mature acceptance of your fates".

Private individual's virtue would produce public rewards. If, as an individual, you engaged solely in acts of high moral character, then any success you achieved was wholly ethical, as God was simply dispensing his rewards. The so-called "Divine Economy" of the South was simply God's economy, where good actions led to God's rewards. A demonstrated successful Southern economy, therefore, was an all-telling sign that "all was right". Furthermore, "it was sheer tyranny to interfere" with the "Divine Economy", as heretics in the North were preaching. Individual benefits, as well as national or sectional benefits (whether economic, political, or even religious), were received in direct correspondence to one's degree of alignment with God's will. God was in control, and it was his system. Man was wrong to change God's plan; if it needed change, God would fix it...not man.

The proslavery advocate could admit that slavery never constituted a "positive good". But, moral individuals were more powerful than any institution. Though slavery was historically evil, and evil slaveholders were bad men, slaveholders who were moral men could achieve wealth which was untainted, despite its source being dependant upon slavery. They argued, how could it be evil, when God has allowed slavery to exist since Biblical times, and in fact, blessed the South with 'King Cotton' and a rice economy of unparalleled success?

Biblical references were used extensively to support slavery. In fact, 40%-70% of Southern ministers held slaves, although in many cases, the slaves were obtained through marriages. Abolitionism constituted heresy. The issue within religions became so intense, that churches split between factions in the North, and separate factions in the South: the Presbyterians, in 1837; the Methodists, in 1844; and, the Baptists, in 1845. By 1845, any constructive exchange of ideas between ministers ended. Southern ministers preached proslavery from their pulpits, and denounced abolitionists. Just the reverse occurred from Northern pulpits.

Other changes occurred as the 1850's began...changes that escalated the looming confrontation several notches higher. For one, John C. Calhoun's death in April 1850 signaled the loss of the South's highest ranking statesman, a man who enjoyed huge political clout in Washington, DC. John C. Calhoun said that slavery was 'good', and the leaders in Charleston and throughout the South listened, and believed. Then, the foremost political voice championing slavery was silent. John C. Calhoun died.

In Charleston, the funeral cortege assembled in Marion Square, just alongside the Citadel, with honor guards and distinguished pall bearers, including Jefferson Davis. A stillness and somber gloom filled the air, as the funeral procession moved through the streets, with onlookers lined several persons deep, in mourning, and many weeping visibly. The cortege moved down King Street, left onto Hasell Street to Meeting Street, and then down Meeting Street to the Battery, and turned back up East Bay Street to Broad Street, and onto City Hall. The next day, a procession moved his body to St. Philip's Church, where it was interred in the west cemetery of St. Philip's. Today, a towering statute of John C. Calhoun looks down upon passersby at Marion Square, along the street renamed for him, 'Calhoun Street'.

Almost coincident with Calhoun's death, the slavery debate began to take on new dimensions, which ultimately would create a tinderbox of emotions. Up until the 1850's, ironically, the debate had been most heated, and vocal, among religious leaders, and ministers who fired up their congregations in both the North and the South. For the most part, political and economic clout had stayed on the sidelines. With the 1850's, the politicians jumped into the fray. Throughout the North, a new band of political figures were touting "free labor" and capitalism as measures on which to base an economy; from these beginnings, the new Republican Party was formed in 1854.

In 1860, Abraham Lincoln's nomination as the Republican Party's candidate for President of the United States accelerated the confrontation. Lincoln's position was clear. He detested slavery, but he accepted the principle that each state had a right to decide for itself, without interference from the federal government. But, though Lincoln did not want to disturb slavery where it presently existed, he was strongly determined to prevent its expansion. New frontier lands west of the Mississippi River were up for grabs, but Lincoln and the Republican Party believed that new land should not be available to slaveholders. The South's view was that the North, and Lincoln, were trying to tie God's hands and steal his bounty for themselves.

(Meanwhile, in a twist of irony, at nearly the same time of Lincoln's nomination, in Charleston March 20th, 1860, Edwin Booth was making his first acting appearance of the season at the Charleston Theatre in the play "Iago". The city newspaper, **_The Mercury_**, reported that though Edwin Booth was somewhat tired from his journey to the city, the "well filled house" seemed "evidently pleased to welcome an old favorite". Edwin Booth's brother was the later infamous John Wilkes Booth.)

Meanwhile, the Democratic Party convened their nominating convention in Charleston in 1860. Delegates were bitterly divided over the issues, and the leading contender for the party's nomination for President was Stephen A. Douglas. The convention was divisive, tensions ran high among the delegates, and emotion spread into the streets of the city. The convention deadlocked, and adjourned, without naming a nominee. Later, Douglas was nominated in Baltimore, and then defeated by Abraham Lincoln in the national election.

To the South, Lincoln's election signaled a deliberate attempt to interfere with the natural development of God's plan...a so-called "great fight between good and evil" was brewing.

The abolitionists were fighting to right a racial wrong, whereas the South and its defenders of slavery were fighting to protect their very livelihood, because slavery was the linchpin of their wealth and economy; how could they let go of slavery? In fact, many in the South, and in Charleston, believed the North would never go to war, and they could stare down the nation. As the argument went, Great Britain would intercede before it came to war, to protect its supply of cotton. They believed, "cotton is King", and 80% of the South's cotton was shipped to Europe. Senator James Henry Hammond of South Carolina wrote: "I firmly believe that the slave-holding South is now the controlling power of the world—that no other power would face us in hostility". He went on, "cotton, rice, tobacco, and naval stores command the world...the North without us would be a motherless calf, bleating about, and die of mange and starvation".

Secession talk grew to a frenzy, fueled by Lincoln's election. In a wildly euphoric, romantic view, secession to the South opened a new opportunity for prosperity, expansion, and power, harkening back to similar exuberant 'radical' feelings of Revolution during the birth of the new nation in 1776. The South believed God would be on their side. Later, Jefferson Davis would say, "Ours is not a revolution", but secession was the means "to save ourselves from revolution" based upon the "terrible designs" of the Republican Party.

In Charleston, the city celebrated when the General Assembly passed a bill calling for a secession convention. The city newspaper *The Mercury* reported on November 10th that celebrations occurred "with wine flowing, palmetto flags flying, and hot-heads reveling in martial display".

On December 17, 1860, a convention of state delegates assembled in the capital in Columbia, SC, to debate whether the state of South Carolina should be the first state to secede from the Union. By then, a groundswell had developed of the opinion that the Federal government could not tell South Carolina what it must do. Hastily, because of reports of an outbreak of smallpox, the meeting was transferred to Charleston.

In Charleston, on December 20, 1860, the city was tense with rumors of possible slave revolt, but no one really expected war. As the delegates arrived by train, they were greeted by a cheering crowd, and a 15-gun salute with each volley representing the number of slave states. On that day, the state Secession Convention met at St. Andrews Hall at Broad and Legare Streets, and voted without debate to secede. The State of South Carolina became the first state to secede from the Union.

With word of secession, the city celebrated with parades, demonstrations, and bon fires that blazed in the streets and burned into the night. The Citadel fired its cannons. The church bells of St. Michael's rang out in celebration (these were the very same bells that were stolen by the British as they evacuated the city at the Revolution; subsequently, the bells were returned to the church from England). Taverns were overcrowded, and boisterous revelers tumbled out into the streets. Firecrackers boomed into the night, and rockets blazed across the sky, an eerie scene and sound that would portend events soon to come.

But, as the prominent Charleston attorney, James L. Petigru heard the bells ringing from St. Michael's Church steeple, and was told it was not a fire, but that South Carolina had seceded from the Union, he said: "I tell you there is a fire; they have this day set a blazing torch to the temple of constitutional liberty, and, please God, we shall have no more peace forever".

At Fort Moultrie, a mere four miles of saltwater and harbor separated from the city, a tiny garrison of 32 enlisted men under the command of Major Robert Anderson heard the sounds from the city echoing across the water, and watched the flares light the night sky. Major Anderson had arrived in

Charleston on November 15th, just a month earlier, to assume command at Fort Moultrie and preserve the Union…ironically, at the very same fort his father had defended as a Patriot soldier in creating the 'Union' during the Revolution.

The crisis, however, was wearing on the tiny garrison of soldiers sworn to defend the United States, but fearing that mob violence or the state militia could overrun them.   The situation had grown desperate.   Within six short days, Major Robert Anderson, under threat, would move his Federal troops, from Fort Moultrie to Fort Sumter.   The South Carolina militia would move to occupy, and raise the Palmetto flag over forts Castle Pinckney, Fort Johnson, and Fort Moultrie.   Lying just 3 miles off the wharves of the city, Fort Sumter was perched in the mouth of the harbor as a lonely, isolated hostile presence.

Mary Chestnut would write in her diary, "why did that green goose Anderson go to Fort Sumter…then everything began to go wrong".

FORT SUMTER BECOMES THE SPARK IN THE TINDERBOX: CHAPTER 23

Major Robert Anderson had been ordered to Charleston, and arrived just a month prior, to assume command at Fort Moultrie, because the Federal government in Washington knew the situation was deteriorating rapidly. Just that Summer and Fall before, Robert Anderson was commissioned at West Point with his friend, Jefferson Davis, working together to examine the curriculum and discipline at the prestigious military academy. Major Anderson's credentials were strong. His father had served at Fort Moultrie, then under George Washington at the Battle of Trenton, and later served as aide to General Lafayette at Yorktown.

Major Anderson had graduated from West Point with Jefferson Davis, and they had remained friends. He had become a protégé of General Winfield Scott. He taught artillery at West Point, with his student's including: William Tecumseh Sherman, George Meade, Joseph Hooker, and Braxton Bragg who would become a Confederate general. In fact, a teaching assistant had been Pierre Beauregard, who would face Major Anderson head-to-head as a Confederate defender of Charleston.

Fort Moultrie was located on Sullivan's Island, known mostly as a summer resort for some of Charleston's elite families. The Huger's, Pettigru's, and Ravenel's all owned cottages on the island. In the summer, the ferry boats to the island were usually crowded with people seeking the cooler ocean breezes on the island. Many were toting bags and picnic baskets as they tumbled from the ferry and strode the wharf, making their way to the nearby sandy beaches. From the wharf, a narrow sandy lane led to the Moultrie House, one of the South's most well known and exclusive resorts. Here the elite and genteel could enjoy the Moultrie House's extensive offering of billiards, bowling, shooting, and horseback riding, as well as lavish dining and dancing. The young officers, stationed at Fort Moultrie, would often arrive, dashing in their fine uniforms, to dance and work their magic on the young daughters and relatives of the island's residents or hotel guests. The night would last long with dances of the polka, waltz, and other dance steps in vogue at that time.

But, these swashbuckling times were not available to the 32 enlisted men of Company E, Fort Moultrie. Although only a few hundred feet of sandy parade ground separated the enlisted men's barracks from the officer's quarters, a huge social gulf separated the men and their families. In the social climate of the mid-1800's, enlisted soldiers were viewed by the public with disdain, as they were thought of as slovenly, lazy men who relied on the army for their well-being because they could not succeed outside of its regimen. Therefore, genteel society was off limits to these enlisted men.

Fort Moultrie's 171-Year History

Two centuries of seacoast defense can be relived today with a visit to this restored fort which has guarded the shores and harbor of Charleston for so long. This is the same fort on Sullivan's Island which was incomplete at the onset of the Revolutionary War in June 1776, when British Admiral Sir Peter Parker and nine warships attacked the city's colonial defenders with 200 guns. The defenders, lead by their commander, General William Moultrie, and their 30 smoothbore cannon repulsed the British for the Revolutionaries' first victory of the war. From that time, the fort was named for its first commander, 'Fort Moultrie'.

That original fort was left to neglect and ruin until a second Fort Moultrie was completed in 1798, as part of America's first coastal defense system, only to be destroyed in 1804 by a hurricane.

Fort Moultrie III was completed in 1809, and remained relatively unchanged through 1860, until it played its role in the onset of the Civil War. For 138 years this fort would serve as an active cog in the country's shoreline defense, its armaments changing with the times from smoothbore canon, to breech loading disappearing rifles, to anti-aircraft and anti-submarine weapons.

Captain Abner Doubleday was the next highest ranking officer to Major Anderson at Fort Moultrie in 1860. This is the same man to whom many sports people today attribute invention of the game of baseball, although Doubleday never laid claim to the myth himself. His wife, Mary

Doubleday, lived with her husband at Fort Moultrie, as she preferred to follow him from post to post. During the Civil War, Mary became a frequent visitor to the White House, often accompanying President and Mrs. Lincoln on carriage rides about Washington.

In future years, two other notable persons would spend time at Fort Moultrie. Edgar Allan Poe, as a soldier, would be stationed at the fort for a year, and would be heavily influenced by these islands, and utilize his experiences in his writings. The Seminole Indian Chief Oceola was captured in Florida, and held prisoner at Fort Moultrie in 1838, where he reportedly died of a broken heart from captivity, and his remains are buried there today.

In addition to Fort Moultrie and Fort Sumter, Charleston's harbor in 1860 had two other forts guarding it...Fort Johnson across the harbor's mouth from Fort's Sumter and Moultrie, and a small fortification known as Fort Pinckney situated on a boggy reef just outside the mouth of the Cooper River and less than a mile off the city's wharves.

As Major Anderson arrived in Charleston in November 1860, tensions were running hot and near hysteria. Secessionists in the city were voicing threats against Fort Moultrie. Major Anderson wrote his superiors in Washington that, "the storm may break upon us at any moment".

Work was underway to hastily buildup physical defenses at both Fort Moultrie and Fort Sumter. Repeatedly, Anderson pleaded to Washington for more men and materials, if bloodshed were to be avoided. But, the mails were slow, and had to be taken by boat to the post office in Charleston, then moved by city wagon to slow trains, before the mail arrived in

Washington at army headquarters, the process taking days at best and often much longer.

But, President James Buchanan's term in office was drawing to a close in the next months. "Old Buck" as he was known, was deafened in his last days by the drumbeat of secession, and he grew more and more reluctant to take any action. No clear directions were given to Major Anderson, although the threat of mob attack grew stronger each day. Even Anderson's wife, Eba, protested to President Buchanan on behalf of her husband's precarious position. "Old Buck" later recalled his confrontational meeting with Mrs. Anderson as "painful", but he did nothing but agonize.

Then, South Carolina seceded on December 20th, 1860. Francis Pickens was elected Governor of the newly seceded state, setting up his office on the 2nd floor of the City Hall at the corner of Broad and Meeting Streets, and taking residency in the Charleston Hotel a few blocks away. In an impatient and ill-advised move, Pickens quickly wrote his friend President Buchanan that Federal guns were being re-directed inward toward the city from the forts in the harbor, and therefore, he requested permission for the South Carolina state militia to occupy Fort Sumter to protect the city. President Buchanan was offended by Pickens' clumsy request, and pressure. Still, President Buchanan did nothing.

Major Anderson decided to take matters into his own hands. He had been working on a bold, secret plan for some weeks. He would move his troops to Fort Sumter, out of harm's way from unruly citizen mobs, to avoid bloodshed, until Washington could make amends peacefully with South Carolina and the South. On the evening of December 26th, the temperature was a chilling 40 degrees, as a misty rain fell. A fog moved in from the beach, making it nearly impossible to see across the short expanse of water to Fort Sumter. Major Anderson decided this was the right time to move his garrison to Fort Sumter. Hastily, the men were called into small boats, as men, materials, and rations were moved in convoys through the darkness of that dreary evening. The plan succeeded, but this bold move would change history in a monumental way.

As the citizens of Charleston awoke that next morning to Anderson's coup, the city and its leaders were aghast and outraged. For, you see, they and Governor Pickens were of the opinion that all forts in Charleston harbor belonged to South Carolina, and were merely being occupied on loan as it were to Washington. This was an open threat, meaning South Carolina would have to take action, and sooner rather than later.

That very first day on Fort Sumter, December 27th, at about noon, Major Anderson had his men raise the U.S. flag, the "star-spangled banner", over the fort. From the very moment the flag began to flap in the wind, it fanned strong emotions on both sides, and soon became a glaring symbol of the national issue at hand. The citizens of Charleston gazed across the harbor that morning on the 'stars and stripes' fluttering against the sky and great expanse of water beyond. Emotions erupted in anger and outrage, and swept through the city like a great fire fanned by the breezes blowing in from the ocean, and the tiny fort visible from the Battery. Anderson's surreptitious move to Fort Sumter, and his raising of the flag over Charleston harbor, was an act of defiance which embarrassed the citizens, and Governor Pickens in particular.

And, Governor Pickens acted hastily, and without much forethought. He ordered the citizen-soldiers, who comprised the militia, to assemble post-haste on the Citadel's parade ground (which is now Marion Square), with the intent of seizing the fort at Castle Pinckney. The small militia marched to a wharf on the Cooper River, where a crowd had assembled to view Fort Sumter in the distance. As the militia approached, the crowd broke simultaneously into a boisterous, noisy greeting for the citizen-soldiers. As the militia passed, strutting their new-found importance, the crowd slapped their backs with encouragement, shouted cheers, and waved handkerchiefs in the charged air of the afternoon. It must have been a remarkable scene.

Fueled by the giddy euphoria of the moment, the militia clambered into a boat which was pushed off the wharf at about 4:00 PM, and within 30 minutes it bumped against the wharf at Castle Pinckney. As Major Anderson watched through a spy-glass from nearby Fort Sumter, the South Carolina militia marched into the fort, lowered the American flag, and in its place, raised the Palmetto flag of South Carolina. Soon, Lt. Meade and his small band of Federal soldiers boarded boats and retreated to Fort Sumter. In stark contrast to the carnage that would come, this first military action, occurred without a shot being fired or single casualty. Reacting to his success, Governor Pickens ordered the militia to seize the federal Custom House on Bay Street downtown, and the vacated Fort Moultrie. As daylight passed that evening, the Palmetto flag was flying over Fort Moultrie as well.

In the North, Major Anderson's actions and Governor Pickens' response were viewed much differently. Newspapers in the North, such as *Harper's Weekly*, billed Anderson's clandestine movement of his troops, and particularly the raising of the American flag over Fort Sumter, as stirring actions of national patriotism. This only served to fan emotions to even higher levels, on both sides. The gulf between sides was ever widening.

In effect, Anderson's move would handcuff, first President Buchanen, and later President Lincoln, while forcing Governor Pickens to retaliate, and increasing the political pressure on both sides. Neither side was ready for war, but Governor Pickens and his advisers were deeply concerned that Washington would now be forced to move quickly and reinforce

Major Anderson, who was now isolated on a tiny sandbar at Fort Sumter.

Fort Sumter

As Marilyn and I stood on the dock on a Saturday afternoon waiting for the tour boat to take us to Fort Sumter, we looked out over Charleston harbor to see the reef that once was Castle Pinckney, and beyond on the horizon stood Fort Sumter, with its flagstaff visible before us. The January air was crisp, and a breeze was blowing in from the ocean, as we tried to imagine what the harbor scene was like in December of 1860.

Fort Sumter was conceived as an additional defense of Charleston harbor, providing crossfire from Fort Moultrie or Fort Johnson to any ship entering the harbor. Castle Pinckney, located within the harbor, would be a secondary last vestige of defense.

In 1827, engineers determined that a large sandbar, stretching northward from Morris Island in the mouth of the harbor, with a proper foundation, could be the site for erection of a fort. The project was referred to as "Fort Sumter" in recognition of the Revolutionary War general from South Carolina. Work started in 1829, but moved very slowly, as there was no real urgency; then, work stopped. In 1836, the Army resumed work, when it decided Fort Sumter could be an important garrison, to be built to the latest thinking in military ideas.

It would be built on 2 ½ acres, with huge boulders brought in to serve as its foundation on the sandy base. With thick, high walls, it could garrison 1,000 men and 140 guns.

Over years, the citizens of Charleston watched from across the harbor as the building of Fort Sumter took place. They watched its progress as it began to rise, silhouetted against the harbor's horizon, and its construction became a part of the city's life and vista for two decades. One can begin to understand why its occupation by Major Anderson became such an emotional jolt to the citizens of the city.

As our tour boat approached the wharf, Marilyn and I could see Fort Sumter's walls rising high above us. A tingling sensation sent small shivers through us, because gazing upon it, and then walking into the fort, is an emotionally charged experience even today.

The fort was like a pentagon with five sides of nearly equal size. It contained two large barracks on either side of a three-story building which contained offices and officer's barracks. Each building had its own catch basins and cistern for water supply. Around its perimeter and outside walls, massive boulders wrapped around and extended to the water's edge. It is wonderful that, though the fort received such a pounding and was virtually left to rubble by the war's end, major efforts to restore much of the fort now provide a vivid, moving experience for today's visitors.

Fort Sumter's face, and strongest side, was oriented east to the ocean; its weakest side was rearward, called the "Gorge", and faced Morris Island. Military thinking at the time of its conception was that the greatest threat would come from hostile ships at sea. A 170 foot long stone wharf extended outward on its Gorge side, designed to receive small boats that would carry supplies directly from Charleston, as small boats could reach it from the city in 50 minutes. One entered the fort from the wharf, through its main gate, walking through a long, dark stone and brick passageway, opening onto a 1-acre parade ground at the fort's center. Its towering walls blocked out sunlight and offered no direct views of the outside world; standing within, Marilyn and I could feel the aura of a prison complex, isolated from the outside world. And, that's some of the feeling Major Anderson and his men must have had as they became virtual prisoners within their own fortress in late-December 1860.

Neither side knew quite how to act, both were under tremendous pressure, and yet, neither side was really ready to consider the other side the 'enemy'. A series of extraordinary events occurred next. Officers from Fort Sumter crossed by boat to ask the South Carolina militia occupying Fort Moultrie whether they could retrieve winter coats left behind upon their hasty, clandestine evacuation of the fort, and whether they would be allowed to carry back coal for fuel to help them fend off the winter's chill. They were allowed to do so.

In another episode a short time later, an officer and four enlisted men left Fort Sumter via boat to Charleston, where they purchased meat and other supplies. The officer held an amicable meeting with Governor Pickens at the Mills House Hotel, where Governor Pickens agreed that women and children would be permitted to leave their men at Fort Sumter, and move from danger to Sullivan's Island. Likewise, Pickens concurred that a boat from the fort would be allowed each day to pick up the mail from the city, although no longer would he allow food or supplies to be taken back to Fort Sumter.

In early January, a younger brother of Major Anderson, Larry, was allowed to visit at Fort Sumter. With his visit, he carried news to the Major that the move to Fort Sumter was viewed across the North as an act of patriotism and bravery "to enforce the laws and preserve the Union". Anderson's wife, Eba, also returned to Charleston, stayed at the Mills House Hotel, and, with Governor Pickens' permission, visited her husband at Fort Sumter. After a short time, however, she returned with other officer's wives, and departed on a train to the North, finding Charleston less than hospitable.

It has been said that these 'civil' acts may have been the last acts of civility in what would later be named the Civil War. But, in the South to this day, if you refer to the great conflict as the "Civil War", you will quickly be recognized with some scorn as just a "Northerner" or "Yankee", because the Southerner will remind you there was "nothing civil about it". Instead, the war is called by many names in the South: the "War of Secession", the "Confederate War", the "late unpleasantness", the "War of Northern Aggression", or the "War for Southern Independence".

Though neither side was ready for war, or willing to accept its inevitability, Governor Pickens moved quickly to strengthen the city's defenses. He believed that Anderson would not take the first hostile action, but if Federal reinforcements arrived and were fired upon, Anderson would be forced to retaliate. December 31st dawned a cold, blustery winter day, and we can imagine standing on the Battery with crowds of curious onlookers, watching the bustle of activity on the city's wharves, as steamers moved in the harbor to and from Morris Island, ferrying soldiers, slaves, munitions, and supplies. Governor Pickens had assigned young cadets from the Citadel to Morris

Island. The Citadel had been formed in the 1840's to train young men in military skills. Some 40-50 Citadel cadets had been recalled from Christmas vacation to install a battery of 24-pound cannons on Morris Island, facing east toward the ocean, and protected and concealed by sand dunes and sandbags.

Anderson's men on Fort Sumter were also busy, working feverishly to shore up the fort's defenses and relocate canons to their best defensive locations.

Within days, rumors were circulating in the city that reinforcements were headed to Charleston. *The Mercury* newspaper riled the citizens with a report that a merchant ship, "Star of the West", had departed New York City's docks headed for Charleston, carrying troops. Reports reached the city from everywhere. Telegraph lines literally hummed with activity. And, Governor Pickens ordered ships on scouting missions to watch for any ships approaching the harbor. A signal system was devised whereby lantern signals would report approaching ships, and if the ship did not identify itself properly, rockets were to be shot-off, and the batteries at Fort Moultrie and Morris Island were to open fire.

As the "Star of the West" steamed toward Charleston, the Federal soldiers passing time on deck enjoyed the clear, balmy weather and sea breezes, as if they were on a vacation cruise. While the ship anchored off Myrtle Beach, about 10 hours run from Charleston, so it could arrive at nightfall, some soldiers fished off its deck. The atmosphere was hardly one of anxious soldiers heading off to battle.

After pulling anchor and resuming its journey, the merchant ship reached Charleston harbor under darkness, about 1:30 AM in the early hours of January 9th. Although the night sky was clear, no moon shone overhead to light the path, and no known beacon lights or land markings could be seen, except for a faint light that was reported, probably coming from Fort

Sumter. The "Star of the West" had no alternative but to wait for daybreak to find its way into harbor.

The morning of January 9th 1861 dawned with a glorious "Carolina blue" sky, as seabirds swooped in the air amid a light breeze. Faint misty haze hung over the harbor, with the promise it would quickly burn away in the glistening morning sun, and drive temperature into the sixties that day. It was ideal weather for the militia's patrol boat to spot a large ship on the horizon. They could tell she was a merchant ship by her silhouette, but was she friendly? Their patrol task was not an easy one. Was she part of the day's routine harbor traffic, because ten ships would arrive that particular day at the city's wharves, while seven ships would depart carrying goods to ports in the West Indies, Europe, and New York, for business had to carry on despite all the uneasiness concerning Fort Sumter. In fact, even the Bank of Charleston continued its usual business with northern banks until late in 1862, well into the war.

A sentry at the Citadel cadets' camp on Morris Island spotted the signal rocket of the patrol boat, and the approach of the "Star". The eager, and nervous, cadets awaited no orders, but took action into their own hands. The cadet commander aimed canon at the bow of the approaching "Star", and ordered "commence firing". With the order, a young cadet, named Edward Haynesworth, nicknamed "Tuck", fired the canon, and some have argued the first shot of the war.

Aboard the "Star", the American flag was hurriedly run up the flagstaff, and dipped as a signal of distress to Major Anderson on Fort Sumter. The cadets on Morris Island took this as an act of defiance, and fired again and again. Fortunately, their marksmanship was not very good. Only two shots hit the "Star", striking her hull and bouncing off with a dull thud, without any damage. One shot tore through her rigging, while the rest

241

missed their target. The "Star" hastily retreated out of canon range, and beat a retreat back to New York.

The entire skirmish was witnessed by Major Anderson and his men at Fort Sumter, but rather than open fire from Fort Sumter, Anderson decided to wait. On the "Star of the West", an officer reportedly recalled, with some humor, "The people of Charleston pride themselves upon their hospitality, but it exceeded my expectations. They gave us several 'balls' before we landed!".

In the city, all became a frenzy. With the sounds of the first canon shot echoing over the city, rumors were passed from street to street. Occupants streamed from their homes to see what was happening. People were running everywhere to gain a vantage point, women in their cumbersome long skirts, and men on horseback galloping toward the harbor. Each strained to catch a glimpse of the action some six miles off shore, some with spyglass or opera glass. Then, quickly, it was over.

Within two days, orders were given to sink five old hulks of ships in the main channel of entry to the harbor to protect against entry by Federal navy warships. The ships that were sunk were gifts from the city of Savannah, bearing granite rock that was planned for use at the new Custom House, then under construction.

The long period of waiting, and isolation, began on Fort Sumter. It would last 3 ½ months.

FORT SUMTER: AWAITING THE UNTHINKABLE: CHAPTER 24

During February and March, 1861, rains and storms lashed out with a fury, pounding the fortress, and further working on the minds of the men within Fort Sumter, virtual hostages in isolation.

February 11th, 1861, dawned dank, gray, and windy at Fort Sumter. At the same moment, 7:30 AM, in Springfield, Illinois, a special train pulled away from the station, carrying a then beardless Abraham Lincoln on its journey to Lincoln's presidential inauguration in Washington, DC. At 6'4" in height, with the sleeves of his black dress coat two inches too short, and his too-short trousers exposing his large feet, Lincoln stood on the train depot platform ready to board. He was about to be handed the problem in Charleston.

Meanwhile, the South was preparing for a possible clash with the soon-to-be president, Abraham Lincoln. On February 22nd, Jefferson Davis, a West Point friend of Major Anderson, was inaugurated President of the Confederacy. Through the South, states had reacted similarly. Seven states followed South Carolina to secede, and vast numbers of weapons, ordinance, and property were being seized by the secessionists. On March 6th, President Jefferson Davis called for 100,000 volunteers to serve for 12 months. Within weeks, the Confederates outnumbered the U.S. Army by 3:1.

In late February, P.T. Beauregard was called to Montgomery, Alabama, to meet with the new President of the Confederacy, Jefferson Davis. The Confederacy needed help in Charleston; Beauregard was sent to Charleston to prepare her defenses. It was critical to the infant Confederacy to hold Charleston, because any loss could prove devastating to the morale of the new Confederacy.

P.T. Beauregard was born into Creole aristocracy, to a family of New Orleans sugar planters, and he retained a Creole accent in his speech. In fact, he spoke better French than English. Beauregard was a diminutive 5'7" in height, but strutted a muscular 150 pound body. With black hair that he vainly maintained with hair dye, and sporting a mustache, and olive skin, he was handsome, and enjoyed thoroughly the attention of the ladies, and the game of charming them. He would soon win over the ladies of Charleston.

He had been trained at West Point, where a favorite teacher of artillery was Robert Anderson. Anderson enjoyed Beauregard, and Anderson kept him on at West Point after graduation as his teaching assistant. The teacher and his pupil, now friends, would enter a deadly chess game with each other in the months ahead, across Charleston Harbor.

Meanwhile, in Washington, DC, following his inauguration ceremony, the first thing handed President Lincoln, as he entered the Executive Mansion on March 3rd, was a letter from Major Anderson, pleading for provisions, supplies, and additional soldiers to fortify and hold Fort Sumter. The situation was bleak. By then, Fort Sumter's lonely defenders included ten officers, 75 enlisted men (8 of whom were musicians), and 55 civilian soldiers. Time was running out, and Anderson could not hold out much longer. Lincoln's chief military adviser, General Winfield Scott, had annotated on the report in his handwriting, "I see no alternative but a surrender". Lincoln needed more information.

In Charleston, in early March, each day passed with batteries on all sides of the harbor practicing loading, and firing their artillery. At Fort Sumter, Major Anderson and his officers would watch to assess the number and size of the canons and their locations. At about 8:00 AM, March 8th, they noticed canon on Morris Island about to fire, and these guns were especially important as they were aimed at Fort Sumter's weakest side, her Gorge or main gate. Two guns fired, and then a third; but, this was different. One gun was loaded with a canon ball, not just practice shot. In horror, Anderson and his men watched the canon ball as it arched toward them in the sky, soaring in-flight toward their main gate at Fort Sumter. But, it arrived short, ricocheted off the water, caromed toward the main gate, smashed into the gate, but then bounced back harmlessly into the water. As Anderson and his men caught their breaths, and regained their composure, across the water they could see men in shock on the beach of Morris Island scurrying for cover behind sand dunes, in fear that Fort Sumter would fire in retaliation. Realizing that the incident was a colossal error, Anderson and his men broke into laughter...perhaps their last bit of mirth for some time. Soon, a boat arrived with a Confederate officer bringing an explanation and apology for the incident.

General P.T. Beauregard, at the same time, was taking charge of the Confederate militia, building his forces at Morris Island, Fort Moultrie, and Castle Pinckney. The city was crowded with wagons, horses, people, and soldiers massing. Charleston harbor was flooded with boats transporting troops. By now, more than 6,000 Confederate soldiers surrounded Major Anderson's small band of men isolated at Fort Sumter.

On March 19th, the weather turned unusually cold, and large, wet snowflakes began to fall. It only snows on Charleston maybe once a decade, but then, over two inches of snow fell. The men suffered on Fort Sumter. Huddled together in the cold, dark chill of Fort Sumter's huge and imposing brick and stucco walls, their fuel, food, and other supplies dwindled. Discomfort and fear of the unknown were their daily regimen. To make matters worse, in February, the small group of women and children were evacuated, with only the soldiers remaining to ponder their destiny. They were hostages of an undeclared 'enemy'.

In contrast to the edginess of the soldiers, in the city of Charleston the weeks passed with most citizens going about their business, and the social calendar being maintained. The elite partied and enjoyed life. Race Week, perhaps the grandest celebration of the season, went on as if nothing were happening. The wealthy continued their parties, and entertained lavishly. Dancing and drinking went on into the late hours of the next mornings. On the plantations, the fox hunts, fishing, card games, and dances went on as usual. One planter's wife wrote, "If there is no war…we mean to have a gay Spring". Mary Chestnut wrote in her diary, "the maddest, merriest dinner we have had yet. Men were audaciously wise and witty. We had an unspoken foreboding that it was to be our last pleasant meeting".

Meanwhile, Lincoln was taking steps to get his large feet firmly on the ground, before he took action. From the very beginning, Lincoln's position was clear, and remained so...he wanted to save the Union, irrespective of whether or not slavery endured or was destroyed. In late March, he sent Stephen Hurlbut to Charleston to assess the atmosphere within the city. Hurlbut was a native Charlestonian, born in the city, and a resident for thirty years. He arrived on a Sunday, March 24th, and immediately visited an old friend of his, Judge Petigru, with whom he spent the evening. The next day he returned North.

Soon after, another emissary was dispatched to Charleston, Lincoln's law partner, Ward Hill Lamon. Lamon met with Governor Pickens, and received agreement to go to Fort Sumter and meet with Major Anderson.

Putting a positive spin on all of this, the leaders and citizens celebrated, thinking that Lincoln was about to order the evacuation of Fort Sumter. But, unknown to them, Lincoln had a different plan. Already the wheels were in motion to prepare an "expedition" to relieve Anderson's desperate situation, which grew bleaker with each passing day. Lincoln sent Gustavus Fox to meet Anderson at Fort Sumter. Major Anderson gave his assessment to Fox; food would only last a few more days, and a relief expedition would be blasted from all sides by Beauregard's batteries, all guns now drawing aim onto Fort Sumter perched precariously in the harbor. Anderson reasoned to Fox that the only alternative was withdrawal from the fort.

Here history becomes cloudy. Either Fox failed to report the dire situation to Lincoln, or perhaps, Lincoln decided to goad President Davis and the Confederacy into the first action of war. Either way, at the end of March, Lincoln ordered an expeditionary force to be ready by April 6th to re-supply Fort Sumter and land 200 men to reinforce the garrison. By April 3rd, Anderson's men were on half rations, and bread would only last another five days. Without receiving additional supplies, and soon, Anderson would have no choice but to evacuate or surrender the fort.

April 6th was a Saturday, and market day in Charleston. The people went about their business as usual, although the mood was apprehensive. It was raining heavily, "but did not discourage the crowds milling about beneath the roof and stalls on Market Street, searching for freshly butchered meats, fresh vegetables, and new blooms of flowers, gardenias, wisteria, and azaleas". Citizens, as well as the Governor of the state and Confederate leaders, all were confident that Lincoln would choose to vacate Fort Sumter, rather than fight.

On Sunday, April 7th, Anderson received a written order from Lincoln, explaining the planned expedition. Anderson could not believe what he read, "hold out, if possible, til the arrival of the expedition", but if "in your judgment, to save yourself and your command, capitulation becomes a necessity, you are authorized to make it".

Anderson was aghast. Quickly he wrote a report to Washington, and a second letter addressed to a friend in Washington. Neither would reach Washington. The correspondence was intercepted at the post office in Charleston, and rushed to the desk of Governor Pickens, who read it, along with his aide, and General Beauregard. The intercepted messages did not divulge the number of men Lincoln was planning to send. Pickens and Beauregard miscalculated, judging that Lincoln had from 2,600 to 4,000

Federal troops on their way to Charleston, with a landing probable on Morris Island. In defense, Beauregard had 2,000 men on Morris Island, although many more were in-place in the city and around the harbor.

It was still raining that Sunday, April 7th, and the churches were filled with parishioners praying for God's continued blessing over their beloved city. In town, soldiers were told to gather with their weapons, if the bells of St. Michael's Church should begin to toll. The city's fire companies were ordered to alert, in case arson was attempted by unruly slaves. War was getting closer and closer on people's minds, but still no one really expected it to come to that.

On Monday, April 8th, with Washington unaware of Anderson's intercepted messages, two emissaries from Lincoln arrived by train in Charleston, and proceeded immediately to Governor Pickens' headquarters at the Mills House Hotel. The messengers carried a short, terse message from Lincoln to Pickens...it read, "an attempt will be made to supply Fort Sumter with provisions only; and that, if such attempt be not resisted, no effort to throw in men, arms, or ammunition will be made, without further notice, or in case of an attack upon the fort".

Governor Pickens was stunned, and speechless, because this gave the Confederacy and South Carolina no viable alternative. Either they would have to yield and suffer disgrace to the new and fragile Confederacy, or attack Fort Sumter as the aggressor, which would clearly unite the fragmented North behind Lincoln. Lincoln would win under either choice. As Pickens shared the note with General Beauregard, Beauregard suggested the two emissaries from Washington leave the city immediately, and they were escorted to the train, and soon left for the North.

Now the city sprang into action. At midnight, April 8th, the bells of St. Michael's Church sounded the call for reserves. The Citadel signaled with a seven gun volley. For the next several days, the streets were bustling with Beauregard's messengers darting in all directions, on foot and on horseback. Uniformed soldiers were on the move. Boats were launched to batteries at all points around the harbor. The telegraph wires were humming hot with messages into and out of the city. You can imagine the emotional frenzy as the citizens of the city watched this unfold, and as rumors darted from street to street.

By Thursday, April 11th, a plan had been formulated. In the afternoon, Beauregard sent aides with a handwritten note asking Anderson to evacuate Fort Sumter, without bloodshed. After all, Beauregard was a close friend of Major Anderson, his mentor. Furthermore, Major Anderson was well known and had many friends in the city of Charleston. Many of the city's citizens knew Anderson's soldiers and their families; they were men who had been stationed some months earlier on Sullivan's Island, who, with their families, had shopped in Charleston, ate in the restaurants, and had good times with residents of the city, perhaps sharing drinks and good-time conversation in the city's pubs. The people of Charleston did not consider these men, or Major Anderson, the 'enemy'. Instead, it was the outsiders from Washington who were threatening them...they were the 'enemy', and especially Abraham Lincoln.

At 3:45 PM, the small boat carrying Beauregard's three emissaries bumped up against the rocky shores and wharf at Fort Sumter with their message for Anderson. Within forty-five minutes, at 4:30 PM, Anderson returned to the three aides with his answer to Beauregard. As the aides boarded their boat, and prepared to push off from the wharf, Anderson asked, "Will General Beauregard open his batteries without further notice to me?" James Chestnut, the most senior aide, replied, "I think not". Anderson called out, one last time, "Gentlemen, if you do not batter the fort to pieces about us, we shall be starved out in a few days". These words would be Anderson's last plea to avoid a terrible 'un-Civil' war.

Mary Chestnut

James Chestnut, the leader of that mission to Major Anderson, had accepted an appointment to General Beauregard's staff, and reported back to Charleston with his wife, Mary Chestnut.

Mary Chestnut would keep a diary of the ensuing struggle, which would become a powerful, and insightful, history from an observer and first-hand witness. Mary Chestnut was a true 'Southern Belle', who embodied the 'Southern Cause', desperately loyal to her husband and the Confederacy he served. Her diary would capture her enthusiasm, though fearful, of the first events of the war, which would then turn to the awful realism of the horrors that would follow the war's progression.

Young Mary first came to Charleston as a 12-year old in 1835, to attend one of the finest boarding schools for girls. Only the wealthy could afford to send their daughter to this elite finishing school, run by Madame Talvande. It was located near the corner of Tradd and Legare Streets, in a home at 32 Legare Street now referred to as the 'Sword Gate' house, because of the sword and spear design on its massive wrought iron gate, which can still be seen today.

While in school, at the age of just 15 years, Mary fell in love with James Chestnut, who was 23 years old, and a recent graduate of Princeton law school. James was one of Charleston's most eligible bachelors, reading law in the offices of one of the city's most prominent attorneys and politicians, James L. Petigru. After a romance of two years, Mary married James Chestnut in 1840 in a ceremony in Mt. Pleasant, and the newly weds moved to the Chestnut family Mulberry Plantation, outside Charleston.

James Chestnut began a successful career that led to his election to the U.S. Senate. Within three days of President Lincoln's election, James became the first U.S. senator to resign his seat in protest.

Mary, and her husband, returned to Charleston, and were present in December 1860 at the secession convention in the city. Following secession, James left the city for Montgomery, Alabama, to help with formation of the Confederacy. Then, James Chestnut, and Mary, returned to Charleston so he could join General Beauregard's staff.

On the evening of April 11th, Mary Chestnut had gone to bed at the Mills House Hotel, where she and James were staying. She had retired restless, and worried for her husband, because she knew he had gone to Anderson that afternoon, and she and other residents of the city had heard the rumors, that bombardment was about to begin. That evening, onlookers had been drifting down toward the Battery to join the growing crowd positioning themselves for a best view of the harbor, and the rumored events that could begin at any moment. Other onlookers took to the rooftops of buildings near the Battery, some with lanterns and carpets to sit upon, even chairs and tables, and beverages and picnic baskets. Charlestonians were known for their parties, and no one wanted to miss this one. Homeowners, and their guests, partied and waited, and laughter could be heard on the streets below coming from the rooftop gatherings.

Tossing and turning in her sleep, Mary Chestnut was awakened at 4:00 AM that morning of April 12th, by the bells tolling from the church spire at St. Michael's. She hurried to the roof of the hotel to watch events unfold, along with many others already gathered. By a twist of irony, another guest that night in the Mills House Hotel happened to be Robert E. Lee.

And, then, at 4:30 AM, Beauregard opened fire on Fort Sumter. In the night's sky, the first mortar shell, quite visible with its fuse glowing in the darkness and bright streamers trailing in the shell's wake, arched high in the sky toward Fort Sumter. The crowds of onlookers in the city saw it explode, and heard its loud boom, like a 4th of July fireworks display, although the shell exploded harmlessly 100 feet over its target. Pandemonium broke out on the rooftops and in the streets of Charleston. The streets, and wharves, quickly filled with people, scurrying everywhere to gain the best vantage point. Cheers went up for the Confederacy.

Mary Chestnut wrote later in her diary, "The women were wild, there on the housetop"; she wrote of worry that husband James was "rowing about in a boat somewhere in that dark bay". Fort Sumter, Mary went on, "did not fire a shot".

Other batteries opened up around the harbor, encircling Fort Sumter. Beauregard's plan was for 43 canons circling the harbor to fire, one at a time, moving in a counterclockwise pattern, in a precise rhythm, with a new shot every two minutes. One eyewitness wrote, "came the brilliant flash of exploding shells from batteries all around the bay, while the deep harsh tones of talking cannons echoed over the waters, the scene was sublimely grand".

Morning rose over Charleston that April 12th, with clouds and a heavy mist hanging over the harbor, concealing visibility of the batteries on the surrounding islands. By 6:30 AM, Fort Sumter still had not returned fire, although Beauregard's guns had fired about 200 cannon shots by then. The fort was taking a terrific beating, and the breakout of fire within the fort was a constant danger.

Then, Anderson's guns began to return fire. Through the morning hours, the crowds of onlookers in the city maintained a high level of excitement, as the spectacle played out before them. By mid-morning, the rains fell, and crowds began to disperse. It was as if the sky were crying, its tears falling as rainfall, over the city and the combatants, as if knowing the horrific price and suffering that would be sustained by both sides, throughout this long, terrible 'un-Civil' war.

By 1:00 PM, the Federal fleet sent by Washington with men and supplies to reinforce the garrison began to arrive, but stayed back out of cannon range. Anderson assumed they were waiting for darkness. The Federal fleet out on the horizon could be seen by onlookers in the city, and fear and alarm spread quickly through the crowds. But, over the next several hours, the distant ships made no move to come closer into harm's way. By 7:00 PM, the storm had grown worse, with heavy rain and howling winds, making artillery fire difficult. Anderson ordered a cease fire until morning to conserve precious ammunition. Likewise, Beauregard's guns reduced their fire. Evening of the first day settled in over the city.

The second day of the conflict, April 13th, dawned with a clear blue sky, as the rain had stopped, but April's breeze whipped the beleaguered U.S. flag flying atop Fort Sumter. Action from the batteries resumed slowly, until 7:30 AM when a mortar shell crashed and exploded through the roof of the officer's quarters at Fort Sumter, and fire broke out. The fire was quickly fanned by the gusting winds, and soon a major conflagration was being battled by the exhausted men within the fort.

From the city, onlookers could see the flames rising above the fort's high brick walls, as billowing gray smoke drifted upward high into the early morning sky. Large crowds once again hurriedly assembled about the Battery and wharves of the city to witness the burning carcass of a once proud garrison. Most stood silently in awe and disbelief; others celebrated the beating being inflicted; nearly all shared a knot in their stomachs for Major Anderson and his brave men caught within its walls, battling that distant inferno, while being shelled in a continuous barrage, and not able to even fire back as their ammunition was dwindling to nearly nothing. Not long ago, these men had been their friends.

Yet, sensing the kill, Beauregard increased the artillery assault from all batteries surrounding the beleaguered fort, simply pummeling the fort that was now without defense.

The next day, a Sunday, April 14th, Beauregard sent a messenger to Fort Sumter, saying to an exhausted and beaten Major Anderson, "General Beauregard wishes to stop this". Anderson knew hope was gone. Anderson replied that they would evacuate (but, not surrender), if they could leave the fort with their belongings, be allowed transportation to the North, and salute the flag as they left. Minutes later, a white signal cloth was raised over Fort Sumter, which could be seen by the spectators in the city, and cheers erupted from the crowds. Firing from all batteries around the harbor ceased. After 34 hours of bombardment, the awful ordeal was nearly over.

Confederate guns had fired about 3,000 shells, and Anderson's men had returned nearly 700 shots; but, remarkably, not one life was lost in the bombardment, and only 3 men received minor cuts within the fort. However, the walls of the fort were badly damaged, and the once raging fire left charred wood, and traces of smoke drifting from the debris, and its pungent odor lingered in the air. In a twist of irony, the only fatality occurred at the U.S. flag lowering ceremony, when sparks from a 100-gun salute caused an explosion in the ammunition supply area. One man died, and five were injured from the ill-planned ceremony, marking the only casualties of this first historic conflict of the war. When all was over, Major Anderson walked out of the fort carrying the tattered U.S. flag that had flown over the fort.

Major Anderson would return again to Fort Sumter, and he would bring that same tattered flag back, to raise it once again, but it would take four long years to the very day for it to happen.

Charleston went wild with excitement and jubilation. Revelers celebrated, and crowded the city's streets. Citizens crowded the harbor in small boats, wanting to get a closer look at Fort Sumter, scene of the Confederacy's first victory. In Montgomery, Alabama, however, the Confederate leaders were less exuberant in their celebration, as they tried to anticipate what Washington's response would be. The South had stood up against Lincoln's alternatives, but Lincoln had succeeded in goading the Confederacy into taking the first artillery shot. With that first shot on Fort Sumter, Confederate officials knew a hesitant North would explode with anger at this flagrant affront to national honor, and unite behind Lincoln.

On April 15th, 1861, Major Anderson and his men boarded a steamer in Charleston harbor, and headed back to New York. The leaders of Charleston, and its citizens, began preparations and hunkered down for war.

(On May 6th, the local Charleston newspaper reported that a number of the city's ladies had marshaled their efforts to design and make a flag for the local militia group, the Palmetto Guard. The flag was presented in a ceremony at Institute Hall. On one side of the flag was a Palmetto tree with the Latin motto of the company in gold letters above, and on the other side a wreath of oak and laurel leaves with the name and date of the company's formation.

Two days later, the newspaper reported that the members of the Palmetto Guard serenaded the household of Emma Holmes for her and the other ladies' work on their company flag.)

ENJOYING LIFE IN THE CITY AT 29 ½: CHAPTER 25

Life in Charleston offers a widely divergent choice of activities. Marilyn and I are constantly amazed just how much is going on in this town, at all times of the year. The problem is choosing. It is a wonderful problem…too many great things to do, and not nearly as much time as we would like to experience them.

College of Charleston 'Cougar' Basketball

It's a Sunday afternoon late in February, and the College of Charleston 'Cougar' basketball team is playing on ESPN TV trying to win the final playoff basketball game in its first year in the Southern Conference. I am nervous and on edge as the game against unheralded Appalachian State is tied with just minutes to go. This year, "the College", as local gadflies refer to the team, is rated No. 17 among top teams in the country, and has run the table in its new, tougher conference, going 16-0 in conference play and 27-2 overall. Coach John Kresse has built a remarkable basketball program for a small school, virtually

258

unknown nationally for its sports, until recent years.

I have thoroughly enjoyed watching games this year at the "Kresse" Arena at the Johnson Center on campus. Walking to the games just seems right. I leave our home at 29 ½ Montagu, turn east two blocks on Montagu Street, left onto Coming Street one block, and then right through the campus on George Street past King Street, to the arena which is between King and Meeting Streets. It is just a comfortable 15-minute brisk walk, often at night with a bit of chill in the air on a winter evening.

Kresse Arena, one of the few arenas in the country bearing the name of a then active head coach, is a cozy building which holds just under 4,000 fans. The arena has the feel of a small high school gymnasium, but that coziness makes the enthusiasm and support of the loyal hometown fans and students even more intense, and fun. Everyone just seems like "family", and this is the program that Coach Kresse, the master motivator, has tried to build over his more than twenty-year reign. Fans, cheerleaders, coach, and team are family, supporting one another, with each member doing their own special part to win and fulfill their dreams of success. Sounds a lot like the resilient, old city of Charleston, and its never-say-die spirit, doesn't it?

For today, I wish I could be at the game, but the conference playoffs are in Greenville, SC, this year, so television is the next best thing. This afternoon I have watched anxiously from my patented 'luge position' (lying on my back, hands to each side, toes up, practicing as I like to call it for the Olympic luge event), on the couch in our second floor study (we have dubbed the "West Room"). As today's game progresses, the College of Charleston makes a patented run of 19-2 points, and ends its first conference season with a victory 77-67. The final score does not reflect the tense moments of the game, and the outstanding effort expended by Appalachian State to deflate the banner year of "the College".

With this victory, the College of Charleston 'Cougars' will win an invitation to the 'Big Dance', the year-ending NCAA tournament of the country's top 64 teams. Just qualifying for this most prestigious tournament field will help Coach Kresse's goal of building an ever better, more recognized program for the school that was founded in 1790.

Dock Street Theatre

The Dock Street Theatre offers a series of outstanding plays, featuring a changing array of very talented actors, many of whom are local players, working with highly talented production companies. In addition to enjoying a variety of good stage plays, theatergoers become part of the rich tapestry of this grand old theatre, and the history of acclaim achieved by Charleston's artists.

The Dock Street Theatre, located on Church Street, just around the corner from Queen Street, opened in 1937. It is a replica of London theatres of the 1730's, and was built inside the old, antebellum Planter's Hotel, keeping its old façade, entry, and iron balcony intact. By the 1920's Charleston had reestablished itself as home to acclaimed writers, poets, artists, and theatre. Artists in varying venues began to portray Charleston's past, present, its people, and its culture.

The opera "Porgy and Bess" reflected life in Charleston, as did the original 1937 movie "Gone with the Wind". The author of the novel "Porgy", Dubose Heyward, lived at 76 Church Street. The black tenement building, a few blocks away, known locally as 'Cabbage Row' became immortalized as "Catfish Row" in the later opera by George Gershwin. Gershwin wrote the opera "Porgy and Bess" while staying on Folly Beach, just west of peninsular Charleston across the Ashley River. In the opera, the great hurricane of 1911 achieved lasting notoriety in Gershwin's words and music, which portrayed the feelings of Charleston's survivors of that storm.

Black Charlestonians achieved acclaim in the Jazz Age, and some claim the 'Roaring 20's' dance sensation, "The Charleston", originated on King Street.

Art Walk

Sophisticated, and fun, describes the Art Walk which is becoming a bigger and bigger citywide social happening each March. It started in 1990 with several small art galleries coordinating their openings to promote business. Since, it has grown to become a wonderful way to spend a

261

social evening touring art galleries in the historic district.

This year, 31 art galleries opened their doors to showcase their art from 5 PM to 8 PM to all visitors, enticing them with hors d'oeuvres and refreshments. One of the gallery owner's has said, "it's a cocktail party on the move, and art is the entertainment". People come to gather, meet friends, wander, and talk streetside.

The art galleries are centered in a borough called the 'French Quarter' off East Bay Street. The Art Walk is just that…a walking tour, and many of the local artists are available to chat. It is a fun night out, and Marilyn and I took the opportunity to hobnob with the artsy folk. We wandered casually, in and out, from gallery to gallery for a couple hours. A few glasses of wine along the way, and the conversations flowed effortlessly.

The galleries get sought after exposure, and art aficionados can jostle with sometime art lovers, and everyone has a good time.

Sweet Grass Basket Weaving

Weathered and battered wooden sheds or stands line Highway 17, as the roadway falls from the heights of the Cooper River Bridge and works its way north through the boutique bedroom community of Mt. Pleasant which adjoins peninsular Charleston, exposing tourists to a unique aspect of lowcountry culture. Here artisans ply the skills their ancestors have passed-down from generation to generation to construct intricate straw baskets, bowls, plates, and all other creative objects.

Basket weaving dates back 300 years as an art-form to West Africa, and knowledge of the craft was brought here by the slaves to the plantations. The strands of straw, or "sweet grass", come from the reed-like shoots of sweet grass plants, which grow naturally and in abundance in the many marshes which border the Lowcountry's labyrinth of tidal creeks and waterways.

About 40 of these basket weaving stands remain along the East Cooper highway, where 150 stands existed in its heyday. The roughly 8'x8' stands are crudely built structures, built of wood pieces that have been located somewhere as leftovers, with open slatted sides and a modest roof overhead to shade the basket sellers and weavers from the intense heat and humidity of summer. Though often dilapidated, the sheds are survivors, as they stand silhouetted against the backdrop of modern Mt. Pleasant, pleasant and charming reminders of the area's historic past. Numerous baskets hang on display from the walls of each stand, and the basket weavers wrap themselves casually in chairs or rockers in the shade of the stand, as they weave, waiting until the next tourist drives up to chat.

Likewise, some 40 sweet grass weaving artisans ply their trade in the city of Charleston, most prominently along the sidewalks at the corners of Meeting and Broad Streets, and in the Market area. Their baskets line the sidewalks, as they weave yet another treasure for someone. Marilyn and I spend time, off to the side, just watching in fascination as these artisans ply their craft, and interchange graciously with tourists who express interest in their products.

The warmth and friendliness of these craftsmen, and the charm of their stands and selling presence, are part of the allure of the sweet grass baskets to the tourist. Charleston Mayor Joseph Riley, Jr. has said that it is an art-form that should not be lost, but he is worried that families continue to weave, and modern development's push not destroy their source of sweet grass. "We must ensure that the grass (for weaving) continues to grow", he said, and "the fact that we're worried about it is a good sign".

Spoleto Festival

An institution in the city is the Spoleto Festival. Through more than three weeks in late May/early June, the arts festival takes place, showcasing over 800 events with over 5,000 performers, in venues throughout downtown Charleston.

The Spoleto Festival has now weathered more than 25 years since its inaugural in 1976, becoming an annual extravaganza attracting visitors from all over the world, as well as an enthusiastic local following. Plays, operas, musical performances, ballet, circus, and art are on display.

In 2002, on a Friday afternoon, at the steps of the City Hall on Broad Street, Marilyn and I joined 1,200 other people gathered to kick-off the year's

Festival and enjoy a brief taste of the events that would come over the next 17 days.

Mayor Joseph Riley, Jr., without whom the Spoleto Festival would not exist, stated in his welcoming remarks, "It is my annual wish that the Spoleto Festival USA will exist in Charleston as long as our citizens search for beauty and truth. And may that be forever".

Lowcountry Oyster Roasts

No one does oyster roasts like the Lowcountry. Outsiders who witness their first oyster roast are sometimes taken aback. Perhaps these outsiders are used to their oysters being served 'on the half shell', or perhaps with a touch of butter and lemon. Others prefer cocktail sauce. But the true Lowcountry aficionado will tell you there is only one way to eat an oyster...cold, raw, and freshly cracked, popping open from its shell.

Whatever your preference, there is plenty of opportunity to enjoy the Lowcountry's favorite mussel. Major oyster roasts occur throughout the area, most in January, although September-April is oyster season.

The so-called Lowcountry Oyster Festival is dubbed by its organizer's "the world's largest oyster roast". It is held at the Boone Hall Plantation, in Mt. Pleasant, for the last 20 years, and more than 10,000 people show up, and consume 65,000 pounds of oysters. Live music and a collection of other foods are also available.

The oyster roasts are a tradition that predates the first European settlers to the area. American Indians would use steam to crack the shells and knives to open them. Imagine the natives sitting around the campfire, shucking the shells, and slurping down the salty delicacies. Remember, it was mounds of discarded oyster shells, piled high and glistening in the sun, which first greeted Charles Towne's first settlers in 1670 on the ship "Carolina" as it passed along the Ashley River's banks, and led to the designation of 'Oyster Point' and later 'White Point' at the Battery.

The 'Angel Oak' Tree

Magnificent 'live oak' trees are everywhere in the area, many with limbs draped majestically with Spanish moss. The 'live oaks' have thrived over the centuries, because they seem to be genetically coded to grow along the Lowcountry coast. The tree has a low, spreading, open branch structure which seems to withstand the tropical storms. Its roots are shallow, but spread two to three times out beyond the tree's canopy, so their base is extremely sturdy.

None is more magnificent than the 'Angel Oak' which stands on property off Bohicket Road on John's Island, to the west of the Ashley River. It is not more than twenty minutes away, so Marilyn and I climbed into our car on a sunny afternoon to see one of the grandest of the 'live oaks'. The 'Angel Oak' stands 65 feet tall, with a trunk 25 feet in circumference; its canopy shades 17,000 sq. feet, and when you see it, the spectacle takes your breath away.

Tourists, and some locals, say it is 1,400 years old...but, Charlestonians love to perpetuate myths. Urban forestry experts believe it is between 350 to 500 years old!

The property around the tree was granted to Abraham Waight in 1717, and received its name 'Angel' when a descendant of the property owner, Martha Waight, married Justis Angel in 1810.

But African beliefs hold that spirits live in trees, and move through the trees. Septima Clark is a well known Charleston civil rights activist and educator born in 1898, and she told the story:

> "The people declared that angels would appear in the form of a ghost at the oak. The killings that happened around the tree during slavery time were seen by people with a 'call'. The spirits were around the tree and it was a live oak and they considered that the angels brought the spirits there".

'Southern Heritage'

As a 'Northerner' it is quite enjoyable to get to understand and appreciate the locals who were born and raised, many over generations, and have as they call it 'roots' that run deep. Just 'being Southern' is the most wonderful thing in the world. They wear it on their sleeve, though with an attitude and lifestyle that is laid back and easy-going. They ooze charm, and friendliness...but they get the job done.

They exude 'Southern heritage', from their heads to their toes. Southern heritage permeates the South, and the Southerner takes great pride in it. For Sunday church, their men are dressed in bow ties, and blue and white-striped seersucker suits; their ladies still don long skirts, and wear wide-brimmed, floppy straw hats.

Their mouths water over a big pot of boiling collard greens. They eat macaroni and cheese for breakfast, lunch, and dinner. Deep down, they really think salt and fried chicken are good for you. 'Matoes (tomatoes) and grits' can make a meal all by itself. They eat 'hoppin John' on New Year's Day for good luck. Shrimp and grits, with brown gravy, is a favorite, even for breakfast. And, rice...they eat all kinds of rice. They invented 'sweet tea'.

Everyone knows the song words to "Dixie", and given the choice, the sight of Lowcountry marshlands and beaches is preferred any day to the gorgeous vistas of the Caribbean islands.

Do not be offended, if when walking down the street, you pass a local and they make direct eye contact with you, and greet you with a big smile, and 'hi ya-all'. They just enjoy being friendly...that is the way they were raised.

One such Southern family was portrayed in an article in **_The Post and Courier_** newspaper in February 2000. Mildred Bell was 80 years-old, and still living in the plantation house in which she was born. Her daughter, Kathleen Husky, was born there as well, and was still living with her mother in their family homestead.

Mildred Bell lived among reminders of her family's heritage in a 160 year-old plantation house, filled with antiques crafted by slaves, and furnishings some of which date back to the Revolution.

Mildred Bell said, "I am humbly grateful that we have this history, and that the house has been preserved for future generations".

Her home was once surrounded by slave cabins, but now only a smokehouse built by slaves during the Civil War endures. Her grandmother had buried her jewelry in the log building's dirt floor to hide it from roaming Yankee soldiers.

The plantation house is a beautiful 10-room building, with towering columns and soaring ceilings, built in 1830 for Bell's great grandparents for $250. It is constructed of heart pine, joined by wooden pegs, or handmade nails.

The family's founder, Joel Lipscomb, came to America three centuries ago, after being forced to flee England after participating in a failed attempt to help a friend, the Duke of Monmouth, take the British throne. In addition to the family's founder being an exiled pretender to the British throne, Mildred Bell counts her ancestors as a murdered American Patriot from the Revolution, and a cunning Confederate courier. Her grandfather, Edward Lipscomb, was a Confederate courier who bluffed his way past enemy Union lines to deliver a message. Such are the treasures that are bound so tightly in Mildred Bell's family history and tradition.

Their 'family tree' is like the grand old live oak trees that adorn their property, with grace and dignity. Their trunks are wide, both the 'family tree' and the live oak trees, to anchor them to the ground they share, with their roots going deep, over three centuries. Though buffeted by the years, they both stand tall and proud, branch after branch, generation after generation, limbs reaching toward the sky.

A TRELLIS FOR 29 ½'s GARDEN: CHAPTER 26

It is January, and I have just completed building a trellis for espalier of a Camellia plant Marilyn and I purchased with a Christmas gift from my parents, Les and Fern Funk, who live in Palm Harbor, Florida, near Tampa. Each of my parents' gifts from the last several seasons have gone to purchase a plant, because Marilyn and I believe nothing can be more lasting than to invest in the long term beauty of a garden. Gorgeous plants are so readily available, and inexpensive, as they are easily grown in the semi-tropical climate along the ocean coastline around Charleston.

This year we also purchased a Confederate Jasmine vine that will climb to conceal unsightly pipes that go up the outside wall at the corner of our sunroom. A wire mesh form was constructed to envelop the pipes at the corner of two walls, while serving as a form upon which the vine could climb. I am now 'training' the vine every few days, by carefully placing and tying its new growth in the desired direction and position on the wire form, so it will grow in a managed way up the side of the house.

Confederate Jasmine is an evergreen vine, with leaves of a glossy green, and its profusion in early Spring of fragrant, tubular, white flowers is one of the glories of living in the South. Sometimes it will bloom well into Summer, and we wanted its sweet aroma to be one of the first pleasant experiences as one entered our gate from Montagu Street, and walked the narrow brick pathway to our rear garden and entry door. Its sister plant, the Carolina Jasmine, has yellow flowers, and we are training several of these plants to grow up and over our arbor.

To provide an inviting place to sit and enjoy the garden, we purchased a wonderful concrete bench. It looks old, and just right under the shade of the arbor, next to our pond.

The new Camellia plant, we decided, would also be perfect to complement the narrow walkway from our streetside gate to the rear enclosed courtyard. The Camellia blooms have a chaste and sculptured beauty that few other flowers possess. Camellias have been grown and cherished on the great plantations of the South for nearly two centuries. The Camellia is a native of Eastern Asia, but introduced into this country via Europe in about 1820. It is an evergreen shrub with dark, glossy foliage. A variety of flower colors ranges from white to cream, through shades of pink, to brilliant shades of scarlet and red. It thrives in the semi-tropical, humid climates of the South, and is abundant in gardens all around Charleston.

The north wall of our house, with semi-shade, was going to be perfect for the Camellia. We wanted to espalier the Camellia tight to the wall of the 4-foot wide walkway. Anything left to grow naturally would become too large and intrude upon the walkway. Treated leftover 2"x2" wood scraps from my worksite would be just right for construction of the trellis, which would mount to the stucco wall and serve as a form upon which the plant could grow. The trellis would reach about 7-feet high and fan out like a sunburst to a width of 6-feet at top. The old 18" thick stucco and brick house walls provided no problem, as anchors were drilled into the walls, and the trellis would be mounted standing off about 3"-4" from the wall.

The trellis was completed in one evening, and now just had to be painted..."Charleston Green" was the color, of course. The color "Charleston Green" was invented here, so the story goes, and is made by combining approximately equal parts of green and black paint. After a couple coats of paint, Marilyn helped me mount the trellis to the wall with wood block spacers, and then we planted the Camellia.

The plant from the nursery had already been started on a small trellis in espalier fashion, so its branches could easily be secured to the new, larger trellis with garden ties. All of this labor made a fabulous 75-degree day in January all the more enjoyable. Our next-door neighbor, George, watched and threw an occasional verbal barb from his veranda, perched high above us in elegant fashion, overlooking our courtyard below. This elevated position was apropos for George, because the 'command' position above us always seemed to fit his persona.

As work was completed, Marilyn and I took a few quiet moments to listen to the special sounds we could hear from our courtyard...the repetitive symphony of water falling from our fountain within the pond, the occasional clip-clop of horses' hooves as a carriage with visitors passed along the street, or merely the pleasant sounds of the wind causing a rush of limbs high overhead in the ancient Ligustrum tree which overhangs our sunroom.

Popping into our minds was the future vision of the newly planted Camellia growing skyward, with blossoms of double pink flowers, offering a fragrance that would welcome anyone entering our gate. It was still January, and 'Winter' in the Lowcountry had another six weeks or so to go, but Spring was just around the corner. You see, March in Charleston is like nowhere else…just imagine the Azaleas, and then the Crepe Myrtle, in all their beauty!

Taking time to enjoy our work.

CHARLESTON HUNKERS DOWN FOR WAR: CHAPTER 27

With the evacuation of Fort Sumter by Federal forces, Charleston became an armed camp preparing for war. Troops were in movement constantly. Fortifications were built with urgency, surrounding the city. Confederate minds tried to anticipate Lincoln's next move.

On June 25th, 1861, the newspaper reported that 'Abraham Lincoln' was hanged in effigy on Archdale Street, opposite Market Street.

(Even Charleston's private citizens began to prepare for war. Emma Holmes wrote in her diary, September 16th, 1861, that she finds herself able to make flannel shirts and drawers, this being her principal occupation since the beginning of the war. In addition, she said, she can knit stockings and load and clean pistols.)

Lincoln acted by requesting Union states for a militia of 75,000 men to be called to duty for 90 days, to counter the Confederate threat, and force the secessionists to back down and return to reason. But, the opposite occurred. The Confederacy considered the call-up of militia Lincoln's declaration of war, and responded by gearing their defenses for the threat of invasion.

Furthermore, four more states seceded, including Virginia; now eleven states comprised the Confederacy, with a population of over 9 million persons.

But the direct taste of war would skirt Charleston for some time. The city had a host of natural geographic defenses…the vast expanse of tidal rivers and creeks, the salt marshes, and the pluff mud, all posed problems for any enemy contemplating a landed attack on the city. Natural barriers were strengthened by artillery batteries constructed on Morris Island and James Island to protect land access routes into the city from its most vulnerable western side.

But, the Union did attempt a naval blockade to prevent port access for supplies or war material to enter or leave the city. The effect of the blockade was more an economic pinch, than militarily significant. Cotton began to backup on the wharves of the city. Blockade running became the lifeline sustaining the city, and private citizens were encouraged to become blockade runners. Blockade running became a business, and a number of runners were successful, making large fortunes from its profits in the early years of the war. In the famous novel *"Gone With the Wind"*, its author, Margaret Mitchell, created the principal character, Rhett Butler, and explained, "I made him a Charlestonian because I had to make him a blockade runner".

(But not everyone was so swashbuckling. Emma Holmes wrote in her diary on October 14th, 1861, that the government had sequestered the property of Edmund Gibbes "for refusing to do military service, or pay his fine", as well as writing "an insulting answer to the summons". She described Mr. Gibbes as "an infidel and a notoriously wicked man". "His only redeeming quality was his love for his mother", she wrote.)

And, as if in keeping with the unbridled free spirit of the blockade runner, the social elite of Charleston maintained their inclination to party. As if in a surreal mockery of their wartime plight, parties were held at Fort Sumter, with bands, drinking, and dancing into the night. Boats would ferry guests to the fort; but, if they partied too late, the tide would go out, leaving their boats marooned in the mud, forcing everyone to spend the rest of the evening on their boat until the tide returned to free the boat.

Then, in November 1861, 13,000 Federal troops landed at Port Royal, a mere 50 miles to the southwest of Charleston, near Beaufort, South Carolina. The news sent shock waves throughout Charleston. Many prepared to move inland from the city, while others moved to the city fleeing the Port Royal area. Charleston resident, Emma Holmes wrote in her diary on November 11th that her 85-year-old aunt, and her cousins, Eliza and Mary, arrived in the city "running from the Yankees and dreadfully scared".

At that same time, a change was made, as Jefferson Davis appointed a then little known commander to oversee the defense of South Carolina, Georgia, and Florida. Until then, his military record had been less than stellar with early defeats in western Virginia, which led to his transfer south to a post in Charleston. That commander's name was Robert E. Lee, of

Virginia. In his short stay in Charleston, Lee strengthened the harbor's defenses, and its railroad links to the South. On November 26th, the city's Mayor, Charles Macbeth, gave public notice that, pursuant to General Lee's instructions, no person would be allowed to leave the city without the mayor's permission.

But, as if war were not enough, another disaster was about to strike the city.

The "Great Fire" of 1861

On a Wednesday evening, December 11th, 1861, Robert E. Lee was dining at the Mills House Hotel, after inspecting the city's defenses that day, when cries of "fire" could be heard, with the clanging of alarm bells interrupting his evening meal.

Slave refugees had started a campfire, which got out of control near a factory on Hasell Street, just east of East Bay Street toward the Cooper River. The fire raced to the Market, and then onto Meeting Street, fanned by a wind which had just kicked up. Flames soared into the night sky, as the inferno cut its swath down Meeting Street, and then moved west along Queen Street, as the high winds moved it ever faster and out of control.

Robert E. Lee had climbed to the roof of the Mills House to watch its horror. More than a third of the city was under fire, and in its path lay smoking ruins. As the heat and fire threatened the Mills House, Lee and his party fled for safety to the Edmonston-Alston House at 21 East Battery.

Robert E. Lee fled for safety to the Edmonston-Alston house,
21 East Battery Street, during the 'Great Fire of 1861'.

Then, the fire turned west along Tradd Street, heading toward the Ashley River. By late morning, December 12th, the fire had consumed itself, after devastating 540 acres of the city, and

279

destroying 575 homes. In its path, lay the ruins of five churches, including the Circular Congregational Church on Meeting Street, St. Andrew's Hall where the secession had recently been voted upon, and the Pinckney mansion on East Bay Street.

It would be the worst fire in Charleston's history. For years, its swath could be seen in charred and blackened remains from the Cooper to the Ashley River. Fortunately, one of the few buildings in its path to escape was the Mills House Hotel.

Imagine was it was like to live in Charleston. Enemy troops were poised just outside the city, the city was under naval blockade in a wartime stranglehold, and then, the most devastating of fires destroyed a third of the city. Once again, only great character and the tenacity of its citizens would allow the city to survive. But, even greater tests were yet to come.

Edmonston-Alston House

The great home at 21 East Battery Street, to which Robert E. Lee fled for safety in the 'Great Fire of 1861', is today a museum which offers the public a wonderful glimpse into the city's antebellum past.

In 1817, Charles Edmondston, a successful merchant, purchased a lot and began to build one of the first dwellings on what was known as the 'High Battery'. The home was completed in 1825, but economic depressions in the 1820's and

1830's reduced his resources, and the 'Panic of 1837' forced the home's sale in 1838.

The buyer was Charles Alston, brother of Mary Motte Alston Pringle, who lived nearby at the family mansion at 27 King Street. Charles Alston made several changes to the exterior of the home to conform to the popular Greek Revival-style of the period. He added a third floor piazza, and roof top parapet emblazoned with the Alston family coat of arms.

An elegant chandelier in the Front Hall was made in Philadelphia, and Alston's home was one of the first to be piped for gas, after gas introduction within the city in December of 1846.

A portrait, painted in Paris in 1856, hangs in the Ladies' Withdrawing Room, and can be seen today of Susan Pringle Alston (1832-1921), daughter of Charles Alston, who continued to live in the house until her death. Fine furnishings, china, silver, artwork, chandeliers, telescope, hunting rifle, and a three-generation family library collection of some 2,000 books can be seen today via guided tours of the home.

As Marilyn and I toured the home on a Saturday afternoon, we imagined Robert E. Lee bursting through the double doors, thrust open for him. He stood on the top floor piazza, enjoying the crisp sea breeze, gazing at the magnificent panorama of Charleston harbor before him, the harbor bustling with military activity, the moonlit night playing upon its waters. Below him, small groups of people gathered on the Battery, engaged in frenzied conversation concerning the raging inferno that was ravaging their city that evening.

Even the great Robert E. Lee must have felt chills racing down his spine as he recalled the tumult of events he had witnessed, just months ago, across the water, toward the ocean, at that tiny speck of land perched on the horizon, called Fort Sumter.

After four months in charge of Charleston's defenses, Robert E. Lee returned to Richmond, Virginia, to advise Jefferson Davis. In March, 1862, General John C. Pemberton replaced Lee, and the situation became grave. Federal troops started toward Charleston from Port Royal, and eventually made their way onto James Island, just on the doorstep to the west, across the Ashley River from the city.

The Pringles Prepare for War

Like many other Charleston families, by Fall 1861, the Pringle family prepared their home at 27 King Street, and themselves, for the unpleasantness of war. Silver and other valuable belongings were packed and sent inland to Columbia for safer keeping.

In December, their magnificent home was under immediate threat from the "Great Fire", but was just spared from the path of the fire.

In January, William Pringle decided to evacuate his slaves, and move them inland.

By April, 1862, one year after Fort Sumter, the Pringles decided the city was too dangerous to return from the plantations, as they had each

Spring. By June, throngs of people were fleeing the city. Caravans of carts lined the exit roadways from the city, piled high with furniture and any belongings that they could carry away. The Pringles had no alternative but to move further inland as well.

In June, Mary Motte Alston Pringle and her daughters returned to Charleston, to pack their best furniture, linens, china, and servants for a move inland to better safety. The Pringles leased a plantation near Society Hill, South Carolina, about 110 miles northwest of Charleston; they paid $2,000 per year to lease the plantation. They, like so many others, were now a family of war refugees.

In May 1862, Harriott Middleton would write to her cousin, "Do you not hope that Charleston may be saved. I don't mind our house but I can't bear to give up the old streets and buildings, and the churches". With the approach of Yankee troops causing great anxiety among the city's residents, the members of St. Michael's Church decided to take down the church's steeple bells and send them inland to Columbia for safer keeping. (Remember, these same steeple bells had been lost to the British, as they evacuated the city following the Revolution, some 80 years earlier.)

In June 1862, the Federals decided to launch an attempt to enter and capture Charleston. Federal troops clashed with Confederate defenders in bitter and bloody hand-to-hand battle in the fields, to be known thereafter as the 'Battle of Secessionville'. The Union lost 700 men; the Confederates lost 200 men, but won the day, as the Federals retreated back to Port Royal. The Union forces, in defeat, were convinced for the time being that Charleston could not be captured by a land assault. Charleston was spared, at least for another year.

Re-Enactment of the 'Battle of Secessionville'

Annual re-enactment of the 'Battle of Secessionville' reoccurs each year at the Boone Hall Plantation, located in Mt. Pleasant. Marilyn and I have attended this event several times.

As we strolled down the remnant of the old entry roadway, lined with huge overhanging live oaks throwing shade everywhere under their massive canopies, toward the main plantation house, we found it easy to fall back in time to those antebellum days in Charleston.

Vendors are set up along the tree-lined dirt avenue, with tents and booths displaying period keepsakes to be purchased…everything from dresses, hats, and full costumes from the period, to Civil War guns and weapons, and much more. The vendors are dressed in period costumes lending an aura of authenticity to the spectacle.

Off the sides of the avenue, are the remains of slave cabins, which we entered to experience momentarily the awful conditions these people endured, while their owner's lived lavishly mere hundreds of yards away.

Most interesting are the tented campsites of the re-enactors. Some people are fanatical about this 'hobby' of re-enactment, and their families accompany them driving great distances throughout the South, devoting their free-time to their passion, 're-enactment' of Civil War times and skirmishes.

As we wandered amid the tent-city, everyone, including the children, was in period dress. Families were cooking, or just sitting in groups around campfires. We could overhear their discussions of the 'enemy approaching', or some such banter. You see, 're-enactment' means that they try to spend their entire time 'acting' as if they truly were back in time.

Then, the re-enactment of the 'Battle of Secessionville' began. We were joined by hundreds in the crowd, lined up at one side of an open field. From within the woods bordering the field, the Federal forces moved into the clearing. Some soldiers were on horseback; others marched forward to a drummer's beat. Off to the sides, various artillery teams prepped their canons. The battle erupted.

Canons exploded, belching white smoke charges into the air (the white smoke was really flour exploded into the air to simulate real canon fire), as the artillery crews hurriedly reacted to reload. Federal troops moved forward, and approached the Confederate defenders who lay lurking behind earthen berms at one end of the field of battle. Rifle sharpshooters opened fire; and, re-enactors fell, feigning mortal wounds. Soon, the field was strewn with 'casualties', until one side fell back in retreat, and the battle was over.

The crowd erupted in cheers for the 'actors', because the 're-enactment' gave everyone a precious glimpse back in history.

As the Summer of 1862 wore on, with Yankee troops in the area, and Federal warships silhouetted on the harbor's horizon, the city's citizens began to experience shortages of many products, including coffee. *The Courier* newspaper suggested in an article to its readers that English chicory root be substituted for the "difficult to obtain java" bean. When chicory was roasted and ground, the article went to say, it is "decidedly good".

In a later article, the newspaper even reported its shortage of ink supply. The article announced that the newspaper had received an ink substitute, developed by druggists Pratt, Dowie & James at 153 Meeting Street, made from "ink nuts". The newspaper reported that it planned to give the substitute a try, and suggested that others do so as well.

In mid-September 1862, General Pemberton was reassigned to the defense of Vicksburg, and the popular General P.T. Beauregard returned to head the defense of Charleston. Beauregard was not an enthusiastic supporter of Jefferson Davis as President of the Confederacy. So, Jefferson Davis tried to remove Beauregard from direct war action by placing him on the sidelines, defending Charleston. Beauregard was back in the city of his first triumph, where he caused Federal forces the humiliating evacuation of Fort Sumter. In the next months, Washington would grow more and more anxious to capture Charleston, and if that proved impossible, to destroy it as punishment for its indiscretion in leading the secession movement.

A HOUSE AND GARDEN TOUR AT 29 ½: CHAPTER 28

The first seasonal bloom of our Amaryllis plant opened on a late January morning, basking in the sunshine from its windowsill perch in our sunroom. Alongside, an old mason jar was mothering newly grown root shoots in water, nurtured from clippings of a Carolina Morning Glory, which Marilyn and I surreptitiously snipped on one of our walks around the city. The Amaryllis bulb was given to Marilyn as a gift from her friend Marian Motley for working on the Thursday ladies' day golf tournament committee at Snee Farm Golf Club. We planted, and nurtured the bulb's growth, cheering it all along the way. Excitement occurs when new things spring to life, as that is what makes gardening so much fun. And, this first bloom was a glorious moment for us.

The longevity of Amaryllis bulbs is a constant source of amazement to gardeners, because when handled properly a bulb can produce flowers for 50 to 75 years, and may become almost an heirloom within a family. The blooms of the Amaryllis are borne on tall, straight flower stalks, 12"-18" above the green, long-leafed foliage at the base of the plant.

Three open, trumpet-shaped flowers suddenly burst open on our plant, and a fourth was still tightly closed, but held promise. The flowers were deep red, popping from a stalk 12" high, with the largest flower shaped like an old gramophone, with pedals that stretched for the luscious sunlight. Multiple red stamens reached out proudly from its heart, and the pods of yellow seeds (some already falling) held promise for the renewal of new generations. In mild climates, like Charleston, the plants can thrive out-of-doors and be used with dramatic effect in the garden as a foreground planting in a shrub border. This plant will find its way to our courtyard this Spring.

Spring Arrives in Charleston

Now it is March, and just outside our pair of French doors leading from the sunroom to the rear courtyard, we planted an Azalea shrub the preceding Fall.

The Azaleas are a botanical form of the Rhododendron, and are among the most beautiful of flowering shrubs. The Azalea was native to Eastern Asia, imported to Southern Europe, and then brought over to America in colonial times. Since then, Azaleas have become abundant and thrive in gardens all over Charleston. With a wide range of colors and varieties, their blooms can be depended upon year after year to provide a glorious profusion of beauty and color each Spring in Charleston.

Spring brings a rainbow of colors to the Lowcountry landscape. Dogwood, Wisteria, and Azaleas are the South's Spring glory, and if it's a Spring when their blooms peak in unison, it simply takes your breath away. Dogwoods spread their white clouds of delicate beauty. Purple Wisteria drapes gracefully from high and low. But, none is more brilliantly beautiful than the mass plantings of Azaleas, with their blooms of purple, magenta, rose, pinks, orange-reds, reds, and white. Azaleas thrive as under-story shrubs, often preferring to live under tall weathered and magnificent old live oak trees. And, when the filtered-light of a sunny, clear Spring day plays its light shafts on the glorious Azalea blooms, it is truly a spectacular visual display.

After planting, and then loving care and nurturing, we are excited to see our Azalea's first buds burst forth with fresh, shining and delicate, red flowers. Nothing exists better than watching something new fulfill its promise. We planted with thought and care, with our hands in the soil, then watered and fertilized, waited, and watched. Then, all effort is rewarded by these first flowers. First blooms seem to say all work is worthwhile, while knowing that this is just the start of our enjoyment. More will come as the plant matures over the years...continuing rewards to anticipate. And so, this single Azalea captured such feeling for us. We enjoyed sharing the exhilaration, and just as we grow stronger together, so does our beautiful, robust Azalea plant.

As March moved onward, each day presented new opportunities for joy as we watched new growth beginning to awaken from winter's dormancy, responding to the sunlight and warmer days, as Spring approached. The Carolina Jasmine on our arbor began to show yellow buds, each day getting a little larger. We took notice each day of new growth on each plant, and moments of fun occur, when we take moments to share our excitement with each other.

Another bell ringer of Spring in Charleston is the start of house tours. Just as sure as the blooming of the Azaleas, the opportunity arrives to step through the gates and peek into some of the city's finest private residences. The tradition of touring grand homes and gardens is long established in the Lowcountry. The house and garden tours are wonderful for everyone, tourists and residents alike. Even longtime residents constantly tell of seeing something new, especially from a walk down a secluded alley where a charming home comes into view that was never noticed, or a peek through the slats of a garden gate reveals a glorious glimpse beyond, or we gaze and simply imagine what the people were like who lived and partied in these homes so many years ago. What was their everyday life like? What did they wear? Who were their friends? We want to get to know them better.

Taking advantage of the house tours lets tourists and the city's residents look inside the houses and gardens, and often learn some of the answers to their curiosity. The granddaddy of house tours is the Spring "Historic Charleston Foundation's Festival of Houses and Gardens".

For over fifty years the Foundation has been putting on these tours of some of the greatest homes and gardens in the city's Historic District. It has become nationally acclaimed, as visitors from all over the country, even the world, plan their trips to Charleston around these tour dates. For a whole month there is a daily tour, some under the stars by candlelight, focusing each year on different areas of downtown Charleston. About 15,000 tickets are sold each year. Proceeds from revenues also go to a good cause, continuing the Foundation's rehabilitation and preservation programs to foster the city's historic architectural heritage.

Nearly 700 local volunteers guide the tours, and Marilyn has volunteered to be a 'docent' in different homes through several tours. The tours are made possible through the generosity of the owners of the private residences who share their treasures with visitors. As the tours wind down, a "Plantation Oyster Roast" at Drayton Hall introduces guests to the culinary traditions of the Lowcountry, including steamed oysters, barbeque chicken, red rice, and coleslaw. Drayton Hall is the only plantation house on the historic Ashley River to have escaped destruction during the Civil War, and stands as one of the finest examples of colonial architecture in America.

Each year, "The Garden Club of Charleston" also sponsors its walking tours of "Private Homes and Gardens" to raise money to maintain some of the city's special gardens, like the Manigault House, and the Heyward-Washington House, among others. Sites are within walking distance of each other. But when you go, wear comfortable walking shoes, so you don't mar the beautiful old heart pine wood floors of the homes, or twist an ankle walking the not-so-smooth old bluestone sidewalk surfaces throughout the city.

Charleston today is remarkable because it is alone among American cities, with treasures of surviving and irreplaceable buildings, streetscapes, churches, and public spaces. Its ambience of centuries-old beautiful structures and lush gardens are woven throughout the fabric of this enchanting port city. Earlier generations built, what has so fortunately survived, to educate and inspire us today.

But, preservation is always a work in progress, never finished; it is a message that beckons each of us who stroll the city's historic streets, and admire its historic neighborhoods. A wonderful motto was used by the "Historic Charleston Foundation" several years ago, and reads, "We will protect only what we love, we will love only what we understand, and we will understand only what we are taught".

A House and Garden Tour Visits 29 ½ Montagu

Marilyn and I were honored and proud that we were asked by "The Garden Club of Charleston" to host a tour of our home and recently restored

291

carriage house and garden at 29 ½ Montagu Street. Marilyn was fortunate to be asked to join the 'Garden Club'.

The tour was a true reward for all the work that both of us put into our new home, and at the same time, we were nervous and anxious, because of the years of success and tradition behind such tours in the city.

We wanted everything to go just right, and to prove worthy of such an honor and distinction. And, yet, in the weeks preceding the afternoon tour, we wrung our hands with trepidation, wondering aloud to each other at times, "why did we say 'yes'?".

Nevertheless, the tour was finalized, tour pamphlets printed, and there was no turning back. A few days before the event, two 'Garden Club' ladies with lead roles in the tour paid a last visit to our carriage house. They check on arrangements, organize the plan for controlling the flow of visitors through our tiny, narrow three-story passage ways, and decide upon floral centerpiece arrangements that the 'Garden Club' would provide to accent the home's display. They encouraged us that all would go well, and guides would be able to handle the traffic. They told us we simply had to stand back, and enjoy. Well, somehow that was not entirely true!

We worked our little tails off in the last few days before the big event. Everything had to be cleaned to a spotless condition, and furnishings arranged precisely, if possible. You can imagine the 'angst' we shared, back and forth...but somehow, our marriage survived. Last days were spent pruning, sweeping, and raking our garden courtyard, as well. In fact, we were still putting last minute touches upon everything almost to the minute first guests arrived.

Then, finally, the magical Saturday afternoon in April arrived. We were blessed. The day was gorgeous, with clear skies, sunshine, and pleasant shirt-sleeve temperature. Our flowers in the garden were at their peaks, even the last days of bloom for the Azalea. Our fountain was creating a wonderful sound, peaceful and calming, as the water splashed below amid the water lilies in bloom. The '52 Smith Street' neighbor's huge Mock Orange tree (it was very old, and the shrub had literally become a tree) was giving off its very strong, delightful orange-like aroma, enveloping our courtyard below with the sweet smells that added to the ambience.

Marilyn and I just finished our last second tidying up, just in time to change clothes, and greet the two tour guides who were going to handle the afternoon's three-hour open house. One would be streetside on Montagu Street to usher visitors through our narrow gate bearing the old brass numbers *'29 ½'*. One would be just outside our French doors to greet visitors and direct them into our home.

The first visitors arrived. Soon, to our complete surprise, throngs of people were lined up, queuing down the block to get into our gate and rear courtyard. The weather was perfect, crowds were large at all venues, and particularly the crowd to see our quaint, charming 150-year old carriage house.   This was especially the case because word had spread that this was home for a time to Charles Kuralt, as he wrote his chapter about Charleston, and our carriage house, in his book *Charles Kuralt's AMERICA*.   In fact, as we lived in the home, we often would listen as tourist-laden horse carriages clopped their way by us on Montagu Street, with their guides relating the story of Charles Kuralt's stay in our carriage house.

Because of the excessive crowds, Marilyn and I were pressed into action. Marilyn took over to do a wonderful, enthusiastic job of greeting people at our doorway, and holding them in check until the house cleared sufficiently to allow more people inside.   She told stories, and simply enjoyed mingling with the warm, friendly visitors who expressed pleasure in the opportunity to view our home.

The   Garden   Club's   guide   worked   inside, answering   questions   and   relaying   historic information of interest concerning the house to the visitors, while directing traffic in a one-way serpentine pattern through the house and out the entry   door   off   the   kitchen   into   the   garden courtyard.

Meanwhile, I drifted back and forth, helping to direct people between the courtyard and the gate out front.   By this time, the line of expectant visitors had formed and extended far down the sidewalk along the street. Our narrow brick 4-ft. wide pathway from the gate to the rear courtyard was   packed;   but,   everyone   was   considerate, friendly, and courteous as they waited patiently in line.

Like no time at all, the three hours of tour passed, and the last of the visitors made their way through our home. The guides left and thanked us, and it was over.

Marilyn and I were still on such a high as we sat back and tried to capture our thoughts from the day's experience. We were elated. Everyone had been so kind, expressing many wonderful words to us concerning our home and garden. And, we were sure they had thoroughly enjoyed themselves as well.

It was an unforgettable, rewarding experience. All the work we expended to restore our carriage house, and the final result, was all worthwhile. Local gadflies have been known to define 'preservation' as "the act of restoring to a level of grandeur, it never before enjoyed". Well, perhaps we had accomplished just that!

Oh, and yes, we need to tell you about one last harbinger of Spring in the Lowcountry. It is not the tulip trees, red bud or Bradford pear trees, dogwood, wisteria, or azaleas bursting into bloom. Nor is it the cackling call of the marsh hen, or the romantic pairing of birds high above in the trees just now beginning to sprout their new buds.

Neither is it the bevy of skateboarders or roller blade skaters wending their way along the walkway encircling Colonial Lake, dodging the young and older couples holding hands as they enjoy a stroll in the warm afternoon sunshine.

It is not the cherubic young coeds of the College of Charleston, showing their pretty legs from the shorts they have eagerly donned for the warm afternoon, as they do their homework perched on the lawns of the campus or down at Whitepoint Garden on the Battery. Nor is it the young men passing them by, trying to act nonchalant, pretending not to notice.

Furthermore, it is not the clip-clopping of horse drawn carriages, frequently over laden with tourists eager to experience 'Charleston' on a delightful afternoon. Nor is it the myriad of crumpled, dry oak leaves which have fallen to the ground, and swirl about our feet in the gentle wind of a gorgeous Spring day.

No, one could say tongue-in-cheek of course, the real harbingers of Spring in the Lowcountry are the so-called 'no-see-ums', those nasty little gnats that assault our faces, eyes, ears, and every exposed area of skin we offer, with a ferociousness that far outweighs their infinitesimal size. But, they will soon be gone…as the locals say, "the mosquitoes will eat them"!

CHARLESTON UNDER SIEGE, 1863: CHAPTER 29

I often stand in our garden, looking up toward the sky, as I imagine what it must have been like in 1863, about 140 years ago, in Charleston. What would life have been like in those desperate days with your city under siege. Think of the fear, trying to live day-to-day with incoming shells piercing the sky with their awful, frightful sounds as they arched overhead, and landed in horrendous explosions, debris becoming further projectiles in the air. Imagine your beloved city being torn apart, and the threat to your own property, that is, what is left. Although, most residents evacuated their homes and businesses below Calhoun Street, by then desolate, and only a military presence remained. I think of our carriage house, built in 1850, standing those days in harm's way. But, I am getting ahead of the story.

The siege of Charleston began in April 1863. In the North, a growing movement developed for the capture of Charleston. Public opinion gravitated toward that prize, spurred on by the newspapers. Lincoln viewed the capture of Charleston as a necessary moral, political, and symbolic victory. Charleston was symbolically more important than the capture of Richmond, capital of the Confederacy, because Charleston was the birthplace, or 'Cradle of Secession', and rebellion.

Militarily, Charleston was an important port, and a home to blockade runners, supplying arms and munitions to the Confederacy. The port was also a lifeline for the South to Europe, and particularly the city's commercial links to Great Britain. Great Britain, furthermore, was partial to the Confederacy, and her larger firms made large profits by shipping supplies from Europe to the Confederacy, thru Charleston. Also, Charleston utilized excellent railroad connections to distribute supplies inland throughout the South.

Moreover, if Charleston were taken, military strategists in the North saw Charleston as a good launch point for an invasion of Union forces into the South's heartland. And, not unimportant to their thinking, military leaders saw Fort Sumter's loss as an embarrassment, and they were eager to redeem themselves.

Accordingly, plans were developed in Washington to launch ironclad warships against Charleston. In the Spring of 1863, ironclads were ordered to assemble just off the mouth of Charleston harbor, a mere 600-800 yards off Fort Sumter. Simultaneously, as the plan went, Federal troops based in Port Royal near Hilton Head Island would move toward Charleston for an invasion onto Morris Island, just across the southern mouth of Charleston harbor.

(Meanwhile, on May 5th, *The Mercury* newspaper in Charleston informed its readers of another "great victory in Virginia" near Chancellorsville, where Longstreet "beat back the advancing columns" and "the daring (Stonewall) Jackson" attacked from the rear. The newspaper reported that further details were limited due to the "mischief of Yankee cavalry to the wires and railroads", including news of the "heroic and skillful" Jackson being wounded.

In an article of somewhat different flavor the preceding day, the newspaper reported the gratitude of soldiers of Battery Bee on Sullivan's Island to "Miss Gadsden and the ladies of Charleston" for the "sugar and coffee as refreshments after the late engagement in this harbor".)

For the same reasons that the Federals wanted Charleston, the Confederacy wanted to keep her. Confederate leaders determined that Charleston would "be defended at any cost of life or property". Robert E. Lee ordered that its defenders fight "street by street and house by house as long as we have a foot of ground to stand upon".

War was about to come to Charleston.

(But, in the meantime, the soldiers were trying to find pleasure during quiet times. The story was reported in the local newspaper on June 10th that two men from the Federal monitor ship "Nahant" took time to go fishing along the North Edisto River. They were surprised by someone spotted in the river's brush, and returned to the ship to gather a search party. After searching the area, two Confederate deserters were captured.)

Over the next weeks, sporadic exchanges occurred between the Union forces digging in on the narrow sandbar beachhead in front of Battery Wagner on Morris Island, and the Confederate defenders in the battery. Battery Wagner was first named 'The Neck Battery' for the narrow strip of land on which it was located. Within the previous six months, it had been renamed 'Battery Wagner' as a tribute to Lt. Col. Thomas M. Wagner, who had died there the previous July in an artillery accident.

On July 15th, a newspaper article reported that Federal sharpshooters were maintaining "their vigorous fire" from their rifle pits dug into the sand, while the Confederate riflemen returned sporadic shots trying to harass the Union soldiers working on gun positions in front of them on the beach. The article went on to say the Union fleet also continues its "usual cannonading".

On July 18th, 1863, Federal forces attacked Battery Wagner on Morris Island, after a tremendous aerial bombardment of the battery from Federal warships just offshore. The 54th Massachusetts, an African-American regiment under the command of Colonel Robert Gould Shaw, led the assault. This assault was immortalized in the recent movie "Glory". When fighting stopped the next day, the Federals had suffered one of the greatest disasters of the war. Federal troops attacking Battery Wagner had numbered 5,000 men; after the gory battle charge, 1,515 were casualties of the one-day assault. Many outfits lost nearly half their men, and many officers were killed. One officer from the 48th New York regiment called the assault the "gate of Hell".

For the South, Battery Wagner and its garrison had held the onslaught. The earthen walls of the battery survived, though blasted repeatedly by one of the largest Federal aerial bombardments of the war. And, its earthen walls protected the Confederate defenders, who received few casualties. Likewise, the Confederates captured a number of Federals, who were held prisoner either at Castle Pinckney, or in the 'Old City Jail' on Franklin Street.

The North paid a great price on that narrow strip of beach and sand dune, and was stopped from advancing on Morris Island, but even more importantly, the South gained time to strengthen Charleston's defenses. Beauregard went to work to beef-up defenses surrounding the city on Sullivan's Island, James Island, and also Fort Sumter. Beauregard now believed that the Federal's strategy would change from assault to siege.

Beauregard was right.

(And the citizens of Charleston were concerned. An article in the **The Courier** newspaper on July 31st encouraged the ladies of Charleston to participate in the "Ladies Gun Boat Raffle", as proceeds were needed "to provide comforts & conveniences for the brave officers and crews". Furthermore, the hospitals and Wayside Home needed corn meal, so planters were encouraged to supply these noble institutions.)

Washington sent 10,000 additional troops to reinforce existing forces. The reinforcements bivouacked on the western end of Folly Island, and during the days, moved to Morris Island where major construction was underway. The Federals were building trenches, bulwarks, and batteries with the objective of beating Fort Sumter and Battery Wagner into submission via an intense artillery bombardment. Working feverishly, despite the stifling heat and humidity of a Lowcountry summer, and constant harassment by Confederate sharpshooters just down the sand dunes at Battery Wagner, as well as sporadic cannon fire from Beauregard's batteries, the job was completed within one month.

(*The Courier* newspaper reported on August 7th, a sultry day in which the temperature reached 92 degrees in the shade, that a Federal gunboat moved close to the shore of Morris Island, and fired 50 shells at the Confederate encampment, wounding two men.

The next day, *The Mercury* newspaper reported a number of "outrageous assaults" by its own Confederate soldiers upon respectable citizens strolling the city's streets. The article encouraged the provost marshal to discourage these assaults by making examples of these "irrepressible sons of Mars".

On August 10th, it was reported as quiet most of the day, until late afternoon "when a heavy fire was opened again" between Union land batteries on Morris Island and Confederate positions at nearby Battery Gregg, Battery Simpkins, and the guns at Fort Sumter. The exchange reportedly continued through the night, heavy at times. In another article, the Wayside Home, which was setup to provide meals and accommodations for soldiers, provided a meal for the 28th Georgia Regiment.

On August 11th, *The Courier* announced that an agent for the city and army, Mr. J.N. Robson, had departed for North Carolina to purchase "flour at the lowest possible rates". His mission was described as "one of grave moment", as the supply of flour had dwindled to only a few days. No new supplies of flour had reached the city since the Yankee Morris Island campaign had started. In the same paper, an acknowledgement appeared from two Mt. Pleasant hospitals for contributions received; the article went on to encourage further contributions, as one of the hospitals depended "entirely...upon the citizens", as it was caring for 25 sick or wounded North Carolinians who were engaged in the defense of Battery Wagner.

On August 15th, the newspaper included suggestions from E.T. Winkler, chaplain of the area hospitals, on how the public could best "serve the brave defenders of our country". He suggested donations of tea, coffee, sugar, stimulants, writing paper, or money to buy such articles. He continued, clothing of any type is needed, for many soldiers have "not had a change of underclothing for a month". He also requested containers to transport water to Morris Island, where many soldiers had become sick drinking the putrid and brackish water.)

Then, at 5:00 AM, the morning of August 17th, 1863, Federal guns opened fire. The bombardment came not only from the recently completed land batteries on Morris Island, but also from a fleet of wooden ships and ironclads just outside the harbor. The Federal bombardment was devastating, particularly from the monster 10-inch 'Parrot' cannon. The

'Parrot' fired 250-pound shells, which would arch their way in the sky 2 ½ miles and reach Fort Sumter in 18 seconds. Observers claimed that the repercussions from each cannon blast were so massive as to cause vibrations as far away as Folly Island. The explosions from these massive 250-pound shells wreaked havoc and destruction. The shells battered huge openings in Fort Sumter's walls, sending deadly shrapnel fragments of brick and masonry hurtling through the air. It must have been sheer hell for the men inside Fort Sumter. They were left no alternative but to hunker down during the day's bombardment; at night, Colonel Alfred Rhett's men did their best to make repairs to the fort while bombardment was at a lull.

(*__The Courier__* reported that during the shelling of Fort Sumter, surgeon James McCauley was struck on the forehead and cheek and thigh by a shell fragment "while discharging his duties". A few days later, he was reported to be doing well and still performing his duties.)

After five days of punishing gunfire, on August 22nd, General Beauregard inspected the ravaged and crippled structure of what remained of Fort Sumter. He judged the fort still defensible, but decided to change strategy. Instead of Fort Sumter, the batteries along the Sullivan's Island side of the channel would become the main defense against a possible naval assault from Federal ironclads trying to enter Charleston harbor.

About this same time, Beauregard received a note from Union forces demanding his evacuation of forces on Morris Island and Fort Sumter, or "…Union guns would open fire on the city of Charleston itself". Washington, and Lincoln, believed the city and its citizens were a legitimate target by then existing rules of warfare. They rationalized that the city was a fortified armed camp, in which a number of munitions factories were located, and its wharves served blockade runners who transported war supplies and munitions. Besides, the city was the 'Cradle of Secession', and deserved punishment.

But, Beauregard would not capitulate.

At 1:30 AM, in the first hours of August 22nd, 1863, and under Lincoln's orders, the gunnery crew of an 8-inch 'Parrot' gun dubbed the "Swamp Angel" on Morris Island sighted down their barrel, and took dead aim on the steeple of St. Michael's Church looming above Charleston in the night sky. And, they opened fire. At the Charleston Hotel, terrified, barely clothed, patrons streaked through the hotel lobby and into the street. Pandemonium broke out. Soon, flames rising from the city could be seen across the harbor by the Federals on Morris Island. And, some Federal soldiers recalled that they could hear the bells clanking from the city's fire brigades as they dashed through the streets, from one area of mayhem to the next. At the Mills House Hotel, a visiting British journalist reported that two men wagered through hours of bombardment as to where the next shell would land.

(After firing 36 shells, the overheated breech of the "Swamp Angel" cannon exploded, injuring three of its gunners, and the gun was never rebuilt for the ensuing Morris Island action.

On August 31st, a Confederate cavalry detachment of seven men arrived on Morris Island to replace the detachment that had been delivering mail on horseback between Battery

Wagner and Battery Gregg. One of the departing cavalrymen shared his views of the place he was departing, by telling his replacements, "I thank God I'm getting away from this place. I tell you it is hell, hell!".)

Federal forces continued their push to capture the city. On September 4th, *The Mercury* published an editorial entitled, "A Grand Example", praising the city and its citizens as an inspiration and example for the Confederacy, saying: "The spectacle presented at and around Charleston has revived the hopes and strengthened the courage of the faint and despondent. A glow of enthusiastic and patriotic pride warms our hearts as we know that Charleston, the cradle of the 'rebellion', will never, as a city, be held and occupied by the hireling Yankee horde."

The next day, Federal forces began bombing Battery Wagner in preparation for what they hoped would be their third and final assault on the position. Both the army's land batteries and naval artillery began a bombardment that would last 30 hours. It was described that the Union ironclad "New Ironsides" "kept a constant stream of shells from her eight gun broadsides ricocheting over the water against the parapet of Wagner, whence, rebounding upward, they dropped nearly vertically, exploding in and over the work and searching every part of it".

In the next few days, Confederate defenders would be forced to evacuate both Battery Wagner and Battery Gregg to the onslaught of the Federal forces.

On September 10th, with Morris Island in the hands of Union forces, *The Mercury* published an article reporting the advance of the enemy surrounding the city. "Yes, they have reduced Fort Sumter to a pile of rubble, making it an infantry outpost instead of an artillery fort, but it still remains strong, manned by the

Charleston Battalion of Light Infantry. They have compelled the evacuation of Morris Island, but in the process have lost 6,000 men to our 800. While the enemy has made some material progress, we have made greater moral progress." The editorial went on to say, "...the next thing our enemies will do, will be the shelling of our city. We are prepared for that too."

The Federal siege, and bombardment of the city, would last for 587 days.

Though Morris Island had fallen, the shelling of the city itself fueled the anger and resolve of its defenders. Throughout the South, eyes were on Charleston, with much anticipation. With earlier losses at Gettysburg and Vicksburg, the South badly needed a morale boost. Despite taking a pounding, holding Charleston was important to regain the South's confidence.

Within the city, though many civilians had left the city before the shelling began, others moved north within the city, and out of reach of the range of Federal guns. The city below Calhoun Street became a virtual ghost town. The city's manufacturing and industrial activity stumbled on, but shifted upriver.

The Pringles Suffer with everyone

During this time, William and Mary Pringle and their family were suffering great losses, as were so many others.

By February, 1863, the Pringles were forced to sell their beloved country retreat at Runnymede on the Ashley River. The selling price was $59,000, but in Confederate currency. They

307

received $20,000 for the property, and $39,000 for its slaves. And, as their financial plight grew worse, they were forced to sell more and more of their once immense assets.

But, like other families, the war tore apart their family itself. Their most successful son, Julius, was a cotton plantation owner of great wealth in New Orleans. To the great shock of his family, he chose to reach an alliance with the Union army, rather than risk his fortune or lands. The family could never forgive him for his disloyalty to the Confederacy.

Again, like most southern families, most of the sons of the Pringles joined and served the Confederate army, most with positions in and around Charleston. In August 1863, the Pringles received the most devastating news. Their son, Robert, received mortal wounds and died in the Union shelling of Battery Wagner on Morris Island. To make matters worse, the family in exile could not return to Charleston for Robert's funeral. His body was returned to the family mansion at 27 King Street, and the funeral was held in the south parlor of his home, with his brothers that were serving in Charleston the only family who could attend.

Through the end of September, Federal forces kept up steady fire on Fort Sumter, while they continued their work constructing new earthworks on Morris Island. As they worked, the Confederate batteries on Sullivan's Island and nearby James Island kept peppering the Union workers with steady canon fire.

Meanwhile, within the city, all were preparing themselves for further action. **The Mercury** on September 29th summed up the attitude of its defenders, "We await the advent of the enemy's iron messengers of death and destruction, confident that, although he may lay in ashes our beautiful city by the sea, he shall never pollute its site by his tread."

(A secret operation was also being undertaken by the Confederacy...development of a weapon that, hopefully, could turn the tide of war in favor of the Confederacy, or certainly help in the defense of Charleston...what would come to be known as the first submarine. But, on October 15th, 1863, a prototype of "The Hunley" torpedo boat sank in Charleston harbor during a trial run. Eight men aboard the vessel were lost, including its captain and designer, H.L. Hunley.)

By October 18th, the siege and bombardment of Charleston had reached its 100th day. On this day, it was reported that Confederate batteries continued firing with their "usual degree of rapidity", while Union guns were silent. But, Federal guns would not remain silent for long. And, on October 26th, the Federals began a campaign of intense bombardment of Fort Sumter that would last 41 days. By November 2nd, **The Courier** reported that 5,565 shells had been fired at Fort Sumter, with 4,768 shells hitting their target, reducing the fort to a mere pile of rubble.

By November 11th, the 123rd day of siege, **The Mercury** reported that the Federals seemed to be changing their "system of attack", bombing more at night and less during the day, and using lighter artillery rather than the larger guns previously employed. The newspaper reported the first frost of the season, as the city's fuel supply was becoming a serious problem. It went on to report that City Council cancelled its regular weekly day meeting to distribute wood at cost to its citizens, due to the failure of several railroads to fulfill their respective contracts to supply the city.

Within two days, *The Mercury* reported on the number of sick and ailing soldiers who had been given furloughs, but since their homes were overrun by Yankees, they had nowhere to go. The newspaper encouraged local planters to invite these soldiers to their plantations to recover, and reminded them that Virginians extended the same courtesy to many of South Carolina's soldiers.

On the 137th day of siege, *The Mercury* called it a "comparatively quiet day". No Federal shots were directed at the city, but one shell directed at a steamer fell short near Castle Pinckney. But, at Fort Sumter, the enemy fired 21 shots by day, and 242 shots during the night. No casualties were reported.

(The next day, the newspaper demonstrated that life must go on in the city, even the mundane. An article appeared that a brown cow, of medium size "with no horns", was reported strayed or stolen from 6 Palmetto Street, and a reward of $10 for its recovery was offered.

Even the churches adapted to the siege. On November 27th, the newspaper reported that the boards of Bethel and Spring Street Methodist churches invited the congregations of Trinity and Cumberland to worship with them. St. Philip's Church announced it would meet for services at St. Paul's Church, and the Huguenot Church would worship at the Second Presbyterian Church.)

As the city entered the New Year, 1864, there was not much left to celebrate. The city was nearly destroyed. Mrs. Ravenel wrote, "By 1864, the whole life and business of the place were crowded into the few squares above Calhoun Street, and along the Ashley River, where the hospitals and prisoners were and the shells did not reach...to pass from this bustling, crowded scene to the lower part of the town was...like going from life to death".

January, 1864, started with much the same pounding each day. On the 188th day of the siege and bombardment, it was reported that by the enemy's "constant fire on the city, indicating, it is believed, a design to continue it steadily and without intermission", 82 shells hit the city that day, with "no casualties, although some very narrow escapes".

On January 16th, the 191st day of siege, *The Courier* said the day was uneasily quiet at Fort Sumter, but 180 shells hit the city striking its buildings but causing no casualties. An editorial suggested that many of the city's vacant houses be cleared of combustible material and replaced with tubs and barrels of water in case of fire.

The Courier, on January 31st, 1864, the 206th day of siege and bombardment, reported that the bombardment of Fort Sumter was "vigorously maintained" throughout the day. And, the city received more than its share, as 101 shells created "the usual damage to buildings...but no casualties".

THE HUNLEY...AND ITS FATEFUL VOYAGE: CHAPTER 30

February 17th, 1864, the 223rd day of Union siege, saw Charleston continuing to choke from the on-going blockade of the harbor. But, for months, the Confederates had been testing a new weapon...a stealth torpedo boat that could deliver an explosive charge from underwater.

If all went well, Northern newspapers would fan the story of the South's new secret weapon, inciting fear throughout the North. More importantly, it could possibly break the blockade that was stifling Charleston. General Beauregard had remained skeptical, and ready to scrap plans, because two crews were already lost in testing. "I can have nothing more to do with that submarine boat", Beauregard swore, "It's more dangerous to those who use it than the enemy."

This project had started in 1863, back in Mobile, Alabama, by a group of civilian submarine enthusiasts, who worked day and night to make their vision come true. The leader of the project was its namesake, Horace Lawson Hunley, a wealthy New Orleans lawyer, legislator, planter, and merchant. He hated the Yankees, and particularly their blockades, first around New

Orleans, that was killing his profitable merchant interests. Hunley and his engineer and designer, James R. McClintock, had built their first submarine, named 'Pioneer', in 1861; but, it had to be scuttled in New Orleans when Union forces took the city.

The group moved to Mobile, where they built a second model, the 'American Diver', but in February 1863 it sank in heavy seas trying to attack the Union's Mobile Bay blockade. They went back to the drawing boards, and began building the third version, named 'The Hunley'. It measured about 40 ft. in length, 4 ft. in height, and was only a little over 3 ft. wide. Yet, its design was remarkably advanced, and some advanced features would be copied by German U-boat engineers for World War I.

For power, the Hunley utilized manpower. A propeller shaft ran the length of the sub's interior, and a team of eight men were needed to crank the shaft. Turning the propeller shaft must have been exhausting work, and probably in virtual darkness, because the sub's interior lighting was from a single candle. The burning candle also signaled when air was about to run out inside, about every 25 minutes, and the sub would have to resurface for air. The first successful test cruise of The Hunley was in Mobile Bay in July 1863, just days after the Union victory at Gettysburg.

The defeat of Robert E. Lee's forces at Gettysburg stunned the Confederate hierarchy. Now the submarine's role in the war was elevated to urgent. "Please expedite transportation of (the) submarine boat from Mobile here", wrote General Beauregard from Charleston, "It is much needed."

Soon The Hunley was on its way to Charleston, tied onto two flatbed railroad cars and covered with tarpaulins for secrecy. Testing continued in Charleston. One five-man crew was lost in a freak accident, August 29th, 1863, near Fort Johnson when, it is believed, the wake of a passing ship flooded through an open hatch as the ship was moored. Five of the nine crew members drowned. All of the victims of that sinking were believed to be Irish immigrant sailors, who had joined the Confederate navy in New Orleans. One of the drowning victims was probably about 13 years old. Young individuals were not uncommon in the navy, particularly this late in the war. Also, the sub's tiny space for its 9-man crew made small stature preferable, if not mandatory.

The bodies of these victims were discovered in 1999, during a dig beneath what is now the Citadel college's football stadium. The site had apparently been a mariner's cemetery during the Civil War, and covered over inadvertently when the stadium was built in 1948. Some of the recovered bodies were dis-membered, and showed hack and cut marks.

Historians believe that the bodies were not recovered until well after the freak accident and sinking in 1863; they became bloated and had to be hacked by saw and hatchet to remove them through the sub's tiny hatch. They were buried in anonymity because of the wartime secrecy of their mission.

After the Hunley was raised and refitted from its first accident, a second Hunley crew was lost on October 15th, 1863, including Horace Hunley himself. Hunley took command during a routine training mission in the Cooper River off Calhoun Street. The crew was trying to perfect an attack maneuver that required trailing a floating explosive charge into the side of a mock blockade ship. The sub never returned.

Weeks later the submarine was recovered, and Hunley was found at the sub's forward escape hatch. His right arm was raised above his head, as if his last movements were in trying to push the escape lid open. His left hand clutched an unlit candle. Hunley and his crew were buried in Charleston's Magnolia Cemetery, though secrecy required that the cause of his death not be mentioned in his obituary. His tombstone reads, "Lost his life in the service of his country".

In total, 13 men lost their lives in test maneuvers before the sub ever faced the Yankees in battle. Despite the risks, its new commander, Lt. George E. Dixon was able to find another crew of eager volunteers. Convinced that the trailing floating charge idea was impractical, the design team tried a new approach, consisting of a 90-pound black powder explosive attached to a 20-ft. long bow-mounted iron spar that would ram the charge onto the side of a blockade ship. A saw-toothed spike at the tip of the spar would be driven into the hull of the enemy ship. The Hunley would then backpedal in retreat to a safe 150-ft. distance, leaving the spike in the hull like a stinger. As the sub retreated, the explosive charge would be detonated as the lanyard rope grew taut. An explosive charge of 90-pounds would blow a 12-ft. hole in the side of a wooden ship.

But, confidence in the new sub had plummeted. With this track record, it is easy to understand why General Beauregard was now skeptical of this new secret weapon...more like an iron coffin. But, Lt. George Dixon begged for a last chance, and Beauregard relented.

Lt. Dixon was 25 years old and an engineer from Kentucky, who had joined the Confederate army's 21st Alabama Infantry Regiment in 1861. In 1862, on a misty morning in April, Dixon's infantry outfit, alongside many others, stormed through the rolling pastureland in western Tennessee, known as Shiloh. Dixon was among the thousands wounded at the bloody battle of Shiloh. His leg had been saved from amputation by a U.S. $20 eagle gold coin that he carried in his pocket, a gift from his sweetheart; the Yankee ball had smashed into the coin, but from then on he carried the coin as his lucky piece. Later, he had it inscribed with the words, "My life Preserver".

He partially recovered from his leg wound, but walked with a limp the rest of his life. After convalescing, he was transferred, or probably volunteered, and was promoted as commander of the experimental torpedo boat project.

A former company commander reportedly wrote of Lt. Dixon, "Very handsome, fair, nearly six feet tall, and of most attractive presence…I never knew a better man; and there was never a braver man in any service of any army". But, the Hunley project had moved from training in Charleston to offshore patrols from Sullivan's Island. Dixon hated life on Sullivan's Island, partly because he was separated from his sweetheart, Queenie Bennett, who lived in Mobile, Alabama. "My headquarters are on Sullivan's Island", Dixon wrote to a friend. "And a more uncomfortable place could not be found in the Confederacy." In his last letter, Dixon wrote of Charleston, "If you wish to see war every day and night, this is the place to see it".

Lt. Dixon and his crew had taken the sub on as many as 20 nighttime cruises, as much as 6-7 miles out to sea, in search of Union blockade ships. The Union warships kept criss-crossing the outer reaches off Charleston harbor, watching for blockade runners or Confederate patrol boats. Out to sea, The Hunley would have to surface often to take on air. Lt. Dixon would pop his head out of the hatch to check for enemy ships, much like a prairie dog popping out of its hole.

Once, Dixon had been close enough to a Union ship to hear the sailors singing. By the early months of 1864, word had leaked to Union blockade commanders of the South's new 'secret weapon'. Union captains had been ordered to move their ships farther off shore at night, and to post special watch for mysterious 'diving torpedo' boats.

The moon was bright in the clear night sky on February 17th, 1864. Lt. Dixon would have preferred it be cloudy. One by one The Hunley's 9-man crew squeezed through the sub's circular turrets, with the last to enter being Dixon. Perhaps he had spent his last moments on shore rubbing his fingers on his lucky $20 gold coin, for he carried it that evening with him in his left trouser pocket. At about 7 PM the sub left its wharf behind Battery Marshall, not far from Breech Inlet on Sullivan's Island. That night's mission would last until about midnight when the sub would catch an incoming tide back to the safety at Breech Inlet. Dixon waved goodbye to the sentries, and pulled the hatch cover closed overhead.

Traveling a few feet under water, like a shark hunting its prey, the cast iron, hand-cranked, torpedo boat rode the outgoing tide. At about 8:45 PM, nearly 4 miles off shore, the sub targeted the Federal warship USS Housatonic carelessly anchored too close to shore. One of the Housatonic's deckhands saw what he thought was a dolphin; another thought he saw a log floating half submerged in the water. And, then, they realized it was a vessel, and suspicion turned to alarm. The crew opened fire on The Hunley with handguns, cut their anchor and tried to steam away from the collision. But it was too late.

The Hunley crew propelled the torpedo boat toward the Housatonic, and plunged the explosive-packed 20-ft. spar and spike and 90-pounds of black powder charge into the Housatonic's starboard hull. As The Hunley's crew feverishly backpedaled in reverse to flee, about 50-80 ft. away from the Housatonic (far less than the planned 150-ft. detonation distance), a massive explosion ripped a 10-ft. hole in the hull of the sloop Housatonic. Timbers and splinters were thrown skyward, and waters rushed into the gaping hole in the mortally wounded warship. Within 3-5 minutes, the ship sank.

Five men from the Housatonic's 160-man crew perished, while others escaped in lifeboats, or stayed bobbing in the icy moonlit waters off the harbor until rescued.

Moments after the explosion, and sinking, Confederates on shore reported seeing a blue light signal, the planned signal of The Hunley's success. Or, was it just a reflection of the lights from a distant ship on the horizon?

The Hunley and its 9-man crew were never seen again. The torpedo ship, the world's first submarine to sink an enemy warship, has rested on the ocean's floor for over 136 years. Today, it and the crew have come home.

That fateful night in 1864, The Hunley and Lt. Dixon and his brave crew proved submarine warfare possible. The future of naval warfare had changed that evening in the waters off Charleston. The next morning, unaware of events out at sea, Charleston's civilians were gleefully distracted by an unusual 1-inch snowfall. Five days later, the successful attack became known, and it was the talk of the city. There was a glimmer of hope, at least for the moment.

> ***The Mercury*** newspaper carried the following, "This glorious success of our little torpedo boat under command of Lt. Dixon of Mobile has raised the hopes of our people and the most sanguine expectations are now entertained of our being able to raise the siege in a way little dreamed of by the enemy".

One year and one day later, after The Hunley's success, Confederate troops would evacuate the city as Sherman bowled his way through South Carolina.

Just over 131 years later, in 1995, The Hunley would be found by divers, resting on her starboard side, buried under 3 feet of sand, and layers of dead oyster and clam shells, a gallant tomb to nine Confederate heroes. She lay entombed just 1,000 yards seaward of her victim. Now, a $20+ million fund raising effort has raised The Hunley, and is restoring it. Protected and preserved by sand and silt, it represents a 19th century time capsule. As a 'secret weapon', details of The Hunley were never widely publicized, and there were next to no drawings.

Now its secrets are being unlocked. Archaeologists want The Hunley to speak to them, revealing clues about the puzzle of what happened that fateful night. Clues that have lied lurking on the murky ocean floor for so long. And, the remains of valiant and courageous crewmen await their final resting place.

The questions at this time are many:

- Did Lt. Dixon really signal a successful mission to the troops on Sullivan's Island, or was the light seen something else?

- Did The Hunley back away far enough to survive the blast, or did the shock waves of the explosion damage the torpedo boat so it took on water and sank?

- Did a Union soldier's handgun shoot out a viewing port window and let water rush in, or did the crew become disoriented in the darkness of that chilly Atlantic night and emotional surge following the explosion and attempted escape?

- And, did the crew decide to wait on the ocean bottom for the change of tide to make their homeward journey easier (explaining why they were 1,000 feet east and seaward of their victim), or did a Union rescue ship strike The Hunley and send it to the ocean floor?

The Hunley was not merely a death trap, a crude submarine. It appears now, with its find and retrieval from the icy waters, that the Confederates knew a lot about nautical engineering. The vessel was much more advanced in technology than most people thought.

On August 9th, 2000, The Hunley broke the ocean's surface at 8:39 AM, after being raised by lift cables from its resting place on the ocean bottom. A little over 40-ft. in length, 4'3" high, and 3'10" wide, its cigar-shaped hull and bow like an icebreaker, caused onlookers to gasp for it was truly an emotional happening.

Marilyn was driving across the Cooper River Bridge, when all traffic stopped, as drivers peered to watch the entourage of boats escorting The Hunley as it passed under the bridge, moving up the Cooper River.

A national television audience also watched, along with some 2,000 spectators on shore, and 300 pleasure boats bobbing in the waters nearby, straining to catch the best glimpse possible of history in the making. Re-enactors donned Confederate, as well as Union, uniforms, while ladies dressed in period 19th century garb. Muskets were fired into the air in salute as the barge bearing The Hunley passed by on the Cooper River.

"Widows" dressed in 19th century black tossed roses into the harbor that morning, in reverence and in memoriam.

DuBose Heyward is arguably Charleston's most celebrated author. Heyward was a multitalented writer. As a novelist, he gave us "Porgy" and "Mamba's Daughters". His folk opera, "Porgy and Bess", brought him lasting fame. Descended from a signer of the Declaration of Independence, Thomas Heyward, DuBose Heyward's family could trace their lineage back to the great rice planters of Charleston. But, it was poverty that would affect most of the great families of Charleston following the Civil War. DuBose Heyward was raised in a family that no longer had money. He wrote of the dire poverty, and abject conditions both blacks and whites endured after 'The War'. It was a time when Charlestonians were "too poor to paint, and too proud to whitewash'.

He was a central figure in what became known in the 1920's and 1930's as the Charleston Literary Renaissance, when a flood of remarkable literature evoked strong images of life in Charleston and her neighborhoods.

In 1922, DuBose Heyward was intrigued by the exploits of The Hunley and its crew. He sought to pay tribute to their naval victory, and the fate of their lost torpedo boat, in a lengthy poem entitled "The Last Crew". Using sweeping lyrical passages, replete with magical words and colorful artistry, he softens the harshness of the little submarine's tragedy. He fashioned a moving and suspenseful tale of sacrifice and victory.

"An early spring came to Charleston in 1864, draping her beauty over the decay and ruins of a despairing city and the shattered 'mounds' in the harbor. Keeping vigil at White Point Gardens were the watchers—the women, the aged, and the lame. While they spoke only of remembered spring nights, their eyes strayed across the bay, where the Hunley waited for its team of lusty young men."

It went on…

"on a pier at the harbor's rim, the crew and a 'chosen few' had gathered…one by one the 'last crew' dropped into the Hunley…the anxious spectators identified with the pain and desperation of the brave men, now huddled in the stifling gloom of the iron craft and heading for their target, the Federal blockader, the Housatonic."

"A sudden flash of moonlight revealed a battered Fort Sumter, the menacing blockade, and then— the arrogant Housatonic. Again darkness enfolded the scene, and an almost palpable certainty silenced all fear, a certainty that Destiny was on the march!"

The climax for the poem is the moment of victory for the craft, as described by an observer on the pier:

"One blinding second out of endless time
Fell, sundering the night.
I saw the Housatonic hurled,
A ship of light,

Out of a molten sea,
Hang an unending pulse-beat,
Glowing, stark;
While the hot clouds flung back a sullen roar,
Then all her pride, so confident and sure,
Went reeling down the dark."

Heyward continued:

"The livid waves thundered and eventually dwindled into pale ripples that, like a winding sheet, covered the grave of the last crew."

"AN EERIE GLOW OVER THE CITY", 1864/1865: CHAPTER 31

Time passed into Spring 1864, and still the incessant daily Union bombardment continued. Just imagine being a resident of the city and enduring such trauma.

- May 19th, 1864: The 316th day of the Siege. 32 shots fired on Fort Sumter, and 25 shots into the city.

- June 22nd: 349th day of Siege. *The Mercury* reported that the Federals fired 35 shots at the city, and another large gun was moved from the lower end of Morris Island to Battery Gregg.

- August 9th: 387th day of Siege. 126 shots fired at Fort Sumter. No shots at the city, but Federal gunners took aim at the stranded steamer "Prince Albert", which ran aground off Sullivan's Island the night before.

- August 10th: **_The Mercury_** reported that the Chisolm brothers were continuing efforts to renovate their rice mill on the Ashley River at the west end of Tradd Street. Also, on their lot was a ginning mill, with the latest machinery, ready to gin cotton "at the very shortest notice".

- October 21st: 470th day of the Siege. 79 shots fired upon Sullivan's Island, 96 shots at Fort Sumter, and 2 shots at the city. The newspaper reported that movements on Morris Island gave hope that Confederate prisoners had been liberated from the "pen" and placed on ship and moved southward. On October 22nd, Mayor Charles Macbeth ordered all people owning slaves between the ages of 16 and 50 years to register them at the city Office of the Council Clerk, so they could be organized to meet labor demands for various city projects.

- October 25th: 474th day of Siege. Bombing of the city began around 7 AM, with some 34 shots falling by 6 PM. With nightfall, "the bombardment became more rapid".

- November 10th: 490th day of Siege. 18 shots fired at the city by day, and 16 shots at night. Enemy forces were observed mounting another gun at Battery Wagner.

- November 13th: 493rd day of Siege. A steady fire was kept up with 100 shots at the city, and 20 shots at Fort Sumter. No casualties were reported in the city, but "a fragment of a 30-pounder Parrot shell" killed two men of Company B 32nd Georgia Regiment, and one member of 1st South Carolina Artillery.

- November 14th: *The Courier* reported the execution of two privates from "Company B. Lucas' Battalion" on James Island on November 11th, who were court-martialed and convicted for desertion and "shot to death by musketry".

- January 15th, 1865: The Federal monitor Patapsco, part of the Union blockade fleet, hit a mine in the harbor between Fort Sumter and Fort Moultrie, sinking the ship and killing 62 persons. Observers from both forts reported hearing the explosion, followed by "confused mingling of shouts and cries of mercy".

But, the end was near. The city had become destitute and lawless. Even Confederate troops looted and ransacked empty houses. Groups of soldiers were the only visitors to the Battery, sometimes wandering down to pass time at night watching the flaming trails of canon shells arching across the night sky. Gloom was everywhere. On January 18th, 1865, *The Courier* carried an article which seemed to foreshadow the inevitable, entitled "The End of All Things".

On January 20th, *The Courier* reported "unusual activity amongst the fleet and troops on Morris Island". The Federal fleet moved two monitors inside the sandbars of the harbor, while eight monitors positioned themselves off Morris Island. The newspaper continued to defend the position of the South, but hinted at the inevitable: "However the war ends...the failure of Republican government will be demonstrated, and force, not free will, asserted as the only basis of government".

By February, General William Tecumseh Sherman's Union forces had captured Atlanta, and then Savannah, only some 60 miles away from Charleston. With Sherman on the doorstep, threatening both Charleston and Columbia, SC, the defense of Charleston was no longer militarily feasible.

On February 17th, 1865, after 587 days of siege and bombardment, Confederate forces evacuated the city and Fort Sumter. As they left, they destroyed anything and everything that could be of use to the enemy, including weapons and munitions that could not be removed, as well as large quantities of cotton and rice stockpiled with no where to go on the wharfs. Even the Ashley River Bridge was destroyed and set afire, creating "an eerie glow over the entire city".

But Sherman bypassed Charleston and headed inland to Columbia. Perhaps the marshes and lowlands which protected Charleston would have slowed Sherman's march; or, perhaps Sherman's longtime fondness for Charleston spared the city from further ravage. History is not clear.

On February 18th, Union forces under Lt. Colonel Augustus Bennett, with members of the 52nd Pennsylvania Volunteers and the Third Rhode Island Artillery, cautiously entered the city and established headquarters at The Citadel. Lt. Colonel Bennett declared martial law, and ordered the 'Stars and Stripes' flag to be flown over all public buildings. Next, he took immediate efforts to distribute food to many, both black and white, who were "utterly destitute, undernourished and near starvation". The next day the Union fleet fired a 100-gun salute, accompanied by a 38-gun salute from a land battery, to celebrate the capture of Charleston. Photographers, meanwhile, scurried about, taking photographs of a city in ruin.

`Mrs. Ravenel wrote, "With the fall of the city and of the Confederacy went out the old life of Charleston". Chaos ruled the city. Fires were set intentionally. Mobs of looters roved the city, and explosions regularly pierced the quiet gloom. As Union troops continued to move into the city, some order was restored, but they also looted. Much of the furniture, furnishings, and artwork or valuables that were left in homes were now lost. General Sherman would write, "Any one who is not satisfied with war, should go and see Charleston, and he will pray louder and deeper than ever that the country may in the long future be spared any more war".

The Pringles are refugees

A destitute Pringle family was in exile to assess its losses. Two sons had been killed in action. One son was suffering severe mental aftereffects. One son was castigated for sympathizing with the Union. While many slaves remained with them, others had run away. Their plantations had been stripped of everything usable. And, then, their unoccupied home in Charleston at 27 King Street was confiscated by Union forces. In a twist of irony, just as had happened during the British occupation of Charleston during the Revolution 85 years earlier, enemy officers now chose their 27 King Street mansion as their headquarters.

The Union forces ordered the citizens of the city to take an oath of allegiance to the United States, without which they would forfeit all rights, including the hope of regaining their ancestral homes. By the summer of 1865, the Pringles began preparations for their return to Charleston.

They saw a city in ruin. The elegance and charm of antebellum Charleston were gone. The Great Fire of 1861, and the war and bombardment of the city below Calhoun Street, had left the city a ghost town of desolation, vacant houses, widowed women, rotting wharves, and deserted warehouses. Charred silhouettes replaced what had been elegant buildings. Gardens, and even the streets, were overgrown with weeds. Piles of debris were everywhere. The once bustling harbor lay empty and fallow, filled only with the hulks of sunken ships. Buzzards filled the city's skyline, or perched in droves upon its charred and scarred rooftops, chimneys, and steeples.

On the once stately plantations, there was nothing. The neglect of three years showed on the rice fields, structures were pillaged, and many burned to the ground. Emancipation of the state's 400,000 slaves ended the labor supply, making rice culture nearly impossible.

Everything was in shambles.

The Pringle family lost 300 slaves through emancipation, a loss of assets of nearly $150,000; moreover, without a labor force, their land was of little value. Investments in Confederate war bonds were worthless, as was Confederate currency. But, they still had their home at 27 King Street, and by September, they were able to regain possession.

Mary Pringle's principal servant and friend, Cretia, chose to stay with the family for wages of $8 per month. And, following war's end at Appomattox, Mary's war weary sons made their way home, one by one, as they were paroled.

William Pringle, at age 65 years, returned to his Richfield plantation to try to rebuild. Mary Pringle, at age 62 years, set about cleaning and restoring their ancestral home at 27 King Street, so it could be reoccupied by the family. Her son, Jacob, wrote of the scene, "As I strolled through the extensive gardens, where huge shells, unexploded, were scattered around and where the rank weeds out-ranked the beautiful flowers— fit emblems of the existing state of affairs—I keenly felt the immense change which like a pall, had spread over the entire country—but in Carolina above the rest".

Mary Pringle wrote in October 1865, "We have slept, again, under our own roof, although it was on a mattress thrown on the floor. We have eaten breakfast on plates borrowed from our Freedwomen, sitting at a narrow old table found in a corner, sitting on boxes turned on their sides".

Pringle Epilogue

In 1871, the family had no alternative but to sell what was left of their Richfield plantation. What had been valued at $200,000 before the war, sold for a mere $10,000.

In December 1881, William Bull Pringle died at his Charleston home at age 82 years. He was buried in the St. Michael's churchyard cemetery. When finally probated in 1885, his estate was valued at $89.00, compared to a value of $500,000 before the war. Mary Pringle died in 1884, in her bed at 27 King Street. She was also 82 years of age at her death, and was buried beside her husband at St. Michael's.

The Pringles' son, Alston, and daughter, Susan, were living in the 27 King Street mansion when the August 31st, 1886 earthquake struck Charleston at 9:51 PM. The old house suffered minor damage, but fortunately, was spared. Daughter Susan continued to live in the home until her death in 1917. At her death, the home and lot combined were appraised at $45,000, plus $1,250 for the grand chandelier and various accessories.

After nearly a century of neglect, without funds available to the family for proper care, the once-splendid ancestral home suffered badly. Then, in 1987, its descendant-owner, Peter Manigault (publisher of today's Charleston newspaper *The Post & Courier*) and his family, started its restoration. Today, the home stands once again as a splendid example showcasing the grandeur and charm that comprise block after block of downtown Charleston.

On April 14th, 1865, Major Anderson returned to Charleston to raise over Fort Sumter, once again, the very same tattered U.S.

flag that he had lowered that very same date four years earlier. Following that flag raising ceremony, he raised a toast at the celebration dinner at the Charleston Hotel. As he was raising his glass at 10:00 PM, almost at the very same moment, in Washington, DC, John Wilkes Booth was pointing a gun at the head of Abraham Lincoln, and pulling the trigger!

With defeats throughout the South, Mary Chestnut wrote in April 1865, "Richmond has fallen…and I have no heart about it…with this storm of woe impending, we snatched a moment of reckless gaiety…".

She went on to describe the reckless feeling that led civilian elite to throw parties, and entertain at dinners, until right up to the war's end: "I think we are more like sailors who break into the spirits closet when they find the ship must sink. There seems to be for the first time a resolute feeling to enjoy the brief hour and never look beyond the day".

Mary Chestnut captured her feeling of despair, as she returned home to her own ransacked and desolate plantation, sapped of all her personal strength, as she wrote, "We are scattered—stunned—the remnant of the heart left alive with us, filled with brotherly hate…a feeling of sadness hovers over me now, day and night, that no words of mine can express". She had watched a once-cherished way of life come to an end.

Throughout the South, realty set in that all was lost. Mary wrote, "We are cut off from the world—to eat out our own hearts". Personal property and fortunes were gone. For the wealthy, a society that had everything, now had nothing. The South had gambled, and lost. Now, Southern families assessed how far they had fallen. Mary Chestnut wrote, "I can not bear to write the horrible details of our degradation…I thank

God that I am old—and cannot have my life so much longer embittered by this agony". She was only 42 years old, but felt so very much older than her years.

Life would never be the same, but Charleston had survived. In 1865, amid ruins and devastation, observers noted that many of the city's Spring flowers were in bloom, somehow a signal that Charleston, bent but not broken, would come back. Now its people would need to dig deep to find the necessary resilience to rebuild from fire's ashes...that 'fire' would forge Charleston into the gem she is today.

A CITY BEGINS TO REBUILD: CHAPTER 32

After the war ended, reconstruction began. The great wealth of the antebellum period would never return, but the city had survived, and she looked to her future.

It took time, but the economy started to recover. Cotton production restarted. Rice production would resume, but would never be as important or viable, because it was too costly to grow without slave labor. By 1873, some prosperity returned. Activity along East Bay Street picked up, as port activity became busy again. King Street's retail shops began to see shoppers once again. And, lumber exports, and a new business, phosphate mining along the Ashley River, boosted the city's economy.

Phosphate Mining

Founded upon the poverty of a defeated South, a new industry sprang upon in Charleston after the Civil War. It was centered in the Charleston Neck, a flat stretch of land bounded by the Ashley and Cooper Rivers, north of peninsular

Charleston and between what is now North Charleston. Despite creating a legacy of environmental contamination, the burgeoning industry would supply the life blood over the next 100 years to the area struggling to survive, before the industry all but vanished by the 1970's.

Smelly, lumpy phosphate rock, not only revived the city's economy, but rejuvenated the soil of the farms exhausted by years of heavy tilling for cotton. The rock was found along creek beds, dug out, and pulverized. The pulverized rock was mixed with sulfuric acid to produce phosphorous, an essential ingredient of fertilizer.

Phosphate mining sprang up, and by the 1880's, rock from Charleston was being shipped across the United States and to Europe. An 1884 *The News and Courier* newspaper headline read, "There's millions in it", and the article celebrated the "wonderful growth of a great industry". At that time, 3,000 blacks, Italians, and convict laborers toiled in the mines along the upper reaches of the Ashley River. Large wooden sheds, warehouses, and acid chambers were scattered across the Neck. Charleston was the phosphate fertilizer capital of the world, and the blue and yellow smoke rising from the smoke stacks, and the foul rotten-egg odor, became a familiar sight and smell to Charlestonians.

By the turn of the century, area creeks had been depleted of the rock, and more accessible, cheaper, and richer phosphate deposits from Florida ended the mining of rock in Charleston, and the mines were abandoned.

But, fertilizer plants continued to thrive, then relying on imported rock. By 1920, 15 plants employed 5,000 workers, who churned 1.2 million tons of fertilizer out of the plants each year. Sulfur fires burned day and night, as blue and yellow gases belched from the chimneys, polluting the air.

From the 1940's, people became increasingly disturbed by the environmental effects of the industry. Increasingly more stringent environmental regulations raised costs, and ammonia-based fertilizer became more popular, so that by the 1970's, the industry was gone, although its after-effects linger in the soil to this day.

But, Charleston was to be tested again, late in the 19th century…and, this time by nature.

In the early morning hours of August 25th, 1885, winds of 125 mph and torrents of rain pummeled the city. Roofs, doors, windows, fences, and trees were torn loose by nature's fury. A tidal surge inundated the Battery seawall with 3-6 feet of water crashing against the wall and damaging it. By noon, the storm was over. The cyclone of 1885 damaged the Battery seawall, flooded most parts of the city, destroyed or damaged 90% of the homes, and left 21 persons dead.

Even more was to come.

Earthquake of 1886, "The Big One"

Just over a year later, on a Tuesday, August 31st, 1886, the evening was hot and sticky. A few tremors had rumbled under the feet of the city's residents a few days earlier, but few noticed and with little concern. No one knew that these small spasms deep within the earth were forecasting the disaster to come.

That Tuesday evening had started as just another carefree, end-of-summer evening. The bells of St. Michael's Church had tolled three times, just six minutes earlier, to let everyone know it was 9:45 PM in Charleston. It was quiet, and peaceful, in the city. People were getting into their dressing robes and night caps, preparing for a peaceful night's rest.

Then, at 9:51 PM, a barely perceptible tremor began, and quickly strengthened. Moments later its sound mimicked a rushing locomotive with a roar that could be heard across the city...the first shock of a great earthquake. In seconds, movable objects, and those previously thought immovable, began to shake, rattle, and roll. Wave after wave of violent vibration reached the earth's surface, from its epicenter deep in the ground beneath a swamp near Summerville, some 20 miles away.

It was the second shock that killed people. The first shock came, and people ran from their houses into the streets to see what 'on Earth' was happening. With the second shock wave, roofs, steeples, buildings, and 15,000 chimneys toppled to the ground, killing 60 people and injuring many. Cries of panic filled the night air.

Observers saw Meeting Street torn asunder, with geysers of sand spewn 70 feet into the air. The editor of ***The News and Courier*** newspaper was walking down Broad Street when he heard a rumbling behind him. He turned to see the street buckling its way toward him in rolling waves 10 feet tall. Later, a writer for ***The News and Courier*** described the scene, "There was no intermission in the vibration of the mighty subterranean engine. From the first to the last it was a continuous jar, adding force with every moment...it seemed for a few terrible seconds that no work of human hands could possibly survive the shocks".

Then, in 8 minutes it was over, and all went eerily silent. But, soon fires erupted and spread everywhere within the city, from overturned lamps. Drinking water was cut off. And, people surveyed the scene. Rubble was everywhere. Modern scientists estimate the earthquake that hit Charleston that day would register 7.3 on today's Richter scale of measurement. In comparison, the quake that hit San Francisco, California in 1989 registered 6.9 on the Richter scale, and lasted 13 seconds.

If a quake of the magnitude of the 1886 disaster should hit Charleston today, seismologists estimate that: 900 people would be killed, and 45,000 injured; nearly 200,000 people would be displaced from their homes, without water for weeks, or even months; 300,000 homes would be left without electric power; 136,000 buildings would be damaged, including 220 schools, and up to 800 bridges; in all, damage throughout the state would total an estimated $20 billion.

Charleston's residents in 1886 remained in a state of fear for days afterward. Six additional aftershocks were recorded in the city the next day. Had the epicenter been directly under the city, rather than 20 miles away, the disaster could have been even worse. As it was, nobody ventured back into their homes for weeks.

The entire city attempted to live in tents erected in public parks for shelter. A tent-city was erected in Washington Park on Broad Street. Observers reported, tongue-in-cheek, that dowagers brought their oriental rugs, tea service, and servants with them, so as to not interrupt 'civilized behavior' because of a little old earthquake!

Still rebuilding from the ravages of the war, Charleston now lay in total ruin once more. Damages at that time were estimated at $23 million. But, instead of razing the city...virtually tearing everything down, and starting over...there was simply no money to rebuild from scratch. So, in a stroke of good fortune for all of us today, the citizens of the city in 1886 were forced to rebuild the precious old buildings from the rubble that remained.

The rebuilding began, brick by brick, board by board, and piece by piece, fitting everything back together, as if in a massive jigsaw puzzle.

Fortunately, for us today and posterity, what we see now are the actual old buildings, resurrected and rebuilt, much like the 'Phoenix from the ashes'. We can see the long iron rods, placed between each floor, in many of the rebuilt buildings. In the middle of the rods are turnbolts, or turnbuckles. When everything was ready, the turnbuckles were slowly cranked tighter, until the buildings groaned their way back into shape.

Remnants of columns at Cannon Park...a reminder today of the ruins Charleston has endured over three centuries.

Charleston has survived by celebrating her history, her lifestyle, and her treasure of great architecture. Preservation of the old became a way of life in the city. The city seal captures Charleston's spirit of holding onto the old, and precious, "She guards her buildings, customs, and laws".

Today, earthquakes in the Lowcountry are not unusual. Charleston is the major area in the state, where faults are centered. Near Summerville, just north of the city, two active faults cross paths, and seismologists are just beginning to explore offshore faults. Every year about 10-15 tremors are recorded, but most are not even felt. Quakes of 2.4 to 3.0 on the Richter scale are the smallest felt by people. In 1992, the most severe tremor in recent years measured 4.1; and, on a Monday, February 6th, 2002, many people from Charleston to Seabrook Island to the south felt a tremor that measured 3.5.

CHARLESTON TODAY: CHAPTER 33

At the dawning of the new millennium in year 2000, Charleston could look back 100 years, when the city's once bustling port was in shambles. In 1900, the city was still struggling to recover and rebuild from the 'un-Civil' War, fires, earthquakes, and other calamities. Rice production had been wiped out by the lack of slave labor, and devastating hurricanes, and shifted to Louisiana because the Lowcountry was too marshy for planting and harvesting by machinery. Cotton production had succumbed to the tiny, but destructive, boll weevil. And, the newly identified business of phosphate mining was short-lived and on the wane, although the spin-off fertilizer business would thrive for a half-century. Real estate values had plummeted, along with the economy. Revelers at the New Year's celebrations of 1900 had little to revel about.

But, Charleston and her citizens' resilience would be proven over the next century. The picture at New Year's 2000 was painted in entirely different colors…much bolder, and awe inspiring. The city's geography has always been important to its success. Because of the favorable trade winds, the city grew and prospered around its port in the days of the great sailing ships.

By 2000, the region's port system had returned to prominence. It had been reinvigorated to become one of the most productive in the nation. But, nothing has affected the port, and its city, more than the advent of huge, standardized 20-ft. and 40-ft. steel containers for shipping and moving goods. Containers have changed the port's landscape as well. Warehouses were torn down, and replaced by endless storage lots of containers. Giant blue container 'cranes' stretch over water's edge with their large booms, competing in the harbor's sky with the usual array of 'cranes' and other water-loving birds. And, business has 'boomed' as well.

Charleston has become the 4th busiest port in the nation, only behind Long Beach, California, New York City, and Los Angeles. In 1998, the equivalent of 1.3 million containers, holding 10 million tons of cargo valued at $29 billion, passed through Charleston's port, and about one-third of that came from Europe. The port served 140 countries. Forecasts are for that level of activity to triple in the next 15 years.

The farm economy that had once made Charleston one of the country's wealthiest cities was no longer its strength. The farm economy was first replaced by an enormous U.S. naval base. Now the city's strength relies on a robust service economy, and ever increasing diversified industrial base.

The resilience and economic evolution of the city could not have been envisioned 100 years ago. For Charleston's economic growth has not been fueled just from within, but also from a large and growing international presence as well. Of the 82 new businesses which established roots in the city the last four years, 30 of them are headquartered overseas. Thus, once again, Charleston is establishing its role as an international trading partner, much as it was in the city's early history.

King Street is an example. King Street became the city's main thoroughfare in the 1700's, largely because it was high atop a ridge on the peninsula and less likely to flood. It became a retail mecca back then for wagon drivers who plied its muddy, rutty street, while peddling their wares. King Street remains a rarity today among the nation's downtown areas, because it manages to thrive despite national trends to shopping malls located outside the inner cities. For example, the family-owned clothing business of Henry Berlin has survived for more than a century at the corner of King and Broad Streets.

The key to the city's retail success, and King Street's longevity, can be attributed to several astute moves. It has not always been so healthy. But Charleston, as always, fought back. Revitalization occurred in the 1980's, it centerpiece being 'Charleston Place', an upscale hotel and shopping complex. An $80 million vision would transform a sagging business district, and become its engine for growth.

The city's mayor, Joseph P. Riley, Jr., would play a key role in that transformation. Mayor Joseph Riley, Jr. is a native of Charleston, born here in 1943, to a family that was wealthy and influential in the real estate business. Joe Riley attended local Catholic schools, before graduating from The Citadel, and then the University of South Carolina law school. After gaining experience as a lawyer, he was elected in 1968 to the state legislature. At the age of 32 years, Joseph P. Riley, Jr. became the city's youngest mayor when he was elected in 1975. 'Mayor Joe' is still there today, after serving over 27 years. It would be hard to say that Mayor Riley's down home persona, and his demanding vision for the city, have not been instrumental in its resurgence.

Today, tony national names in retail line King Street and the surrounding downtown shopping area. Chains such as Saks Fifth Avenue, Gucci, Ann Taylor, Abercrombie & Fitch, and others have followed, and filled storefronts that previously housed small local merchants. All of this was fueled by the growing tourist business, as visitors have increasingly flocked the city. Insurance monies from Hurricane Hugo in 1989 allowed property owners to restore their homes, gardens, and commercial buildings, often "to grandeur they never before enjoyed", as is the tongue-in-cheek definition given locally for "restoration".

Hurricane Hugo (1989)

In September 1989, a Category 4 hurricane cut a swath across the Atlantic Ocean. On September 21st, 180 miles off the coast, its course turned directly toward Charleston.

By 10:30 PM, rains and high winds started. By midnight, a 12-17 ft. high wall of water swept across the harbor. The barrier islands of Folly Beach, Sullivan's Island, and Isle of Palms were inundated with the tidal surge. Fires erupted from ruptured gas lines. Water rose to over 2 feet above the first floors of mansions along the Battery. Everywhere, observers remembered the sounds that echoed like gunfire, but were really pine trees snapping in the wind's ferocity, and sailing splinters of deadly and devastating wood, like shrapnel through the air.

By 4:00 AM, it was all over. Fallen trees blocked streets oozing with pluff mud, as its unmistakable pungent smell choked the air. Roof tops were gone. There was no electricity, in some areas for weeks. Drinking water was scarce, and food quickly left the shelves of any shops still open for business.

Then, the sounds of chainsaws and hammers filled the air, replacing the roaring, cracking sounds of devastation that had occurred during the hurricane. Charleston began fighting back, once again!

Tourism

Charleston's secret is out. Visitor business booms. The city has enjoyed acclaim as the number 3rd or 4th 'most visited' city in annual national rankings by readers of *Conde Nast Traveler* magazine (this year, trailing only New York City and San Francisco). About 3 million tourists visit Charleston each year. Charleston is a residential city, accessible by walking, and its residents and visitors alike enjoy taking to the sidewalks. This enhances the charm and accessibility of its many architectural treasures. And, it seems 'history' sells; and then, one adds great weather, pretty much year-round, endless sandy beaches that are walker-friendly, superb golf, and a wide array of fine dining choices. The combination is hard to duplicate, and bodes well for the future.

It is not uncommon to see massive cruise ships looming over the city's horizon at the south end of Market Street and the Custom House, although passenger traffic from cruise ships comprise only a small portion of the annual tourist business. In just a few years, however, cruise ship traffic has grown from almost nothing to about 40,000 visitors recently.

Experts say that preserving history gives people a sense of security and belonging, because they are yearning for a sense of their past...they want to know more about their roots.

Marketing the city to tourists becomes sophisticated, and Charleston promotes itself well. But, the challenge has been to balance tourist growth, while maintaining the city's residential character. Because, Charleston is a fun place to live, and managing tourist growth is critical. Mayor Joseph P. Riley, Jr. has said, "We have to be eternally vigilant. The reality is that Charleston is a real city where people live, work, worship, and play, and it has 18th and 19th century buildings that make it attractive. If we lose that, people won't want to come".

The city's future looks robust. Its location, or geography, continues its strength, as more and more people wish to relocate here. Demographics of the aging baby boomer generation holds even more promise. In the next 25 years, the portion of the Charleston area's population over 65 years of age is forecast to double. The "graying of Charleston" is a phenomenon for the city, and the nation, which promises to be good for the local economy. Younger retirees, with substantial disposable income, translate into even more travel and tourists, and relocation growth. Well-heeled retirees mean a boon to service industries, health care, and leisure businesses.

As Mayor Joseph P. Riley, Jr. has said, "As we have begun a new millennium, Charlestonians have never had more reasons to be optimistic...".

ONLY THE BEGINNING: CHAPTER 34

Today, Marilyn and I are reminded how beautiful life can be in Charleston, SC. As we stroll the city's streets, we cherish the beautiful scene looking out from her harbor into the vast ocean and sunset beyond, the gorgeous gardens and fragrant smells of freshness from the new blooming flowers, the church spires rising above her skyline reaching for the 'Carolina blue' sky, and the wonderful historic buildings which are city treasures that remain to remind us of her past. Charleston is truly a 'Holy City'.

We have been fortunate to become a part of such a city...a city which is a national treasure, somehow weathering the storms which have buffeted her for more than three centuries...wars, enemy occupation, fire, disease, and nature's wrath in the form of hurricanes and earthquakes. She has undergone the terror and destruction of two great wars. Twice occupied by enemy forces, her economy has been torn asunder...by war, and by the total collapse of her agrarian way of life. Through it all, the city and its people have remained standing; they have endured.

The city has taken some mighty blows...her landscape left in charred and scarred ruin, buildings collapsed, and at times, death and the horror of destruction were everywhere. When times were most bleak, somehow its citizens dug deep, and with spirit and determination, survived.

Our little carriage house at '29 ½' has witnessed over 150 years of that history, and now we have succeeded in restoring it, and making it ready for its next century. Both Marilyn and I are happily ensconced within its old walls, enjoying the improvements we have made. And, somehow that old mockingbird, and perhaps Charles Kuralt himself, have helped us tell our story. We look forward, like our wonderful city of Charleston, to the next century.

Though city and its peninsula are only four square miles in size, so much has come from this beautiful, landlocked harbor, shaped by rivers, and surrounded by islands. Her bellows has sparked the fires of two revolutions, and her anvil has helped forge a new nation.

Truly, her 'three rivers form an ocean'...an 'ocean' of courage and fortitude, formed within her citizens, causing them time and again to move on, rebuild, and recreate an ever stronger, more vibrant city. Who is to say that her fourth century won't be even better.

SELECTED BIBLIOGRAPHY

- Anderson, Charles R., "Charleston, A Golden Memory", Wyrick & Company, 1992.
- Elgison, Howard, "The Unholy City", B D Publishing co., 1990.
- Bowes, Frederick P., "The Culture of Early Charleston", Greenwood Press, 1978.
- Taylor, Rosser H., "Antebellum South Carolina: A Social and Cultural History", De Capo Press, 1970.
- Rogers, George C., Jr., "Charleston in the Age of the Pinckneys", University of South Carolina Press, 1995.
- O'Brien, Michael, and Moltke-Hansen, David, "Intellectual Life in Antebellum Charleston", The University of Tennessee Press, 1986.
- Garrison, Webb, "Lincoln's Little War", Rutledge Hill Press, 1997.
- Wise, Stephen R., "Gate of Hell—Campaign for Charleston Harbor, 1863", University of South Carolina Press, 1994.
- Bradshaw, Timothy, Jr., "Battery Wagner", Palmetto Historical Works, 1993.
- Beatty, John, "The Citizen Soldier", Wilstach, Baldwin & Co., 1879.

- Weir, Robert M., "Colonial South Carolina", KTO Press, 1983.
- Fraser, Walter J., Jr., "Charleston! Charleston!", University of South Carolina Press, 1989.
- Detzer, David, "Allegiance—Fort Sumter, Charleston and the Beginning of the Civil War", Harcourt, Inc., 2001.
- Rosen, Robert N., "A Short History of Charleston", University of South Carolina Press, 1997.
- Simons, Katherine Drayton, "Stories of Charleston Harbor", The State Company, Columbia, SC, 1930.
- Rosen, Robert N., "Confederate Charleston", University of South Carolina Press, 1994.
- Poston, Jonathon H., "The Buildings of Charleston", University of South Carolina Press, 1997.
- De Credico, Mary A., "Mary Boykin Chestnut: A Confederate Woman's Life", Madison House, 1996.
- Mentzer, Melissa Anne, "Rewriting the Unwritten: The Fictions of Autobiography in the Civil War Journal of Mary Chestnut", University Microfilms International, 1989.
- Haw, James, "John and Edward Rutledge of South Carolina", The University of Georgia Press, 1997.
- *The Post & Courier* Newspaper (various articles).
- Greb, Gregory Allen, "Charleston, South Carolina Merchants, 1815-1860", University Microfilms International, 1978.
- Petit, J. Percival, "Freedom's Four Square Miles", The R.L. Bryan Company, 1964.
- Junior League of Charleston, Inc., "Our Charleston: 1700-1860".
- Daly, John Patrick, "When Slavery Was Called Freedom", The University Press of Kentucky, 2002.
- Cote', Richard N., "Mary's World", Corinthian Books, 2001.

Printed in the United States
40344LVS00004B/249